WITTGENSTEIN ON
MIND AND LANGUAGE

WITTGENSTEIN ON
MIND AND LANGUAGE

DAVID G. STERN

New York   Oxford
OXFORD UNIVERSITY PRESS

Oxford University Press

Oxford   New York
Athens   Auckland   Bangkok   Bogota   Bombay
Buenos Aires   Calcutta   Cape Town   Dar es Salaam
Delhi   Florence   Hong Kong   Istanbul   Karachi
Kuala Lumpur   Madras   Madrid   Melbourne
Mexico City   Nairobi   Paris   Singapore
Taipei   Tokyo   Toronto

and associated companies in

Berlin   Ibadan

Copyright © 1995 by David G. Stern

First published in 1995 by Oxford University Press, Inc.,
198 Madison Avenue, New York, New York 10016

First issued as an Oxford University Press paperback, 1996.

Oxford is a registered trademark of Oxford University Press, Inc.

Library of Congress Cataloging-in-Publication Data
Stern, David G.
Wittgenstein on mind and language / David G. Stern
p.   cm.
Includes bibliographical references and index.
ISBN 0-19-508000-9; ISBN 0-19-511147-8 (pbk.)
1. Wittgenstein, Ludwig, 1889–1951—Contributions in philosophy of
mind.   2. Wittgenstein, Ludwig, 1889–1951—Contributions in
philosophy of language.   3. Philosophy of mind—History—20th
century.   4. Language and languages—Philosophy—History—20th
century.   I. Title.
B3376.W564S876   1995   192—dc20   93-34800

1 3 5 7 9 8 6 4 2

Printed in the United States of America
on acid-free paper

To my grandparents, parents, and brothers

Acknowledgments

This book began as a dissertation written in the philosophy department at the University of California, Berkeley; these acknowledgments are sent from its rhetoric department. But most of it was written while I was a postdoctoral fellow at the University of Alberta, Edmonton, during 1987–1988, and a member of the philosophy department at the University of Iowa, Iowa City, during 1988–1993. All three universities generously supported the writing and research. In 1986, a Berkeley Graduate Humanities Research Grant enabled me to travel to Europe to study the Wittgenstein papers; subsequent research trips to England, Scandinavia, and Austria in 1988 and 1993 were supported by a Killam Postdoctoral Scholarship at the University of Alberta and the University of Iowa's May Brodbeck Humanities Fellowship, respectively. The University of Iowa also provided summer support in 1989, 1990, and 1992, and a sabbatical semester in 1991.

My greatest debt is to Hans Sluga, who chaired the dissertation from which this book originated and who continued to provide invaluable advice throughout the process of writing the book. Angela Blackburn, David Pears, Roger Shiner, and Barry Stroud all offered extremely helpful suggestions concerning how to transform the dissertation into a book. I also want to thank the following people who gave me comments on the work in progress that led up to this book: Richard Bett, Janet Broughton, Elizabeth Calihan, Marianne Constable, Marlena Corcoran, Caitlin Croughan, Jim Duerlinger, Linda Foy, Sabine Gölz, Lars Hertzberg, Jaakko Hintikka, Patrick Maher, Nancy Mullenax, Geeta Patel, David Pears, Maureen Robertson, Ted Schatzki, Roger Shiner, Allan Silverman, Hans Sluga, Fred Stoutland, Barry Stroud, Michael Wrigley, and Guenter Zoeller.

Parts of the book are based on the following journal articles, although each has been considerably revised; the permission of the editors to make use of this material is hereby gratefully acknowledged: "Heraclitus' and Wittgenstein's River Images: Stepping Twice into the Same River," *The Monist* 74 (1991) pp. 579–604; "The 'Middle Wittgenstein': From Logical Atomism to Practice Holism," *Synthese* 87 (1991) pp. 203–226; "Recent work on Wittgenstein, 1980–1990," *Synthese* 98 (1994) 415–458; "A New Exposition of the 'Private Language Argument': Wittgenstein's Notes for the 'Philosophical Lecture,'" *Philosophical Investigations* 17 (1994) 552–565.

I would like to thank the Wittgenstein trustees, Professor G.E.M. Anscombe, Sir Anthony Kenny, Professor Peter Winch, and Professor Georg Henrik von Wright, for their permission to quote from the published and unpublished Wittgenstein writings.

Special thanks are due to Claus Huitfeldt, Alois Pichler, and Ole Letnes at the Wittgenstein Archives at the University of Bergen, Jonathan Smith and David McKitterick at the Wren Library, Trinity College, Cambridge, and Dr. Eva Irblich at the Austrian National Library for their assistance in working with the Wittgenstein papers.

Passages from the *Tractatus Logico-Philosophicus*, by Ludwig Wittgenstein, translated by C. K. Ogden in 1922, and by David Pears and Brian McGuinness in 1961, are reprinted with the permission of Routledge, copyright © 1922, 1961, Routledge and Kegan Paul. Material from Wittgenstein's other books is reprinted by permission of the respective copyright holders. In the UK and Commonwealth, the copyright is controlled by Basil Blackwell, who also retain the world rights to *Zettel*. Acknowledgements for the United States are as follows: Passages from *Philosophical Investigations* by Ludwig Wittgenstein, translated by G.E.M. Anscombe, are reprinted with the permission of Macmillan, copyright © 1953, 1981 by Macmillan College Publishing Company. Passages from *Philosophical Grammar*, by Ludwig Wittgenstein, translated by Rush Rhees, are reprinted with the permission of the University of California Press, copyright © 1974 Basil Blackwell. Passages from *Preliminary Studies for the "Philosophical Investigations" Generally Known as "The Blue and Brown Books,"* by Ludwig Wittgenstein are reprinted by permission of Harper Collins, copyright © 1958.

Passages from the Frank P. Ramsey Papers are referred to by the control number assigned to the manuscript by the Archive for Scientific Philosophy in the Twentieth Century, Department of Special Collections, University of Pittsburgh Libraries. The University of Pittsburgh owns the literary rights to the Ramsey papers.

Note on the Text

Wittgenstein's published works are referred to by title in the footnotes; full references are included in a list of primary sources, preceding the bibliography. Writings by other authors are referred to by title and author in the footnotes; full references are given in the bibliography.

References to Wittgenstein's typescripts (TS) and manuscripts (MS)—the *Nachlass*—use the numbering system in von Wright's catalogue of the Wittgenstein papers, except for TS 213, where I use the name by which it is commonly known, the Big Typescript. References to Wittgenstein's typescripts and manuscripts give a page number whenever possible. References to the Big Typescript cite section number and page number. The translations of previously unpublished quotations from the *Nachlass* are mine; the German text for all quotations from the unpublished papers is given in an appendix. When I have translated only part of a sentence in the English, the full German sentence is given in the appendix, and I have occasionally included an additional sentence in the German when I thought it might assist a reader check my description of the context of the passage.

A number of features of Wittgenstein's writing are somewhat unusual. He usually wrote in the form of remarks, units of writing that could be as short as a single sentence or as long as a sequence of paragraphs spanning several pages, separated from each other by a blank line in a manuscript, or an additional carriage return in a typescript. These line breaks are indicated in the quoted text by a larger than normal gap between one paragraph and the next. Wittgenstein used broken underlining in his typescripts and wavy underlining in his manuscripts to indicate that he was not satisfied with the words in question; in the places where it occurs, such underlining is often an important clue to what is going on. In my quotations and transcriptions, such words or phrases are underlined like this; *italics* correspond to double spacing in a typescript, underlining in a manuscript. Wittgenstein used double slashes (//) to separate variant wordings; single slashes (/) are used to indicate alternate words or expressions that were written in by hand above or next to the main text. Where variant wordings were very close in meaning to the original wording, and the choice of words did not seem particularly significant, I usually translated them by a single expression; but all such variants are indicated in the corresponding transcriptions of the source material. My translations are based on published translations, where available, but often deviate from them, in the interest of a more literal translation, and consistent translation of central terms.

My transcriptions preserve Wittgenstein's orthography, such as his use of "ß" and "ss": in general, he uses "ß" where appropriate in his manuscripts but not in his typescripts. Where Wittgenstein's abbreviations have been completed, or the original was partly illegible, the material that has been added is enclosed by square brackets. I have corrected minor grammatical errors, but I have preserved Wittgenstein's idiosyncratic punctuation, including his very sparing use of commas.

Where possible, I have given the date of the earliest known draft of each passage I quote from Wittgenstein's writings. However, the dating of passages from the Wittgenstein *Nachlass* is problematic, not only because most passages underwent a complex and lengthy process of revision, but also because there is no systematic way of searching the *Nachlass* as a whole at present and because it is not always possible to assign a precise date to any given source. Most of this information is taken from André Maury's lists of the sources of *Zettel* and the *Philosophical Investigations*, and Alois Pichler's list of source manuscripts for *Culture and Value* (full references are given in the bibliography.)

Berkeley, California
February 1994

D. G. S.

Contents

WITTGENSTEIN ON
MIND AND LANGUAGE

1

Introduction

1.1 The Wittgenstein Papers

This book is an exposition of Wittgenstein's early conception of the nature of representation and how his later revision and criticism of that work led to a radically different way of looking at mind and language. Most interpretations of the development of Wittgenstein's philosophy focus on the *Tractatus Logico-Philosophicus* [hereafter called *Tractatus*], written during World War I and published shortly afterward, the *Philosophical Investigations*, written and rewritten during the last twenty years of Wittgenstein's life and published shortly after his death in 1951, and the literature that has grown up around these books. In contrast, my reading of his philosophy of mind and language begins from the initial articulation of his thoughts in his first drafts, conversations, and lectures and the process of revision that led to the published works. Consequently, I quote extensively from such sources as his manuscript notes, notes taken at his lectures in Cambridge, and records of conversations with the members of the Vienna Circle and Frank Ramsey, and I emphasize the importance of the ideas expressed in these passages. This introductory chapter offers an outline of my reasons for taking such an approach and the development of Wittgenstein's philosophy to which it leads.

Because the *Tractatus* and *Philosophical Investigations* were published well before most of Wittgenstein's other published writing became available, interpretation began with these two books. Most interpreters have regarded the *Tractatus*, published in 1922, and the *Philosophical Investigations*, published in 1953, two years after his death, as the only reliable expositions of Wittgenstein's earlier and later philosophy. The *Tractatus* was the only book Wittgenstein published during his lifetime, while the *Philosophical Investigations* was the book he wrote and rewrote for most of the rest of his life. But the compressed and aphoristic character of these works made it particularly easy for interpreters to find their own concerns and commitments in those texts. The obvious differences between the early and the late work, coupled with Wittgenstein's criticism of the *Tractatus* in the *Philosophical Investigations*, gave rise to the view that the early and late Wittgenstein were diametrically opposed. Partly as a result of the diversity and complexity of the material, and partly because so many different readers appropriated Wittgenstein's writings for their own purposes, the literature on Wittgenstein proliferated, consisting for the most part of a series of self-contained debates, often conducted at a considerable distance from the

3

texts under discussion. At the same time, an increasingly intricate body of scholarly writing grew up around each of the new publications from the *Nachlass*—Wittgenstein's papers—which he left to his family and trustees. But while Wittgenstein's posthumously published books do contain much of his most polished writing, and must play a central role in any interpretation of his thought, they are often much more compressed and opaque than the drafts on which they were based and were written in the conscious expectation that very few readers would understand them.

In the first sentence of the preface to the *Tractatus*, Wittgenstein wrote that the book will perhaps only be understood by those who have already had the thoughts expressed in it. Similarly, in a draft of a foreword written in 1930, he states that it is "written for those who are in sympathy with the spirit in which it is written," later adding the observation that "the spirit of a book has to be evident in the book itself and cannot be described. For if a book has been written for just a few readers that will be clear just from the fact that only a few people understand it."[1] Moreover, in the preface to the *Investigations*, Wittgenstein says that the object of the book is not to save us from the trouble of thinking through these problems for ourselves, but to stimulate readers to worthwhile thoughts of their own. If we are to think for ourselves, we may well ask how he conceived of the problems he claimed to solve, or dissolve, in the *Tractatus* and *Philosophical Investigations*. Despite the fact that much of Wittgenstein's work from the 1920s and 1930s has been available for some time, in the form of posthumous books and articles, as well as lecture notes from his classes in Cambridge and transcripts of his discussions with the Vienna Circle, this material has had surprisingly little impact on the general reception of his philosophy.

Some rough figures may be helpful in providing a sense of the scale of the Wittgenstein papers. An electronic edition of all the published Wittgenstein (translations are not included), occupies about 7 megabytes, just under 2,000 published pages containing a little over 1 million words. The *Tractatus* and *Investigations* occupy approximately 1 megabyte between them.[2] Claus Huitfeldt and Viggo Rossvaer, in their report on the Norwegian Wittgenstein Project, an attempt to produce an electronic edition of the entire *Nachlass*, estimated that an electronic version of the complete works would take up about 40 megabytes, or well over 5 million words. While a substantial fraction of this would consist of drafts of published remarks and a representation of every variant, erasure, and rearrangement, there is at least as much material that does not fall into these categories.

Approximately eighty manuscript (MS) volumes, notebooks, and papers, or over 12,000 manuscript pages, covering most of the years from 1929 to 1949, amount to

---

1. *Culture and Value*, pp. 6–7. Source: MS 109, pp. 204 and 208, 6 and 7 November 1930. Subsequent footnotes for Wittgenstein quotations will give source manuscripts and dates, where known, in this format. References to published works by Wittgenstein simply list the title; further details can be found in the bibliography. References to unpublished works by Wittgenstein use the numbering system set out in G. H. von Wright's "The Wittgenstein Papers," with the exception that I follow the usual practice of referring to TS 213 as the Big Typescript.

2. These figures are based on the uncompressed text files in *Wittgenstein's Published Writings in Electronic Form*. The same material has recently been republished in compressed format, with the Folio Views software package, as *The Published Works of Ludwig Wittgenstein*. See Stern, "Review of *The Published Works of Ludwig Wittgenstein*," for further discussion of this material.

a line-by-line record of much of Wittgenstein's later work in progress. Two sequences of volumes—the first numbered from I to XVIII, covering 1929 to 1940; the second lettered up to S, covering the 1940s—comprise the bulk of the manuscript material; the other third includes his last writings, some preparatory material connected with the two main series of volumes, and a number of miscellaneous items. From 1929 to 1949, the manuscript volumes were used to record his first-draft writing and, later, to revise and rearrange that work. These volumes, many of them still unpublished, contain a record of the inner dialogue that was the driving force in the development of Wittgenstein's philosophical work. Many of them, like Wittgenstein's three surviving wartime notebooks, published as *Notebooks 1914–1916*, constitute a sequential record of first-draft writing that might be used or revised in subsequent work. Most remarks in the manuscript volumes were tagged with a sign; many of them were subsequently revised or rewritten. While no key to the signs has been found, some of them were clearly intended to show which paragraphs should be used, or discarded, in a subsequent phase of his work. Selections from the manuscript volumes were typed up, revised, rearranged, and typed up once again. Over forty typescripts (TS) provide a record of the repeated revisions and rearrangements that led from the manuscript volumes to his most polished work. Entries in the manuscript volumes show us Wittgenstein at work, raising questions, rejecting old ideas, and developing new ones; the revisions and the typescripts show which parts he accepted and the uses he made of them.

In principle, most of Wittgenstein's unpublished work has been available to researchers since the late 1960s, in the form of either twenty-two rolls of microfilm or dozens of volumes of bound photocopies. In practice, the copies are far from easy to use. Many are blurry, overexposed, or underexposed. Pages are missing and, in some cases, so are whole manuscripts and typescripts. While Wittgenstein's handwriting becomes more legible with practice, the result of all these obstacles has been that his unpublished notebooks and typescripts have remained inaccessible to almost all his readers.[3]

Studying the development of Wittgenstein's work by making use of his published and unpublished typescripts and manuscripts, records of what he said, and the like, in addition to his later and his earlier masterpieces, can make a substantial contribution to our understanding of those works. It can clarify the problems that led him to

---

3. There have been plans for a complete scholarly edition of the Wittgenstein papers since 1976, when the first project aiming at publication was funded, but so far virtually nothing has been published in such a format, and nothing has been said about the precise form that such an edition would take. For further discussion of plans for a complete edition of the Wittgenstein papers, see Claus Huitfeldt and Viggo Rossvaer, *The Norwegian Wittgenstein Project Report 1988*, and Jaakko Hintikka, "An Impatient Man and His Papers."

The Wittgenstein Archives at the University of Bergen has received permission from the Wittgenstein Trustees to produce an electronic edition of the entire *Nachlass*, and have already developed a suitable transcription protocol; by the summer of 1993, approximately 6,500 pages had been transcribed. It is currently expected that the first installment of their work, which will include the papers from 1929 to 1936 and 1949 to 1951, will be released on a CD-ROM, together with colour facsimiles of the entire *Nachlass*, in 1997. For some information about the Bergen Archives, see the papers by Huitfeldt listed in the bibliography; for further discussion of these issues, see David Stern, "The Availability of Wittgenstein's Philosophy."

write those works, and it can illuminate aspects of his thought that have generated enormous controversy in the secondary literature, by making it clear which positions he opposed and what solutions he had to offer. It is unfortunate that Wittgenstein's method of continually rewriting and rearranging his philosophical work has rarely been given the attention it deserves, for the *Tractatus* and *Philosophical Investigations* are much more readily intelligible within the dialectical context provided by his manuscripts and typescripts. Instead, his other writing has usually been construed as preparatory work or rough notes, useful if it indicates a further development of his ideas, suggests a new reading of a primary text, or confirms a contentious construal, but lacking the authority of the two principal texts. Consequently, the many other books and papers since published under his name are usually treated as being of secondary importance, and the still larger quantity of unpublished manuscripts and typescripts have only been studied by a few determined specialists, so that the work that has been done on the larger corpus of Wittgenstein's writings has actually reinforced the assumption that it is of little interest to a general audience.

Perhaps the principal reason for this state of affairs is that the precise character of the path Wittgenstein took on his return to philosophical writing in 1929 later struck him as a personal idiosyncrasy on which it would be inappropriate for him to dwell. In a manuscript written in 1948, he expressed his conviction that he should not publish a philosophical autobiography in which the specific difficulties he had felt were "chewed over." The real importance of his work for a wider audience, he thought, lay in the "remedies" he had developed, not the particular causes that had occasioned them:

> These difficulties are interesting for me, who am caught up in them, but not necessarily for other people. They are difficulties of *my* thinking, brought about by *my* development. They belong, so to speak, in a diary, not in a book. And even if this diary might be interesting for someone some day, I cannot publish it. My stomach-aches are not what is interesting but the remedies—if any—that I've found for them.[4]

As a result, the *Philosophical Investigations* contain only a few signposts marking the path that led to its composition. However, the difficulties that Wittgenstein faced in revising and then abandoning the logical atomism of the *Tractatus* and the lengthy and detailed early drafts that lead up to the cryptic formulations in the *Investigations* often provide us with a much clearer exposition of his views than does his more polished writing.

The importance of Wittgenstein's *Notebooks 1914–1916*, first published in 1960, for an understanding of the *Tractatus* is now generally recognized. More recently, we have begun to see that his later manuscript volumes, as yet unpublished, document the emergence of his later philosophy, for they are a record of the inner dialogue that was the driving force in Wittgenstein's philosophical work. Wittgenstein rewrote and pruned his first drafts until they had been cut down to a bare minimum. As a result, parts of the *Investigations* are more like miniatures than the "sketches" to which he compares his work in the preface. Fania Pascal, who taught Wittgenstein

---

4. Wittgenstein, quoted by Rush Rhees, "Correspondence and Comment," p. 153. Rhees does not give a precise reference, simply stating that the quotation is taken from a manuscript written in 1948. [German in appendix.]

Russian during the 1930s, has described how Wittgenstein "would devote hours to shaving off tiny slivers from the small photos he took before he would be satisfied with some kind of balance achieved."[5] Often, by the time a picture had reached its final dimensions in Wittgenstein's hands, most of the original photograph had been cut out. Similarly, his succinct and polished final drafts reveal little about the lengthy editorial process in which his first drafts were gradually rewritten. But they draw on a much larger body of work, and often need to be understood in that context. Wittgenstein's absorption in his own inner dialogue left him little sense of which parts of the original picture or draft might be most important to a later audience. His sense of the course of his struggle with his conflicting intuitions was always shaped by the problems that currently occupied him. "Anything your reader can do for himself, leave to him," he once noted at the end of a day's notes on the awareness of different aspects of visual experience.[6]

Much of the power of Wittgenstein's writing arises out of a struggle between opposing intuitions and his attempts to resolve that struggle. One of the strongest currents of thought in his later philosophy is the idea that one cannot dissociate the first impulses toward a philosophical train of thought from its most finished expression, an idea that motivates the fragmentary arguments one finds in the opening sections of the *Investigations*. The debate that animates so much of his writing is a conversation with interlocutory voices that express intuitions and instinctive convictions, not polished philosophical theories.[7] "The interlocutor," the usual term adopted by commentators for the voices that raise objections in Wittgenstein's later writings, is certainly not a straw man; neither is he a representative of other people's views. Rather, he—if it is appropriate here to speak of a separate person at all—is Wittgenstein's alter ego. In his notes from the day after the passage just quoted, Wittgenstein wrote: "Nearly all of my writings are private conversations with myself. Things that I say to myself *tête-à-tête*."[8]

1.2 The Development of Wittgenstein's Philosophy

In both his early and his later philosophy, Wittgenstein aimed to bring about an insight into the nature of our language, an insight that would make it clear that traditional philosophical problems and the solutions that have been proposed to them are literally nonsense. In his early work, he also thought he could show that all language shares an underlying formal structure, and that insight into the form of that structure would show philosophical truths that were, strictly speaking, inexpressible. So while the *Tractatus*, like works of traditional philosophy, consists of sentences that, on the theory of representation he sets out there, are to be condemned as nonsensical, Wittgenstein nevertheless thought that his book, unlike the others, pointed to the truth. The central paradox of the *Tractatus* is that it aims to draw a limit to thought, yet, at

5. Fania Pascal, "Ludwig Wittgenstein, A Personal Memoir," p. 42.

6. *Culture and Value*, p. 77. Source: MS 137, p. 134, 25 December 1948.

7. For a reading of the opening sections of the *Philosophical Investigations* along these lines, see Warren Goldfarb, "I Want You to Bring Me a Slab."

8. *Culture and Value*, p. 77. Source: MS 137, p. 134, 26 December 1948.

the same time, it is supposed to point to philosophical insights that cannot be thought or put into words. Writing to Ludwig von Ficker, an editor he admired, in the hope of persuading him to publish his book, Wittgenstein said:

> The book's point [*Sinn*] is an ethical one. I once meant to include in the preface a sentence which is not in fact there now but which I will write out for you here, because it will perhaps be a key to the work for you. What I meant to write then, was this: My work consists of two parts: the one presented here plus all that I have *not* written. And it is precisely this second part that is the important one. My book draws limits to the sphere of the ethical from the inside as it were, and I am convinced that this is the ONLY *rigourous* way of drawing these limits. . . . I would recommend you to read the *preface* and the *conclusion*, because they contain the most direct expression of the point of the book.[9]

By setting out the nature of language and making clear what can and cannot be said, the book is supposed to make clear the limits of language. In the preface to the *Tractatus*, after stating that the book deals with the problems of philosophy and shows that they depend on misunderstanding the logic of our language, Wittgenstein adds that the "whole sense [*Sinn*] of the book might be summed up in the following words: what can be said at all can be said clearly, and what we cannot talk about we must pass over in silence."[10] These words are a paraphrase of the book's concluding sentence: "What we cannot speak about we must pass over in silence." Yet Wittgenstein was no positivist, for he combined the thesis that only factual and logical uses of language are meaningful with the view that philosophical insights about ethics, aesthetics, and "the mystical" lie *outside* language, despite the fact that any attempt to state these insights will only lead to nonsense. Characteristically, the very fact that he said almost nothing about ethics in the *Tractatus* itself was a product of his overriding concern with the limits of what can be said.

In one of the last remarks of the *Tractatus*, Wittgenstein says that "the correct method in philosophy" would be to avoid talking about philosophy altogether, except when someone else wanted to "say something metaphysical"; on those occasions, one would show the person that some of the signs he or she was using were meaningless. One would have to restrict people to saying what can be said: either empirical or logical statements. "Although it would not be satisfying to the other person—he would not have the feeling that we were teaching him philosophy—*this* method would be the only strictly correct one."[11] But he ends the book by saying that the propositions it contains are an instrument that must be ultimately discarded if his aim is to be achieved:

> My propositions are elucidatory in this way: he who understands me finally recognizes them as nonsensical, when he has climbed out through them, on them, over them. (He must, so to speak, throw away the ladder after he has climbed up it.)
>
> Whereof one cannot speak, thereof one must be silent.[12]

9. Paul Engelmann, *Letters from Ludwig Wittgenstein*, pp. 143–144. The letter was written in 1919.
10. *Tractatus Logico-Philosophicus* [hereafter referred to as *Tractatus*] 7, Pears and McGuinness translation.
11. *Tractatus* 6.53; see also 6.5–7.
12. *Tractatus*, 6.54–7, Ogden translation.

The content of the *Tractatus* is not limited to propositions of natural science, or even to saying what can be said. The book does "say something metaphysical": most of the propositions it contains set out an atomistic ontology and a program of logical analysis. In other words, the strictly incorrect method followed throughout most of the book is to provide an austere outline of a metaphysical system, a canonical analysis of the ultimate structure of any possible system of representation, based on Bertrand Russell's and Gottlob Frege's work in logic and ontology. The account of analysis in the *Tractatus* is so extremely abstract that we are never given fully worked-out examples of analyses of ordinary factual assertions, let alone discourse about visual experience or the self. Instead, the *Tractatus* attempts to show the limits of language without providing such detailed exposition.

The chapters that follow look at Wittgenstein's schematic attempts to develop analyses of the structure of language and experience and his later criticism of the attempt to construct such theories. In this chapter, I concentrate on a preliminary overview of the contrast he drew between "ordinary" and "philosophical" ways of looking at things when he wrote the *Tractatus*, and how that contrast was transformed in his subsequent writing. In October 1916, Wittgenstein discussed a contrast between two ways of looking at a thing: as a "thing among things," part of a larger spatio-temporally extended world, and as a world in itself:

> As a thing among things, each thing is equally insignificant; as a world each one equally significant.
>
> If I have been contemplating the stove, and then am told: but now all you know is the stove, my result does indeed seem trivial. For this represents the matter as if I had studied the stove as one among the many, many things in the world. But if I was contemplating the stove *it* was my world, and everything else colourless by contrast with it. . . .
>
> For it is equally possible to take the bare present image [*Vorstellung*] as the worthless momentary picture in the whole temporal world, and as the true world among shadows.[13]

In other words: if only one looks in the right way, one will see the images one experiences as the "true world," radically different from the ordinary temporal world. The day before, Wittgenstein had distinguished the "usual way of looking at things" that "sees objects as it were from the midst of them" and "the view *sub specie aeternitatis* from outside, [i]n such a way that they have the whole world as background."[14] To see something *sub specie aeternitatis*, "under the form of eternity" is, Wittgenstein proposes, to see it as the world, to see it as "a limited whole." Developing the idea further, he suggests that it involves transcending the spatiotemporal form of ordinary experience, so that space and time are also regarded as objects to be transcended: "Is this it perhaps—in this view the object is seen *together with* space and time instead of *in* space and time."[15] Toward the end of the *Tractatus*, Wittgenstein cryptically connects seeing the world as a limited whole with his notion of the "mystical":

13. *Notebooks 1914–1916*, p. 83, 8 October 1916.
14. *Notebooks 1914–1916*, p. 83, 7 October 1916.
15. *Notebooks 1914–1916*, p. 83, 7 October 1916.

"To see the world *sub specie aeterni* is to see it as a whole—a limited whole. Feeling the world as a limited whole—it is this that is mystical."[16]

The ideas expressed in these fragmentary and cryptic remarks arise out of Wittgenstein's reading of Arthur Schopenhauer's aesthetics. Schopenhauer held that aesthetic contemplation involves a transformation in which one becomes so absorbed in perceptual experience that one loses one's individuality, becoming a pure subject outside space and time that mirrors the object perceived. Schopenhauer even says that this is what Spinoza had in mind when he wrote that the mind is eternal insofar as it conceives things under the form of eternity.[17] These obscure but suggestive ideas about the nature of subject and object, space and time, and their transcendence struck Wittgenstein with the force of a revelation under quite specific circumstances: he was contemplating the stove heating his room, concentrating his attention on it, and arriving at conclusions about the nature of the world and his knowledge of it. The stove, a familiar part of everyday life and a natural focus of attention on an October evening, provided a convenient example of something close at hand, ordinarily quite unproblematic. The stove is an example of what Stanley Cavell calls a "generic object," an object that serves as a concrete example of a material object in a philosophical discussion. Such objects are chosen precisely because they are so familiar that we ordinarily have no problem in recognizing, identifying or describing them. As Cavell puts it, they are objects "about which the only 'problem,' should it arise, would be not to say what they are but to say whether we can know that they exist, are real, are actually there."[18] A generic object is a paradigm of an object that we ordinarily take for granted, items such as René Descartes's slippers or G. E. Moore's hands. In bringing out the role of a generic object as a starting point in epistemological argument, Cavell tries to capture the spirit in which our knowledge of such an object can become the focus of philosophical inquiry. When such an object presents itself to a philosopher, "he is not taking one as opposed to another, interested in its features as peculiar to it and nothing else. . . . What is at stake for him in the object is materiality as such, externality altogether."[19] Focussing his attention on his stove, Wittgenstein became captivated by the intuition that there is a fundamental distinction between the "primary" phenomena—immediate experience understood as the "true world," a timeless, spaceless world—and the spatiotemporal "secondary" world we ordinarily inhabit.

Wittgenstein's conception of the structure of primary experience was the result of tracing out the consequences of the idea that the ordinary world and the world of experience are radically different, and that experience, looked at in the right way, presents one with insights that cannot be put into words. He conceived of the primary phenomena of immediate experience as a self-contained realm, a world out-

16. *Tractatus*, 6.45.

17. Arthur Schopenhauer, *The World as Will and Representation*, i.179; Benedict Spinoza, *Ethics*, Book V, Prop. xxxi Note. See P. M. S. Hacker, *Insight and Illusion*, pp. 95–100.

18. Stanley Cavell, *The Claim of Reason*, p. 52. See also pp. 136–138 and chapter 8 passim, esp. p. 219 ff. In Cavell's terms, the relationship between the primary and the secondary in Wittgenstein's writings is a conflict between claim and non-claim contexts. The secondary is the context in which concrete claims are made; the primary is the context in which philosophical claims are made.

19. Cavell, *The Claim of Reason*, p. 53.

side space and time, in the sense that it contains a "now" and a "here" but no "then" or "there," yet provides the basis for the spatial and temporal empirical world, the secondary system. He was thus committed to the paradoxical view that experiential space and time is radically different from physical space and time, yet somehow related to it.

While we ordinarily take it for granted that the world existed long before anyone now alive was born and will be there after we are all dead, from the primary level, "the world is *my* world . . . at death the world does not alter, but comes to an end."[20] In that world, everything beyond immediate experience is absolutely excluded. Since ordinary notions of past, present, and future; subject and object; cause and effect are part of the scientist's language, they have no application to the primary realm: the world of experience and the world of fact are incommensurable. On this view, one can only apply ordinary language to immediate experience once one steps outside "my world" and conceives of it as part of the world the scientist investigates; considered in its own terms it lies beyond the reach of factual language, "beyond all speaking and contradicting."[21] That may have been what Ramsey meant when he wrote in his notes that "Ludwig's primary world contains no thought."[22] Even though nothing can be said, or even shown, concerning the primary world, however, Wittgenstein still thought its true nature could, under the right circumstances, "show itself." The struggle to express these extralinguistic insights into the nature of experience had led Wittgenstein to write in the *Tractatus* that "the world is *my* world" and in the 1929 manuscripts and the early 1930s, to repeat the Heraclitean dictum that "all is in flux,"[23] in an attempt to describe the evanescent character of the stream of consciousness.

Wittgenstein's examples of primary phenomena are predominantly visual; his conception of the primary world is based on the model of visual space. In part, that is simply because the visual field provides a wide and varied range of phenomena for analysis. But his choice of examples is also motivated by the visual metaphors to which he was drawn, metaphors that suggested a direct insight into the nature of things, unmediated by language. That deeper motivation is an elusive one, for it implies that that the primary level of philosophy is a matter of insight which cannot be put into words. The Wittgenstein of the *Tractatus* holds that solipsism, scepticism, and any other theory that makes subject or experience primary, are all nonsense, misfiring attempts to say something where nothing can be said: "Scepticism is *not* irrefutable but obviously nonsensical, when it tries to raise doubts where no questions can be asked."[24] Sceptical questions about the existence of the external world can be dismissed because they raise possibilities that make no empirical difference. Similarly, in a conversation about epistemological scepticism with the Vienna Circle, he rejected the solipsistic thesis "If I turn away, the stove is gone," describing it as an example of a "loose wheel" in the mechanism of language, because nothing could

20. *Tractatus*, 5.62, 6.431.
21. *Philosophical Remarks*, §74.
22. Frank Ramsey, unpublished manuscript, Pittsburgh catalogue number 003-30-05.
23. *Tractatus* 5.62. *Philosophical Remarks*, §54, and Big Typescript §91, pp. 427 ff. For further discussion, see this volume, chapter 3, section 4 and chapter 6, section 1, respectively.
24. *Tractatus*, 6.51.

possibly count as definitively verifying or falsifying it.[25] The proposition might look meaningful, he said, but "taken in the empirical sense" it fails to pass the test. There is an equally curt treatment of the issue in the *Philosophical Remarks* and Big Typescript:

> If . . . you ask, "Does the box still exist when I'm not looking at it?", the only right answer would be, "Of course, unless someone has taken it away or destroyed it." Naturally, a philosopher would be dissatisfied with this answer, but it would quite rightly reduce his way of formulating the question *ad absurdum*.[26]

Wittgenstein held that the grammar of our everyday language has been shaped by pragmatic concerns, such as the need for a vocabulary suited to describing and manipulating our surroundings, rather than by faithfulness to the full multiplicity of experiential phenomena. Although none of our ordinary words are adequate for the task of describing immediate experience, we cannot help using the convenient approximations that ordinary language provides:

> Describing phenomena by means of the hypothesis of a world of material objects is unavoidable in view of its simplicity when compared with the unmanageably complicated phenomenological description. If I can see different parts of a circle, it's perhaps impossible to give a precise direct description of them, but the statement that they're parts of a circle, which, for reasons which haven't been gone into any further, I don't see as a whole—is simple.[27]

Thus, the earlier passage quoted, dismissing the question whether a box exists when one is not looking at it, continues as follows:

> All our forms of speech are taken from ordinary, physical language and cannot be used in epistemology or phenomenology without casting a distorting light on their objects.
>
> The very expression "I can perceive x" is itself taken from the idioms of physics, and x ought to be a physical object—e.g. a body—here. Things have already gone wrong if this expression is used in phenomenology, where x must refer to a datum. For then "I" and "perceive" also cannot have their previous senses.[28]

The contrast between the primary world of phenomena and the secondary world of physics is summed up in a student's lecture note from the early 1930s: "The world we live in is the world of sense-data, but the world we talk about is the world of physical objects."[29] From that vantage point, the hypotheses that describe the world of the scientific realist are constructions that enable us to see the structure of the experiential world, a world where "all is in flux."

In 1929, Wittgenstein treated everyday descriptions of people and familiar ob-

25. *Ludwig Wittgenstein and the Vienna Circle*, p. 159. Cf. *Philosophical Remarks*, ch. 23.

26. *Philosophical Remarks*, §57. A slightly revised version of the first sentence is repeated in the Big Typescript, §94, p. 438, preceded by these words: "Erroneous application of our physical means of expression to sense data. 'Objects,' i.e. things, bodies in the space of the room—and 'objects' in the visual field; the shadow of a body on the wall as object!" [German in appendix.]

27. *Philosophical Remarks*, §230.

28. *Philosophical Remarks*, §57.

29. *Wittgenstein's Lectures, Cambridge, 1930–1932*, p. 82.

jects, on the one hand, and scientific theories, on the other, along the same lines, for he held that both presuppose hypotheses about the objects in question that go beyond that anything given in immediate experience. These hypotheses enable us to organize our experiential data and to regard them as a perspective on an objective, external world, the world natural science investigates. But an hypothesis has an infinite number of observational consequences and so can never be definitively verified; instead, it plays the role of a law that implies specific observational statements, or simply "propositions," as Wittgenstein called them. In his lectures for 1930–1931 Wittgenstein said that the term "proposition," "as generally understood," covers three distinct categories: not only "what I call propositions," namely statements about direct observation, but also hypotheses and mathematical propositions. Each of these categories has its own grammatical rules, but because the rules for truth-functions apply to all of them, he conceded that there was some legitimacy in the traditional terminology that classifies all of them as propositions. Wittgenstein compared propositions in his sense of the term to points on a graph and hypotheses to a line connecting these points; he also compared observational propositions to two-dimensional sections through a hypothetical three-dimensional body.[30] In each case, the point of the comparison is that the hypothetical entity provides a way of unifying the available data by conceiving of them as partial observations of a larger whole.

In the late 1920s, Wittgenstein distinguished between secondary hypotheses about empirical phenomena, immediate experience as primary, and the mystical by appealing to a logical distinction between what can be said about the phenomena by making factual assertions, what can only be shown by displaying the structure of our language, and what lies beyond the limits of language but nevertheless "shows itself." Frank Ramsey, who found such an attempt to dissolve the problems of philosophy entirely implausible—"[W]hat we can't say we can't say, and we can't whistle it either"[31]—summed up his understanding of that strategy in a cryptic note[32] that refers to different "levels" of Wittgenstein's philosophy:

3 ?   levels of philosophy   *Ludwig's*

        investigating world   = *scientific realism*

        the world *as* fiction   = *phenomenalism*

        mystic   = *transcendentalism*

The two kinds of type in this passage represent two different kinds of writing in the original. The words in plain type were written in a rather uneven hand, perhaps with a pencil; the words in italics are much more even and are written in ink. This information, together with the fact that the italicized words qualify the others, strongly suggests that the italicized words are a later addition. While such a note by itself is too sketchy to show anything more than that Ramsey thought it worthwhile to make

30. See *Philosophical Remarks*, ch. 22; Big Typescript §32, published as Appendix 6 of the *Philosophical Grammar*, pp. 219–223; "Solipsism," *Wittgenstein and the Vienna Circle*, p. 48.

31. Frank Ramsey, *Philosophical Papers*, p. 146. The jibe is in part an allusion to the great importance that Wittgenstein attached to music, and the fact that he was able to whistle, note for note, extensive passages from some of his favourite pieces.

32. Ramsey, unpublished note, Pittsburgh catalogue number 002-25-10.

a note of his construal, taken in context it does provide an elegant summary of the overall shape of Wittgenstein's thought at the time.

Although Ramsey's notes unequivocally record that Wittgenstein told him it was "nonsense to believe in anything not given in experience,"[33] Wittgenstein was never quite so explicit in his writing. Indeed, I think it would be a mistake to read such a view back into the *Tractatus*, for despite the striking passages that I have cited in this section, I shall be arguing that the author of that book deliberately avoided making any such clear-cut ontological commitments. Nevertheless, the view is clearly evident in his discussion of hypothesis and prediction in the *Philosophical Remarks*, where present experience has to give a sense to empirical propositions about anything that is not experientially given:

> What's essential is that I must be able to compare my expectation not only with what is to be regarded as its definitive answer (its verification or falsification), but also with how things stand at present. This alone makes the expectation into a picture.
>
> That is to say: it must make sense *now*.[34]

This phase of Wittgenstein's work is only sketched in the published writings, finding its fullest expression in his manuscripts from 1929 and the early 1930s and in the unpublished chapters of the Big Typescript entitled "Phenomenology" and "Idealism, etc." As a result, his transitional metaphysics of experience, and its subsequent rejection and critique, have not yet received the attention they deserve.

1.3 Wittgenstein's Methods

When Wittgenstein returned to Cambridge at the beginning of 1929, the distinction between the primary, the phenomenal world of experience, and the secondary, the physical world of material objects, must have seemed obvious and unavoidable. But in 1929 he set out to articulate the structure of the primary world, a paradoxical place where our ordinary concepts of objects, causality, self, and temporality no longer apply. That, in turn, led to the reemergence of previously suppressed concerns about the relationship betweeen the true world and the world of appearance, and the closely related problem of the relationship between ordinary language and its analysis.

Wittgenstein's transition from his earlier to his later philosophy is largely a matter of his seeing through the seemingly self-evident conception of philosophical method he had embraced in the *Tractatus* and gradually replacing it by an unsystematic plurality of methods. Though the Tractarian program of analysis is left highly schematic, Wittgenstein believed that, in principle, it could be given a precise and detailed articulation. In 1929 he returned to the task and soon realized that the notion of an elementary proposition, the logically independent atomic elements that would be identified at the end of any analysis, was logically flawed: such an analysis leads

---

33. Ramsey, unpublished manuscript, Pittsburgh catalogue number 004-21-02. The material is quoted in full in chapter 3, p. 78.

34. *Philosophical Remarks*, §229. Elsewhere, Wittgenstein makes a parallel claim about propositions about the past. See chapter 5, pp. 155ff.

to systems of interrelated propositions, not independent atoms. As a result, Wittgenstein rejected the logical atomism of the *Tractatus* for a conception of language as a system of calculi, formal systems characterized by their constitutive rules.

Wittgenstein's subsequent writing in 1929 marks a further break with his early work: in October 1929 he drafted the controversial first paragraph of the *Philosophical Remarks*, declaring that he no longer had "phenomenological language" as his goal. The work that led to that conclusion centred on the problem of understanding how the phenomena of immediate experience, on the one hand, and the physical propositions we produce—e.g., marks on a page, or vibrations in the air—on the other hand, can be directly compared with each other. On the conception of mind and language that had attracted Wittgenstein earlier that year, the significance of language ultimately consists in its connection with present experience. He had hoped to clarify the connection by producing a "phenomenological language," a language solely for the description of immediate experience. But now he became convinced that was impossible, or at least unnecessary.

Merrill Hintikka and Jaakko Hintikka have construed Wittgenstein's rejection of phenomenological language as a matter of replacing one theory of knowledge for another: they maintain that Wittgenstein gave up a phenomenalistic view, on which all significant uses of language are analysable into propositions about experiential phenomena, for the corresponding physicalistic view.[35] But their reading, on which Wittgenstein rejected one traditional epistemological thesis for another, does not do justice to Wittgenstein's methodological commitments. While he was certainly attracted by a number of different analyses during the 1910s, including physicalism, phenomenalism, and solipsism, as the *Notebooks 1914–1916* attest, the *Tractatus* does not lend itself easily to any of these construals, for it studiously avoids specifying the epistemological status of the elementary propositions. Nor does their reading do justice to the radical nature of Wittgenstein's break with the philosophical tradition in 1929. Rather than substituting one familiar kind of analysis for another, it consists in a rejection of the notion that any single analysis should be our goal in philosophy, and it led him to question the Cartesian conception of the mind that is responsible for so many of these problems. Wittgenstein now branded his earlier work as "dogmatic," precisely because he had placed so much weight on the claim that an analysis into elementary propositions was possible, but had failed to carry it out. In a discussion with Friedrich Waismann in 1931, he explained why he could not accept Waismann's *Theses*, an exposition of the *Tractatus* as a set of theses, dogmatically stated:

> I used to believe, for example, that it is the task of logical analysis to discover the elementary propositions . . . the elementary propositions could be specified later on. Only in recent years have I broken away from that error. At the time, I wrote in a manuscript of my book (this is not printed in the *Tractatus*), The answers to philosophical questions must never be surprising. In philosophy you cannot discover anything. I myself, however, had not clearly understood this and offended against it.
>
> The wrong conception which I want to object to in this connexion is the following, that we can hit upon something that we today cannot yet see, that we can

35. Merrill and Jaakko Hintikka, *Investigating Wittgenstein*, ch. 3.

discover something wholly new. The truth of the matter is that we have already got everything, and we have got it actually *present*; we need not wait for anything. We make our moves in the realm of the grammar of ordinary language, and this grammar is already there.[36]

In his post-*Tractatus* work, Wittgenstein recognized that he could not reconcile the Tractarian thesis that he had arrived at discoveries about the nature of our language with the idea that our language is in order as it is; on his later view, the philosopher has no such special dispensation that would allow him or her to operate outside the limits of language. The following passage, also from Wittgenstein's response to Waismann's *Theses*, is a particularly clear statement of his conception of the nature of philosophy:

> As regards your *Theses*, I once wrote, If there were theses in philosophy, they would have to be such that they do not give rise to disputes. For they would have to be put in such a way that everyone would say, Oh yes, that is of course obvious. . . . Controversy always arises through leaving out or failing to state clearly certain steps, so that the impression is given that a claim has been made that could be disputed. I once wrote, The only correct method of doing philosophy consists in not saying anything and leaving it to another person to make a claim. That is the method I now adhere to. What the other person is not able to do is to arrange the rules step by step and in the right order so that all questions are solved automatically.[37]

Wittgenstein immediately went on to offer the example of a rule of formal logic as an illustration of this general statement of his method:

> What I mean by that is the following: when we are talking about negation, for instance, the point is to give the rule "~~p = p." I do not assert anything. I only say that the structure of the grammar of "~" is such that "p" may be substituted for "~~p." Were you not also using the word "not" in that way? If that is admitted, then everything is settled. And that is how it is with grammar in general. The only thing we can do is *to tabulate rules*. If by questioning I have found out concerning a word that the other person at one time recognises these rules and, at another time, those rules, I will tell him, In that case you will have to distinguish exactly *how* you use it; *and there is nothing else I wanted to say*.[38]

The final sentence is in the past tense because Wittgenstein takes himself to be setting out not only his present view, but also what he had been doing in the *Tractatus*: investigating the grammar of our language, the rules we all follow. Our language has an underlying structure; philosophy elucidates that structure. Its results may be unexpected, but in a deeper sense, they cannot be surprising, for anyone who speaks a language knows them.

Wittgenstein aimed to bring about a change in the way philosophers see things, a change in perspective that would make us aware of what we ordinarily take for granted. In the *Philosophical Investigations*, he speaks of "turning our whole exami-

---

36. *Ludwig Wittgenstein and the Vienna Circle*, pp. 182–183, 9 December 1931.
37. *Ludwig Wittgenstein and the Vienna Circle*, pp. 183–184, 9 December 1931.
38. *Ludwig Wittgenstein and the Vienna Circle*, p. 184, 9 December 1931.

nation around,"[39] so that obvious facts about ordinary life and language undermine what other philosophers take for granted when they try to answer philosophical questions. There, Wittgenstein describes his own conception of his approach to philosophy as though he were simply stating incontestable commonplaces, but other philosophers had not recognized their significance. In sections 126–128, Wittgenstein summarizes how his later philosophy depends on drawing the reader's attention to uncontroversial observations about everyday life:

> Philosophy simply puts everything before us, and neither explains nor deduces anything.—Since everything lies open to view there is nothing to explain. For what is hidden, for example, is of no interest to us.
>
> One might also give the name "philosophy" to what is possible *before* all new discoveries and inventions.
>
> The work of the philosopher consists in assembling reminders for a particular purpose.
>
> If one tried to advance *theses* in philosophy, it would never be possible to debate them, because everyone would agree to them.[40]

This conception of philosophy and of philosophical theses, elaborated in the surrounding remarks, forms one of the major threads running through the development of Wittgenstein's work: he contrasts his approach to philosophy, which is not supposed to advance any theses at all, with the controversial theses advanced by most other philosophers.

In holding that there are certain principles implicit in what we ordinarily say and do that can be elucidated by philosophical investigation, Wittgenstein put himself in a philosophical tradition that goes back to the Platonic doctrine of recollection. But unlike Plato, who thought of learning as a matter of remembering doctrines learned in a past life, Wittgenstein holds that philosophy consists in reminding ourselves of the rules of our language, rules we ordinarily follow without thinking about them. The purpose of "assembling reminders" is to combat the urge to misunderstand our language. In this sense, he wrote: "Learning philosophy *really* is recollection. We remember that we really have used the words in this way."[41] For Wittgenstein, philosophy is not a matter of recollecting the forms from a previous life, a metaphysical domain we once knew. Instead, philosophy reminds us of something we already know, but find hard to put into words: it brings us back to the everyday.

Near the beginning of the chapter on "Philosophy" in the Big Typescript, Wittgenstein constrasts what he regards as the traditional understanding of the nature of philosophical problems with his own. On the old conception of philosophy, one drew a sharp line between the timeless and great problems of philosophy on the

39. *Philosophical Investigations*, §108.

40. *Philosophical Investigations*, §§126–128; cf. Big Typescript, §89, pp. 417, 419, 415, 419. The manuscript sources of the three remarks are MS 108, p. 259, 1930; MS 112, p. 235, 1931; MS 110, p. 259, 1931.

41. Big Typescript, §89, p. 419. Wittgenstein "once observed in a lecture that there was a similarity between his conception of philosophy . . . and the Socratic doctrine that knowledge is reminiscence; although he believed there were other things involved in the latter." Norman Malcolm, *Ludwig Wittgenstein: A Memoir*, p. 44.

one hand, and empirical problems on the other: "essential big universal problems and inessential, as it were, accidental problems."[42] He attributes the conception to "the great western philosophers," but it also fits the *Tractatus*. The book aims to solve certain central problems of philosophy, and it does so at an extremely high level of abstraction. He says that he now regards the preoccupation with the great problems of philosophy as a facet of the "dogmatism" of the *Tractatus*. As a result, he rejects the distinction between the "essential" problems and the rest, maintaining that there are no such *"great* essential problems in the scientific sense."[43]

During the early 1930s, Wittgenstein repeatedly stated that he had found a method that made "peaceful progress" possible; one of the sections in the "Philosophy" chapter of the Big Typescript is entitled "Philosophical Method. Possibility of peaceful progress."[44] The reference to "peaceful progress" was echoed in Wittgenstein's lectures. He said he had discovered a "new method," a break as decisive as the emergence of Galilean mechanics or the development of chemistry out of alchemy.[45] As a result "it was now possible for the first time that there should be 'skillful' philosophers, though of course there had in the past been 'great' philosophers."[46]

Wittgenstein's conception of the nature of philosophy in the early 1930s is both summarized and presented in the "Philosophy" chapter of the Big Typescript.[47] Many of the ideas there are familiar from the *Tractatus* and the *Philosophical Investigations*: philosophy is a matter of avoiding the traps language sets for us; it is supposed to point to misleading analogies and aim at a perspicuous representation of our language. Many of the best-known passages on philosophical method in the *Investigations* are already present in the Big Typescript. Wittgenstein states that "the work of the philosopher consists in collecting reminders for a particular purpose";[48] "philosophy may in no way interfere with the actual use of language, it can, therefore, in the end only describe it";[49] "if one tried to advance *theses* in philosophy, it would never be possible to debate them, because everyone would agree to them";[50] "the aspects of things that are most important for us are hidden because of their simplicity and familiarity. . . . [W]e fail to be struck by what, once seen, is most striking and powerful";[51] "a philosophical problem always has the form 'I don't know my way about.'"[52] In fact, such programmatic methodological passages in sections 108–133 of the *In-*

42. Big Typescript, §86, p. 407; *Culture and Value*, p. 10. Source: MS 110, p. 200, 22 June 1931.
43. Big Typescript, §86, p. 407; *Culture and Value*, p. 10. Source: MS 110, p. 200, 22 June 1931.
44. Big Typescript, §92, p. 431.
45. G. E. Moore, "Wittgenstein's Lectures in 1930–33," p. 322. Moore based this series of articles on the copious notes he took at the time.
46. Moore, "Wittgenstein's Lectures in 1930–33," p. 322.
47. Big Typescript, chapter 12, §§86–93 pp. 405–435; first published as "Philosophie . . ." Reprinted in *Philosophical Occasions*, pp. 160–199 with the original pagination shown in the margin.
48. Big Typescript, §89; p. 415; *Philosophical Investigations*, §127. The section is entitled "Method in philosophy: the surveyable representation of grammatical // linguistic // facts. The goal: surveyable arguments. Justice."
49. Big Typescript, §89, p. 417; *Philosophical Investigations*, §124.
50. Big Typescript, §89, p. 419; *Philosophical Investigations*, §128.
51. Big Typescript, §89, p. 419; *Philosophical Investigations*, §129.
52. Big Typescript, §89, p. 421; *Philosophical Investigations*, §123. (The *Investigations* drops the "always.")

vestigations are virtually the only passages from the period that occur in the final version of the *Philosophical Investigations*.[53]

Throughout his writing, Wittgenstein maintained that philosophical problems are due to our "running up against the limits of language." While the *Tractatus* treats these limits as the key to grasping the nature of self and world, Wittgenstein later saw them as a sign that the philosopher has been misled into trying to say something where there is nothing to be said or shown, other than the self-defeating nature of such attempts. In a passage in the Big Typescript that is repeated almost verbatim in the *Philosophical Investigations*, he states:

> The results of philosophy are the discovery of one or another piece of plain nonsense and of bumps that the understanding has got by running up against the limits // end // of language. These bumps make us understand // see // the value of the discovery.[54]

A few pages later, Wittgenstein writes:

> The real discovery is the one that makes me capable of stopping doing philosophy when I want to. —The one that gives philosophy peace, so that it is no longer tormented by questions which bring *itself* into question. —Instead, a method is shown by examples; and the series of examples can be broken off.[55]

This material was drafted in 1931;[56] in the Big Typescript it begins the section entitled "Philosophical Method. Possibility of peaceful progress."[57] There, Wittgenstein likens his old approach to dividing an infinitely long piece of paper lengthwise, producing a small number of infinitely long strips. He compares his new method to dividing the same strip crosswise, into short strips. In other words, he had given up seeing philosophy in terms of a few insoluble problems.[58] Instead, he would divide them into many smaller ones, each of them finite and soluble. The old conception sets us impossible tasks; the new one turns the seemingly central problems into many tasks that can be done piecemeal. The philosopher who looks at things the wrong way around produces

> the *greatest* difficulty. It is as if we wanted to grasp the unlimited strips and complained that it can't be done piecemeal. Of course it can't, if by a piece one means an infinite longitudinal strip. But it may well be done, if one means a cross-strip. —But in that case we never get to the end of our work! —Of course not, for it has no end.

---

53. The whole of *Philosophical Investigations*, §§119, 122–124, 126–129, and parts of §§116, 118, 120, and 133 can be traced back to manuscripts dating from 1930–1931. The only other materials in the *Investigations* dating from the period before 1933 are §§108, 436, and 474 (in parts) and all of §460. Most of the rest of §§89–133 was written in 1937.

54. Big Typescript, §90 p. 425. Cf. MS 108, p. 247, 1930; *Philosophical Investigations*, §119. In the *Investigations*, Wittgenstein omitted the words "end" and "understand."

55. *Philosophical Investigations*, §133.

56. MS 112, p. 93, 25 October 1931.

57. Big Typescript, §92, p. 431.

58. In a passage from the "Notes for Lectures on 'Sense Data' and 'Private Experience'" that was left out of the first published edition of that text, Wittgenstein wrote: "The philosophical puzzle seems insoluble if we are frank with ourselves and *is* insoluble. That is, till we change our question." *Philosophical Occasions*, p. 253.

(We want to replace wild conjectures and explanations by quiet weighing of linguistic facts.)[59]

Wittgenstein retained this passage in his later work; in the Early Investigations, it forms the second half of section 118, following the text of the published section 133, and it also turns up in the *Zettel* collection (section 447.) But his commitment to bringing philosophy under control was counterbalanced by the hold philosophy had over him. In a letter, Rhees recalled a conversation with Wittgenstein that ended in the following way: "As he was leaving, this time, he said to me roughly this: 'In my book I say that I am able to leave off with a problem in philosophy when I want to. But that's a lie; I can't'."[60] Wittgenstein aimed to bring philosophy to an end, yet in doing so, he was continually struggling with philosophical problems. The traces of this struggle are much clearer in his drafts than in his most polished work, however, where many of his readers have only found their own reflections.

If the significance of his work now shifted to the misunderstandings that had misled him, what was there left to do? Wittgenstein's answer was that his philosophy has to clarify the way we actually use language: he aims "to remove particular misunderstandings."[61] The goal of providing a presuppositionless phenomenological language, a description of experience without any hypothetical additions, was replaced by the project of describing our actual use of language, in such a way as to dissolve philosophical problems.

While Wittgenstein gave up the idea that a canonical analysis is possible or desirable in his later work, he still thought of himself as using language to get his readers to see their way out of philosophical problems. But now his aim was to get his readers to give up formal analyses and see alternatives. In section 130 of the *Philosophical Investigations*, Wittgenstein emphasized that his descriptions of "language-games"—real or imaginary ways of using language—were not intended as preliminary studies for a systematic account of language, first approximations to something more systematic. While the picture theory had made use of a few paradigmatic examples to get us to see the essential similarities between propositions and pictures, the point of his use of language-games is precisely to subvert any such systematic conception. By comparing the language-game with what we actually do and say, we are supposed to gain a better understanding of linguistic practice: "The language-games are . . . set up as *objects of comparison* which are meant to throw light on the facts of our language by way not only of similarities, but also of dissimilarities."[62]

In his later work, Wittgenstein insists that it is extremely important that we always give genuine examples in illustrating a logical system, and not qualify our examples by saying "these are not the ideal cases which the calculus really deals with, which we don't yet have."[63] Instead, we have to look at our current use of that calculus; it is no failing of the calculus that it does not capture every aspect of the objects to

59. Big Typescript, §92, pp. 431–432.
60. Garth Hallett, *A Companion to Wittgenstein's "Philosophical Investigations,"* p. 230.
61. *Philosophical Grammar*, p. 115. Cf. Big Typescript, §15, p. 67 and the back of p. 66; MS 114, Part II, pp. 105–106.
62. *Philosophical Investigations*, §130, 1937; cf. MS 157b, p. 33; MS 115, p. 81.
63. Early Investigations, §107 (109). The first number is the actual number in Wittgenstein's typescript; the second is the result of von Wright's renumbering to correct for double counting.

which it is applied. Rather, the real mistake is to "promise that its use lies in the cloudy distance."[64] The point is summarized in the following rough note, jotted down between a lengthy series of examples: "We must be clear that our examples are not preparations to the analysis of the actual meaning of the expression so-and-so (Nicod) but giving them effects that analysis."[65] When Wittgenstein says here that giving his examples effects the analysis, he does not mean that we should think of our language as constructed out of simpler language-games. The point of his examples is rather to help us understand our language by seeing the similarities and dissimilarities between the constructed language-games and our own:

> When I describe certain simple language-games, this is not in order to construct from them gradually the processes of our developed language—or of thinking—which only leads to injustices (Nicod and Russell). I simply set forth the games as what they are, and let them shed their light on the particular problems.[66]

In the later 1940s, he gave the following general reply to complex counterexamples that supposedly undermine his description of simple language-games by showing "that our theory doesn't yet correspond to the facts":

> More involved cases are just more involved cases. For if what were in question were a theory, it might indeed be said: It's no use looking at these special cases, they offer no explanation of *the* most important cases. On the contrary, the simple language-games play a quite different role. They are poles of a description, not the ground-floor of a theory.[67]

Wittgenstein used his examples of actual and possible language-games to get his readers to look more carefully at what we take for granted in our ordinary use of language and so recognize the limitations of systematic analyses. One can apply that observation to his choice of the term "language-game" itself, one of the very few new terms that Wittgenstein introduces in his later philosophical writing: it is designed to bring out certain similarities between language and games, not to identify them. To some critics, to compare our use of language to a game is to trivialize it. But that is to overlook the very point of Wittgenstein's notion of an object of comparison: he is not claiming that language is nothing more than a game, or a loosely related collection of games, but rather that comparing our use of language with certain games, both actual ones and imaginary ones, will help us understand both the similarities and dissimilarities between the games and language. The point of the comparison is to bring out certain analogies between our use of language and playing a game: both are activities, things we do, and both involve the use of rules.

Most of Wittgenstein's real and imagined examples of language-games involve relatively simple everyday activities: bringing and fetching, counting, obeying orders, and the like. He suggests that if we examine such games and compare them with the theories that philosophers ordinarily pursue, we will see that such theories do not

64. Early Investigations, §107 (109).
65. MS 148, p. 21, 1934–1935. In English.
66. Quoted and translated by Rhees in the introduction to the *Blue and Brown Books*, p. viii (no source given). Cf. Early Investigations, §115 (117), and *Philosophical Investigations*, §130.
67. *Remarks on the Philosophy of Psychology*, Vol. 1, §633.

deliver the insights they promise—that their language-games are secondary and derivative when compared with everyday life:

> Our mistake is to look for an explanation where we ought to look at the facts
> as a "proto-phenomenon." That is, where we ought to have said: *this language-
> game is played.*
>
> It's not a matter of explaining a language-game by means of our experiences,
> but of noting a language-game.
>
> . . . —Look on the language-game as *primary.*[68]

This strategy is applied not only to the language we use in everyday life, but also to
the ways of speaking that lead philosophers to distinguish between a primary realm
of immediate experience and a secondary domain of physical objects:

> One says, sense data are more primary than physical objects—but our nota-
> tion in terms of "physical objects" should still in the end refer to sense-data. There-
> fore surely only one *notation* can be primary and one secondary. And why should
> one not call the single notation that has proved itself the primary? Or why talk
> here of primary and secondary at all? For a misunderstanding is at the bottom of
> that. If one says a "physical object" is only a logical construction erected out of
> sense-data, then what one has constructed is after all only a language-game.[69]

In the "Notes for Lectures on 'Sense Data' and 'Private Experience,'" Wittgenstein
writes: "I want to say: 'the visual world is like this . . .'—but why *say* anything?"[70]
Taken out of context, the remark could be read as an example of his earlier strategy
of shifting back and forth between the desire to express his solipsistic intuitions and
recognizing that they cannot be stated, just as the *Tractatus* maintains that while any
attempt to put solipsism into words will lead to nonsense, what the solipsist wants to
say embodies a crucial philosophical insight. Instead, Wittgenstein continues the
discussion by rejecting such an ambivalent attempt at compromise, pointing to the
emptiness of the words he had been tempted to utter:

> But the point is that I don't establish a relation between a person and what is
> seen. All I do is that alternately I point in front of me and to myself.
>
> //Solipsism.// The conception of solipsism does not stretch to games. The other
> can play chess as well as I. I.e., when we play a lang[uage] game we are on the
> same level.[71]

In the *Blue Book*, Wittgenstein maintains that philosophical theses use words that
are meaningless, because, taken out of context, the words in question still *seem* meaningful as they can each be used meaningfully in different contexts: "We are like people
who think that pieces of wood shaped more or less like chess or draught pieces and
standing on a chess board make a game, even if nothing has been said as to how they

---

68. Philosophical Investigations, §§654–656.

69. MS 121, pp. 98–99 (counting from the front), 5 September 1938. [German in appendix.]

70. "Notes for Lectures on 'Sense Data' and 'Private Experience,'" p. 299; *Philosophical Occasions*, p. 258.

71. "Notes for Lectures on 'Sense Data' and 'Private Experience,'" (not included in the version
edited by Rhees); *Philosophical Occasions*, p. 258.

are to be used."[72] So, just because someone says *"This* is what's really seen" with the solipsistic intention of picking out the contents of his or her visual experience, that does not mean that anything significant has been said, for pointing cannot, by itself, ensure that anything has been picked out: "[A]lthough I make the gesture of pointing, I don't point to one thing as opposed to another. This is as when travelling in a car and feeling in a hurry, I instinctively press against something in front of me as though I could push the car from inside."[73] The example of trying to speed a car by pushing from the inside is not only meant to illustrate the point that no effort to point or push can succeed if one does not have an independent place to start from, but is also a way of drawing our attention to the characteristic gestures and tics that accompany such philosophical exercises, akin to the lapses Freud anatomized in his studies of the psychopathology of everyday life.

In a conversation with Malcolm, Wittgenstein summed up his approach in these terms: "In philosophy one feels *forced* to look at a concept in a certain way. What I do is to suggest, or even invent, other ways of looking at it."[74] What Wittgenstein's later philosophy "puts before us" is our use of language: what we ordinarily do and say, how we use words, and what we do with them. But the point of the description, its "particular purpose," is precisely to do away with the philosophical problems that occupy most philosophers' attention.

> When philosophers use a word—"knowledge," "being," "object," "I," "proposition," "name,"—and try to grasp the *essence* of the thing, one must always ask oneself: is the word ever actually used this way in the language[75] which is its original home?
>
> What *we* do is to bring words back from their metaphysical to their everyday use.[76]

Wittgenstein maintained that the doctrines and theses about the nature of knowledge, reality, self, and language that are traditionally debated by philosophers, and the positions they give rise to, such as Socratic analysis, Cartesian dualism, behaviourism, physicalism, phenomenalism, scepticism, and solipsism, arise out of philosophically motivated misunderstandings of everyday language. His principal aim in his later work was to uncover the mistakes that lead people to formulate philosophical theses. He does so by drawing his readers' attention to what they already know as speakers of a language, but do not usually explicitly articulate. According to Wittgenstein, philosophical problems arise out of misunderstanding our ordinary use of language and consist in trying to explain the nature of language when no explanation is possible. The problems are to be dissolved by describing our use of language in a way that enables to see how our language really works. In the *Philosophical*

72. *Blue Book*, p. 72.

73. *Blue Book*, p. 71.

74. Malcolm, *Ludwig Wittgenstein: A Memoir*, p. 43.

75. The German word is simply *Sprache*, language, not *Sprachspiel*, language-game, but the published translation is "language-game." While my quotations from Wittgenstein's published writings are based on the published translations, they are sometimes rather more literal.

76. *Philosophical Investigations*, §116; cf. Big Typescript, §91, p. 430. Source: MS 109, p. 246, 1930.

Investigations, Wittgenstein set out the relationship between his philosophy and the philosophical tradition he wanted to end in the following terms:

> And we may not advance any kind of theory. There must not be anything hypothetical in our considerations. We must do away with all *explanation*, and description alone must take its place. And this description gets its light, that is to say its purpose, from the philosophical problems. These are, of course, not empirical problems; they are solved, rather, by an insight into the workings of our language, and that in such a way as to make us recognize those workings: *in despite of* an urge to misunderstand them. The problems are solved, not by producing a new experience, but by arranging what we have always known. Philosophy is a struggle against the bewitchment of our understanding by means of language.[77]

Here, as in his earlier work, Wittgenstein aims at a nonhypothetical description of the given. But what is "given" to philosophy in his later work is, in the first instance, our ordinary language, not the content of immediate experience. What makes his later investigations radically different from his earlier linguistic phenomenology is his recognition of the difficulties arising from the fact that language is both the means of bewitchment and the means by which we can struggle against bewitchment. The ambiguity is captured in the final sentence of the passage just quoted, which supports both readings equally well.

The following passage summarizes Wittgenstein's conception of the movements that lead the philosophical sceptic to question our knowledge of the world, and then back to "the standpoint of common sense":

> When we think about the relation of the objects surrounding us to our personal experiences of them, we are sometimes tempted to say that these personal experiences are the material of which reality consists. . . . When we think in this way we seem to lose our firm hold on the objects surrounding us. And instead we are left with a lot of separate personal experiences of different individuals. These personal experiences again seem vague and seem to be in constant flux. Our language seems not to have been made to describe them. We are tempted to think that in order to clear up such matters philosophically our ordinary language is too coarse, that we need a more subtle one.
>
> We seem to have made a discovery—which I could describe by saying that the ground on which we stood and which appeared to be firm and reliable was found to be boggy and unsafe.[78]

The "discovery" Wittgenstein describes is the sceptic's discovery that we do not know anything about the external world and that all that is real is the content of experience. Wittgenstein's choice of words also alludes to some of the characteristic aspects of his own engagement with scepticism in the 1930s: he thinks of scepticism as a temptation, a temptation that presents itself as a discovery, the idealistic or solipsistic "discovery" that immediate experience is "primary," all there really is. Echoing Descartes's insistence that his doubts should only be entertained when one has

---

77. *Philosophical Investigations*, §109.
78. *Blue Book*, p. 45. The passage introduces an extended discussion of these topics that occupies the remainder of the book, which was dictated to those who attended his classes during the 1933–1934 academic year.

the time and inclination to meditate, and Hume's inclination to dispel scepticism by returning to social life, Wittgenstein goes on to observe that the uncertainty disappears once we revert to the standpoint of common sense: "—That is, this happens when we philosophize; for as soon as we revert to the standpoint of common sense this *general* uncertainty disappears."[79] Wittgenstein's later response to scepticism is to attack the moves that allow it to get started, to show how the philosophical sceptic is using language in a suspicious way, to bring out the priority of our prephilosophical relation to the world, and to turn to investigating how we were tempted out of it in the first place. As in the *Tractatus* and the early 1930s, Wittgenstein holds that what a sceptic or idealist wants to say is, strictly speaking, senseless. But he no longer simply dismisses it while implicitly endorsing what the solipsist wants to say: instead, he turns to the train of thought that motivated it to understand and treat the sceptical temptation. At one point he wrote: "In philosophy we are deceived by an illusion. But this /an/ illusion is also something, and I must at some time place it completely clearly before my eyes, before I can say that it is only an illusion."[80]

In the early 1930s, Wittgenstein stressed the similarities between his dissolving a philosophical problem and resolving a problem in psychoanalysis: in both cases, the difficulty is primarily emotional, rather than intellectual, and can only be overcome by acknowledging what motivated the problem. On some occasions, Wittgenstein even described himself as a "follower" and "disciple of Freud,"[81] though most of his specific comments on Freud's work are highly critical. The chapter on "Philosophy" in the Big Typescript begins with a discussion of some of these Freudian themes; the first section is entitled "Philosophical difficulty not the intellectual difficulty of the sciences, rather the difficulty of a switchover. Resistance of the *will* has to be overcome."[82] The section begins with a discussion of the observation that there is a sense in which one doesn't really give anything up when one rejects a philosophical thesis. For it isn't as if there is something meaningful that we can no longer say; we simply recognize that a certain combination of words, the words that supposedly expressed the thesis in question, are senseless, and so give up using them. The idea that the philosopher is groping for a way of expressing an esoteric insight that we can't actually say is itself to be given up. In the *Philosophical Grammar*, Wittgenstein writes that the words the philosopher wants to say are "excluded from our language like some arbitrary noise, and the reason for their *explicit* exclusion can only be that *we are tempted* to confuse them with a sentence of our language."[83] But recognizing that a given philosophical thesis makes no sense is only part of what is involved in giving up a philosophical error: one also has to be able to explain why one wanted to say those words. If they are flat-out meaningless, what was responsible for the *appearance* of depth?

Wittgenstein's answer is that one may well have a great deal invested in a certain

79. *Blue Book*, p. 45.
80. MS 110, p. 239, 1931. [German in appendix.]
81. See Rhees, Preface to "Conversations on Freud," in *Lectures and Conversations on Aesthetics, Psychology and Religious Belief.*
82. Big Typescript, §86, p. 406. Section titles in the Big Typescript are double underlined, but that is not reflected in the typeface of this and subsequent quotations.
83. *Philosophical Grammar*, §83; cf. MS 116, p. 78, 1934; *Philosophical Investigations*, §500.

way of seeing things: "It can be hard not use an expression, as it is hard to hold back tears or an outburst of anger."[84] While in one sense one does not give up anything—one does not have to give up *saying* something—one does have to change one's outlook:

> What makes a subject hard to understand—if it's something significant and important—is not that before you can understand it you need to be specially trained in abstruse matters, but the contrast between understanding the subject and what most people *want* to see. Because of this the very things which are most obvious may become the hardest of all to understand. What has to be overcome is a difficulty having to do with the will, rather than the intellect.[85]

And so it is a matter of developing a certain kind of understanding of how one approaches things, and what drives one to do so: "Working in philosophy—like work in architecture in many respects—is really more a working on oneself. On one's own interpretation. On one's way of seeing things. (And what one expects of them.)"[86] The following section in the "Philosophy" chapter of the Big Typescript, entitled "Philosophy points to the misleading analogies in the use of language," sets out Wittgenstein's conception of the crucial role of analogies in philosophy, both in creating philosophical problems and in his own response to those problems.[87] In variant drafts, Wittgenstein speaks of correcting a philosophical error as a matter of "pointing out an analogy which has been followed, and that this analogy does not hold" and "pointing out the analogy along which one has been thinking but which one has not recognised as an analogy."[88] The changeover, if it is to be of any value, cannot simply be a matter of changing one's beliefs, or even one's outlook: it must also include an explicit acknowledgment of where one went wrong. Such an analogy is like an illusion that can still deceive us even after we have recognized that it is an illusion. Wittgenstein offers the example of a thing that appears to be a person when seen from a distance, but when we get closer, is seen to be a tree stump: "We have hardly moved away a little when we put these explanations out of our mind and it looks a certain shape; if we look more closely we see another; now we move away again, etc., etc."[89] He also calls it "a continual struggle and discomfort (a continuous irritation as it were.)"[90] The aim of these striking analogies is to bring the philosophical use of analogy down to earth. Instead of trying to grasp the hidden structure underlying everyday life, Wittgenstein now thinks of himself as getting hold of the analogies that had generated those illusions:

> The philosopher strives to find the liberating word, that is, the word that finally lets us grasp that which, ungraspable, has continually weighed upon our consciousness.

84. Big Typescript, §86, p. 406.
85. Big Typescript, §86, pp. 406–407. *Culture and Value*, p. 17. Source: MS 112, p. 223, 22 November 1931.
86. Big Typescript, §86, p. 407. *Culture and Value*, p. 16. Source: MS 112, p. 47, 14 October 1931.
87. Big Typescript, §87, p. 408.
88. Big Typescript, §87, pp. 408–409.
89. Big Typescript, §87, p. 409.
90. Big Typescript, §87, p. 409.

(It's as if one has a hair on one's tongue; one feels it but can't get hold of //grasp// it and so can't get rid of it.)[91]

Like a psychoanalyst, Wittgenstein aimed to find the words that would go to the root of the problem, making it possible to remove it once and for all:

One of the most important tasks is to express all the false trains of thought so characteristically that the reader says "Yes, that's precisely how I meant it." To copy the physiognomy of this error.

Then of course we can only convict another person of a mistake if he acknowledges that this really is the expresssion of his feeling. //. . .if he (really) acknowledges this expression as the correct expression of his feeling.//

That is to say, it's only if he acknowledges it as such that it *is* the correct expression. (Psychoanalysis.)

What the other acknowledges is the analogy that I offer him as the source of his thought.[92]

In his later philosophy, Wittgenstein came to see that our use of language depends on a background of common behaviour and shared practices, on "forms of life." As a result, he rejected the idea that the philosopher can achieve a privileged vantage point, maintaining that "the place I really have to get to is a place I must already be at now."[93] The point of his later philosophy is still to achieve insight into the nature of our language, but that insight is only supposed to undermine the grammatical illusions that generate philosophical problems, not generate yet another philosophical theory. He gave up the idea that the philosopher can achieve an objective standpoint outside our ordinary lives, a "view from nowhere," as it were, recognizing that the very notion of a standpoint outside language is an illusion, an illusion generated by certain distinctively philosophical ways of speaking and thinking. In other words, he saw that Tractarian attempts to show what cannot be said were ultimately just as flawed as the philosophical tradition the book was supposed to bring to an end. Instead, he turned to showing how traditional philosophers, including the one who had written the *Tractatus*, had misunderstood the working of our language, exposing the protophilosophical moves that lead to the formulation of philosophical theories. His later philosophy "leaves everything as it is":[94] that is, he aims to expose traditional philosophical claims to answer philosophical questions as meaningless, while providing no substantive answers to those questions himself. At one point in

91. Big Typescript, §87, p. 409.

92. Big Typescript, §87, p. 410; Source: MS 110, pp. 230–231; for the paragraphs immediately before and after this passage in MS 110, see chapter 4, p. 105.

93. *Culture and Value*, p. 7. Source: MS 109, p. 207, 6 November 1930. The remark from which it is taken, which is, in turn, part of a draft for an introduction to the book Wittgenstein was writing, reads as follows:

I might say: if the place I want to get to could only be reached by way of a ladder, I would give up trying to get there. For the place I really have to get to is a place I must already be at now.
Anything that I might reach by climbing a ladder does not interest me.

94. *Philosophical Investigations*, §124.

the *Philosophical Investigations*, he summarizes his response to philosophical theorizing in these terms: "What I want to teach: to turn a piece of unclear nonsense into clear nonsense."[95] In the early 1930s, he set out his conception of the relationship between his work and traditional philosophizing in equally stark terms:

> The person with a "healthy human understanding" who reads a former philosopher, thinks (and not without right): "Mere nonsense!" If that person hears me, he thinks—rightly, again—"Nothing but boring truisms!" And so the aspect of philosophy has changed. (I want to say: "this is the way such a thing looks from different standpoints.")[96]

But his insistence that the change of view he aimed to produce was simply a matter of seeing that he was stating obvious truisms was balanced by a recognition that philosophical problems can be extremely complex, and that their solution, like untying a knot, involves undoing all the moves that one made in tying the knot, moves that one took for granted when tying it.

Wittgenstein spoke of the insight into the structure of our language he aimed at as an *Übersicht*. The term plays a central role in his later work, but it is notoriously difficult to translate into English. It literally means an overview, but connotes a more thorough and intimate understanding than the English words suggest; "clear view" is perhaps a better approximation. Anscombe's translation of the *Philosophical Investigations* does not offer a uniform translation for the term, mainly using "surveyable" and "perspicuous"; "surveyable" seems closer to the sense of the German. In the "Philosophy" chapter of the Big Typescript, Wittgenstein writes that

> The concept of a surveyable representation is of fundamental significance for us. It designates the form of account we give, the way we see things. (A kind of "*Weltanschauung*," as is apparently typical of our time. Spengler.)
>
> This surveyable representation produces just that understanding which consists in "seeing connections." Hence the importance of finding *intermediate cases*.[97]

These "intermediate cases" are closely related to Wittgenstein's "objects of comparison": cases whose similarities and dissimilarities to the situations that puzzle us when philosophizing enable us to orient ourselves.

In the *Investigations*, Wittgenstein compared our language with "an ancient city: a maze of little streets and squares, of old and new houses, and of houses with additions from various periods; and this surrounded by a multitude of new boroughs with straight regular streets and uniform houses."[98] His positive contribution to understanding the structure of our language, providing an "overview" of the city, is a matter of getting to know the lay of the land, surveying the twists and turns we habitually and unreflectively make when we go about our everyday business. As Wittgenstein

95. *Philosophical Investigations*, §464.
96. TS 219, p. 6. An appendix to the Big Typescript. "Healthy human understanding" is a fairly literal translation of Wittgenstein's expression "*gesundem Menschenverstand*"; but it is worth noting that on another occasion, he offered the English "common sense" as an alternative to this expression (MS 107, p. 240). [German in appendix.] For a useful discussion of Wittgenstein's notion of the "healthy human understanding," see J. C. Edwards, *Ethics Without Philosophy*.
97. Big Typescript, §89, p. 417. Cf. *Philosophical Investigations*, §122.
98. *Philosophical Investigations*, §18. Probably November or December, 1936.

puts it at one point: "A philosophical problem has the form: 'I don't know my way about.'"[99]

Wittgenstein did not think of philosophical problems as merely technical; he thought of them as a form of intellectual neurosis, calling for self-examination and, above all, treatment. Immediately before some of the central remarks in his discussion of a "language which describes my inner experiences and which only I myself can understand,"[100] he writes:

> What we "are tempted to say" . . . is, of course, not philosophy; but it is its raw material. Thus for example, what a mathematician is inclined to say about the objectivity and reality of mathematical facts, is not a philosophy of mathematics, but something for philosophical treatment.
>
> The philosopher treats a question; like an illness.[101]

The following remark, written during 1942–1943, conveys some sense of the importance he attached to the contrast between health and sickness in his conception of philosophy:

> The philosopher is the man who has to cure himself of many sicknesses of the understanding before he can arrive at the notions of the healthy human understanding.
>
> If in life we are surrounded by death, so in healthy understanding we are surrounded by madness.[102]

Wittgenstein's later treatment of philosophical questions, unlike the approach he takes in the *Tractatus*, does not fall back on an appeal to an inexpressible objective order that supposedly validates a particular view of the world. Instead, he emphasizes aspects of everyday life that we ordinarily take for granted, in order to get us to see that these obvious facts undermine what we take for granted when we try to answer philosophical questions:

> The aspects of things that are most important for us are hidden because of their simplicity and familiarity. (One is unable to notice something—because it is always before one's eyes.) The real foundations of his enquiry do not strike a man at all. Unless *that* fact has at some time struck him. —And this means: we fail to be struck by what, once seen, is most striking and most powerful.[103]

As if to confirm Wittgenstein's insistence that philosophers are unable to recognize what we ordinarily take for granted, there has been very little understanding of what he meant by talking of the "real foundations" of enquiry as simple and obvious. Most expositors refuse to take him at his word, preferring to search for passages that, taken

99. *Philosophical Investigations*, §123.

100. *Philosophical Investigations*, §256. I avoid the term "private language argument" here, a term that occurs nowhere in Wittgenstein's published writing and has given rise to a literature that only makes occasional contact with Wittgenstein's discussion of mind and language.

101. *Philosophical Investigations*, §§254–255.

102. *Remarks on the Foundations of Mathematics*, Part IV, §53, p. 157. Cf. the following passage from MS 150, p. 59, 1935-36, composed in English: "Philosophizing is an illness and we are trying to describe minutely its symptoms, clinical appearance." See also the discussion of *Philosophical Remarks* §§17–18, chapter 6, p. 166.

103. *Philosophical Investigations*, §129. Cf. Big Typescript, §89, p. 419.

out of context, will enable them to find whatever thesis they want hidden in his writing, rather than the change of perspective that he aimed to bring about. For instance, Saul Kripke, in his influential study, *Wittgenstein on Rules and Private Language*, argues that Wittgenstein advocated a new and extremely powerful form of scepticism about meaning, a scepticism on which it is always possible that one's explanations of what one means by one's words may be misunderstood. Characteristically, Kripke lays great stress on Wittgenstein's summing up of "our paradox," in section 201 of the *Philosophical Investigations*—namely, that "no course of action could be determined by a rule, because every course of action can be made out to accord with the rule"—yet he gives very little attention to his initial formulation of the paradox.[104] In section 143, however, where Wittgenstein introduces his discussion of the task of continuing a series of numbers, the basis for Kripke's "sceptical paradox," he does not ask us to imagine that we ourselves do not know how to continue the series. Instead, he provides a number of examples of how communication with a child learning the series might break down. The point of these examples is to get us to see that "our pupil's capacity to learn may come to an end"[105] and so how much "stage-setting" has to be in place in order for one person to get another to follow a rule. Wittgenstein is not arguing that we should ordinarily raise such sceptical doubts, or that a refutation of every conceivable doubt is necessary, for in practice the normal background of training and exhibiting correct behaviour is sufficient for us to say the person understands. Instead, he is trying to show us the importance of the context as a precondition for grasping the rule.[106]

In the next remark, Wittgenstein explains the intended effect of the story he has just told about someone who is learning the natural numbers:

> What do I mean when I say "the pupil's capacity to learn *may* come to an end here"? Do I say this from my own experience? Of course not. (Even if I have had such experience.) Then what I am doing with that proposition? Well, I should like you to say: "Yes, it's true, that's conceivable too, that might happen too!" —But was I trying to draw someone's attention to the fact that he is capable of imagining that? —I wanted to put that picture before him, and his *acceptance* of the picture consists in his now being inclined to regard a given case differently; that is, to compare it with *this* rather than *that* set of pictures. I have changed his *way of looking at things*. (Indian mathematicians: "Look at this.")[107]

In the Early Investigations, Wittgenstein explains the parenthetical allusion: "I once read somewhere that a geometrical figure, with the words 'Look at this', serves as a proof for Indian mathematicians. This looking too effects an alteration in one's way of seeing."[108] Argument is not the only way of changing another's mind, or proving one's point; another method is to present someone with an example or com-

---

104. For further discussion of Kripke's reading of Wittgenstein, see chapter 6, §3.

105. *Philosophical Investigations*, §143, final sentence, taken up again in §144.

106. Significantly, the story of the wayward child follows a lengthy recapitulation of the points about ostension and rule-following that Wittgenstein has been developing since the first section of the *Philosophical Investigations*.

107. *Philosophical Investigations*, §144.

108. Early Investigations, §126 (128.) These words, with "certain" inserted before "Indian," are repeated in *Zettel*, §461.

parison that will change his or her "way of looking at things." Wittgenstein made extensive use of this method in both his earlier and his later work. But while his earlier use of such stories is intended to establish a particular way of seeing things that supposedly cannot be stated directly, in his later work, the point of the examples is precisely to get us to see alternatives to any one way of looking at things. In effect, Wittgenstein takes the idea that an analogy can point to an inexpressible truth and turns it around. The analogy is not a means to an otherwise inexpressible truth; rather, the conviction that the analogy points to an inexpressible truth is itself a product of the analogy's hold over the philosopher. In seeing how that came about, one sees not only how the analogy misled us but also how it concealed itself.

I

WITTGENSTEIN'S
EARLY PHILOSOPHY

2

Logic and Language

2.1 The Picture Theory

In his biographical memoir of Wittgenstein, Georg Henrik von Wright tells the following story about how Wittgenstein arrived at the picture theory of meaning:

> It was in the autumn of 1914, on the Eastern Front. Wittgenstein was reading in a magazine about a lawsuit in Paris concerning an automobile accident. At the trial, a miniature model of the accident was presented before the court. The model here served as a proposition, that is, as a description of a possible state of affairs. It had this function owing to a correspondence between the parts of the model (the miniature houses, cars, people) and things (houses, cars, people) in reality. It now occurred to Wittgenstein that one might reverse the analogy and say that a *proposition* serves as a model or *picture*, by virtue of a similar correspondence between *its* parts and the world.[1]

In other words, Wittgenstein saw that one could, so to speak, take the ordinary way of looking at the model of the accident in the law court as a special kind of statement and turn it around. Instead of treating the model as an unusual type of statement, a particularly graphic way of representing a traffic accident, he was struck by the idea that any statement, regardless of whether it is spoken or thought, must somehow model what it represents. Comparing the nature of a *Satz*—a term that can be translated as "sentence," "statement," or "proposition," depending on the context in which it is used—with the model in the law court was supposed to bring out aspects of the statement that are not ordinarily noticed. Like the model, it can be construed as composed of parts that stand for objects, and the arrangement of those parts as expressing the proposition that the objects in question are arranged in a corresponding manner. And so the model became a paradigm with which to understand the functioning of language.

Wittgenstein used the German word "*Bild*" to talk about the model, a term usually translated as "picture"; as a result, the theory of meaning it inspired is generally known as the picture theory. While both words cover such things as images, film

---

1. G. H. von Wright, "A Biographical Sketch," in Malcolm, *Ludwig Wittgenstein: A Memoir*, p. 8. Malcolm gives a similar report on p. 57. Actually, Wittgenstein could not have been at the Eastern front at the time, as he did not go there until late March, 1916; see Brian McGuinness, *Wittgenstein: A Life. Young Ludwig*, pp. 237–238.

frames, drawings, and paintings, the idea of a three-dimensional model is more readily conveyed by the German "*Bild*" than the English "picture." So while I will follow established usage and not talk of Wittgenstein's "model theory of meaning," it is important not to be misled: the theory involves generalizing from what models, pictures, and the like are supposed to have in common, and treats two-dimensional pictures as just one kind of *Bild*.

Talking later about the overall point of the picture theory, Wittgenstein stressed the use of the picture as a paradigm, a model that was supposed to make clear the essential similarities between propositions, pictures, and any other representation. He explicitly acknowledged that the idea was far from novel:

> The word "picture" has one advantage: it has helped me and many other people to make something clear by indicating a common feature and pointing out: "So that is what matters!" We then have the feeling, "Aha! Now I see, a proposition and a picture are of the same kind."[2]

In a footnote to his retelling of Wittgenstein's story about his moment of insight, von Wright refers to the close analogies between the picture theory and Heinrich Hertz' account of the language of theories in *The Principles of Mechanics*, a book Wittgenstein regarded very highly.[3] In the preface to *The Principles of Mechanics*, Hertz proposed that physics constructs mathematical models (*Bilder*) of reality, representing the essential features of the physical world by the relations that hold in the model; his book provided a reconstruction of classical mechanics along these lines. Hertz' programmatic remarks in the opening pages of the *Principles of Mechanics*, outlining his model theory in quite general terms, contain a passage Wittgenstein often invoked when describing his own conception of philosophical problems and how to solve them. The passage summed up the book's proposed solution to the problem of understanding the role of force in physics, which was to provide a systematic presentation of Newtonian mechanics without using force as a basic concept:

> But we have accumulated around the terms "force" and "electricity" more relations than can be completely reconciled among themselves. We have an obscure feeling of this and want to have things cleared up. Our confused wish finds expression in the confused question as to the nature of force and electricity. But the answer which we want is not really an answer to this question. It is not by finding out more and fresh relations and connections that it can be answered; but by removing the contradictions existing between those already known, and thus perhaps by reducing their number. When these painful contradictions are removed, the question as to the nature of force will not have been answered; but our minds, no longer vexed, will cease to ask illegitimate questions.[4]

2. "On Dogmatism," *Ludwig Wittgenstein and the Vienna Circle*, pp. 182–186, 9 December 1931.

3. Heinrich Hertz, *The Principles of Mechanics*, p. x.

4. Hertz, *Principles of Mechanics*, p. 8. Wittgenstein considered using the last sentence of this passage as a motto for the *Philosophical Investigations*. In the Big Typescript, §89, p. 421, he wrote:

> A philosophical problem always has the form: "I simply don't know my way about."
> As I do philosophy, its entire task consists in expressing myself in such a way that certain troubles //problems// disappear. ((Hertz.))

On the first page of the *Principles of Mechanics*, Hertz sets out a Kantian conception of representation and knowledge: our representations share a common structure with what they represent, one that we actively form for ourselves and that can lead us into irresoluble philosophical debates if unchecked by philosophical criticism. Hertz writes that "we form for ourselves models or symbols of external objects; and the form which we give them is such that the necessary consequents of the images in thought are always the images of the necessary consequents in nature of the things pictured."[5] Ludwig Boltzmann had gone on to work out the implications of the Hertzian programme for other parts of physical theory and before he killed himself in 1906, there had been some discussion of Wittgenstein's studying under him.

But while Hertz and Boltzmann concentrated on developing an account of scientific theories as models, Wittgenstein developed the philosophical implications of the picture theory as the basis for a theory about all meaningful discourse, drawing not on physics, but on Frege's and Russell's pioneering work in formal logic and the foundations of mathematics. In fact, Russell's lectures on logical atomism, delivered in 1918, but based on ideas he had learned from Wittgenstein in 1913–1914, make it clear that they had already discussed such a view about the nature of language before they were separated by the war. Discussing the notion of a logically perfect language, a language that clearly displays its logical structure, Russell said:

> In a logically perfect language the words in a proposition would correspond one by one with the components of the corresponding fact. . . . [T]here will be one word and no more for every simple object, and everything that is not simple will be expressed by a combination of words. . . . A language of that sort will be analytic, and will show at a glance the logical structure of the facts asserted or denied.[6]

If Wittgenstein had acquired the idea that language has a pictorial character from Hertz and Boltzmann, and had already proposed a conception of the proposition on which its parts each correspond to the parts of the fact they represent in his prewar conversations with Russell, how are we to make sense of the story he told von Wright? What had he learned when he read the newspaper article about the Paris courtroom? Crucially, Wittgenstein presented the picture theory neither as a generalization from Hertz' physical theories nor as the conclusion of a philosophical argument, but rather as *emerging from an intuitive insight into how pictures work*. Just as a statement and the state of affairs it purports to represent must have something in common—whatever enables the one to represent the other—so the picture must share that feature also. If only we look in the right way, we can see that the picture and the statement must share all those essential features that enable them to represent.

In the entry in his wartime notebook where he recorded his discovery, Wittgenstein drew two stick figures facing each other, with long sticks in their hands, and wrote:

> If the right-hand figure in this picture represents the man A, and the left-hand one stands for the man B, then the whole might assert, e.g.: "A is fencing with B." The proposition in picture-writing can be true or false. It has a sense independent of its

5. Hertz, *Principles of Mechanics*, p. 1.
6. Bertrand Russell, "The Philosophy of Logical Atomism," pp. 197–198. Cf. Wittgenstein's 1913 "Notes on Logic," in *Notebooks 1914–1916*, p. 94: "The meaning of a proposition is the fact which actually corresponds to it."

truth or falsehood. It must be possible to demonstrate everything essential by considering this case.[7]

What we are supposed to see is that a statement has to work in the same way as a picture, because it must share with the picture all the features that are essential for representation. While a verbal statement such as "A is fencing with B" is perfectly clear as it stands, it conceals its underlying form; that form can be seen by considering what the picture and the statement have in common.

We can see the importance of this idea if we compare the three kinds of representational form that Wittgenstein introduces in his exposition of the picture theory in the *Tractatus*: conventional, pictorial, and logical form. "Conventional form" covers aspects of representation that are the product of an artificial convention, such as the choice of a particular symbolism or the old cinematic practice of using a bluish tinge to show that a memory is being depicted.[8] "Pictorial form" covers aspects that are unavoidable given the medium one is using, such as the use of sounds in speech. In other words, pictorial form is whatever aspects of a particular type of picture that enables it to represent as it does—for instance, a spatial picture can represent anything spatial, a coloured one anything coloured, and so forth.[9] "Logical form" is reserved for those aspects of representation that must appear in any representation whatsoever. Wittgenstein introduces logical form as a generalization of the notion of pictorial form: "What any picture, of whatever form, must have in common with reality, in order to be able to depict it—correctly or incorrectly—in any way at all, is logical form, i.e. the form of reality."[10]

Wittgenstein takes this to imply not only a schematic conception of how our language is constructed, but also that philosophical analysis should uncover that form and so make the precise structure of our language clear to us. If propositions are indeed like pictures, they must ultimately consist of objects that stand for the things that make up the state of affairs they represent, just as the model cars stand for the vehicles in the accident. For instance, the court might have a rule that a particular bright red model sports car can represent any two-door car, but not a four-door car. If the objects in the model are to act as a proxy for the objects they represent, we must establish which features of the objects in the model are relevant—such as, whether the model car has two or four doors—and which are irrelevant—such as, the colour of the model car. In Wittgenstein's terms, the objects that make up the proposition must have the correct logical form—that is, they must have at least the same possibilities of combination as the objects they represent. In this way, the logical structure of the world would be mirrored in the logical structure of language. That is why, in the passage quoted above, Wittgenstein equates logical form with "the form of reality."

Wittgenstein did not think that the relationship between ordinary language and the objects that make up the world would be as simple as the relationship between the model in the law courts and the street accident it represents, however. Instead, he thought that most everyday statements would turn out, on analysis, to correspond to

7. *Notebooks 1914–1916*, p. 7, 29 September 1914.
8. Wittgenstein discusses this convention in MS 107, p. 167, and MS 116, §292.
9. *Tractatus*, 2.171.
10. *Tractatus*, 2.18.

a whole set, possibly an infinite set, of "elementary propositions," each of which functions along the lines suggested by the picture theory. It is these elementary propositions that consist of objects combined in a certain way, thereby representing that the corresponding objects in reality are combined in the same way.

In this chapter, I explore Wittgenstein's articulation of a pictorial conception of representation in his wartime notebooks and its crystallization in the *Tractatus*. It is essential to that conception that the picture theory present itself as an obvious truism, and that is why I have taken it as my starting point. We shall see how the pictorial analogy can lead to a powerful and austerely beautiful philosophical system. But, first, we should briefly consider Wittgenstein's later criticism of the picture theory, for it is typical of his later work that his objections do not depend on an appreciation of the subtleties involved in the detailed development of the picture theory, but are directed at the way it begins. Indeed, from that standpoint, the train of thought I have just set out is a prototypical example of a philosophical mistake.

Puzzled by the nature of the proposition, Wittgenstein had been struck by the observation that verbal reports of a traffic accident can be modelled using puppets and toy cars. That led him to see a promising analogy between assertoric propositions and models in general. Then he leaped to the conclusion that the analogy provided the basis for a quite general solution to the problem of understanding the relationship between language and the world: all meaningful language pictures the world. As a result, he was led to the theory that any proposition, true or false, must have a certain form, namely "logical form, i.e. the form of reality," if it is to represent at all. Thus he came to think of the general form of the proposition, a description of what is essential to the propositions of "*any* sign-language *whatsoever*," as amounting to "This is how things stand."[11] By this he meant that any significant proposition must assert that certain things in the world are arranged in a certain way.

The intuitive obviousness of Wittgenstein's chosen examples, such as the model in the law courts and his drawing of the stick figures, and the apparently straightforward inference to the general theory of the proposition, had kept him from seeing that he had focussed on just one use of language—factual reportage—in the search for the essence of language, and had ignored the possibility that there might be exceptions and counterexamples. Later, he was to blame his shortsightedness on the conception of logic he and Russell had accepted at the time: "The basic evil of Russell's logic, as also of mine in the *Tractatus*, is that what a proposition is is illustrated by a few commonplace examples, and then presupposed as understood in full generality."[12]

It was not only the apparently self-evident character of the pictorial analogy that blinded Wittgenstein to the fact that he had built his theory on the basis of a very few examples. An essential part of the train of thought that led Wittgenstein to the picture theory is that it is not acknowledged as a theory, but is treated as an insight into the nature of things:

> We now have a *theory,* a "dynamic" theory* of the proposition, of language,
> but it does not present itself to us as a theory. For it is the characteristic thing about

11. *Tractatus*, 4.5; cf. 6 ff.
12. *Remarks on the Philosophy of Psychology*, I §38.

such a theory that it looks at a special clearly intuitive case and says: "*That* shows how things are in every case; this case is a proto-picture for *all* cases." —"Of course! It has to be like that" we say, and are satisfied. We have arrived at a form of representation that *strikes us as obvious*. But it as if we had now seen something lying *beneath* the surface.

The tendency to generalise the clear case seems to have a strict justification in logic: here one seems *completely* justified in inferring: "If *one* proposition is a picture, then any proposition must be a picture, for they must all be of the same nature." For we are under the illusion that what is sublime, what is essential, about our investigation consists in grasping *one* comprehensive essence.[13]

No account of the structure of our language and its representational relationship to the world can possibly be put into words: instead, one must simply see the unitary and inexpressible essence of language. As a result, the picture theory gained the status of an insight into the nature of language as a whole, on an entirely different level from ordinary assertions, which are made from within language:

> One person might say "A sentence is the most ordinary thing in the world" and another: "A sentence—that's something very remarkable!"—And the latter cannot simply look and see how sentences function. Because the forms we use in expressing ourselves about sentences and thought stand in his way.
>
> Why do we say a sentence is something remarkable? On the one hand, because of the enormous importance attached to it. (And that is correct.) On the other hand, this importance, together with a misunderstanding of the logic of language, tempts us into thinking that the sentence must achieve something extraordinary, something unique. —A *misunderstanding* makes it look to us as if a sentence *did* something strange.
>
> "A sentence is a remarkable thing!" Here we have in germ the subliming of all representation. The tendency to assume a pure intermediary between the sentential *signs* and the facts. —Or even to try to purify, to sublime, the signs themselves. — For our forms of expression prevent us in all sorts of ways from seeing that nothing out of the ordinary is involved, by sending us in pursuit of chimeras.
>
> "Thought must be something unique." When we say, and *mean*, that such-and-such is the case, we—and our meaning—do not stop anywhere short of the fact; but we mean: *this—is—so*. But this paradox (which has the form of a truism) can also be expressed in this way: One can *think* what is *not* the case.
>
> Other illusions come from various quarters to attach themselves to the special one spoken of here. Thought, language, now appear to us as the unique correlate, picture, of the world. These concepts: proposition, language, thought, world, stand in line one behind the other, each equivalent to each. (But what are these words to be used for now? The language-game in which they are to be applied is missing.)[14]

As Wittgenstein cryptically intimates, the picture theory transmutes the notion of a pictorial relation into a quite general simile for the relationship between any representation and what it represents. But while he had taken the simile and the notion

13. *Zettel*, §444, probably 1936. The asterisk marks the location of a footnote, a device Wittgenstein used very rarely. In it, he observes that "Freud speaks of his 'dynamic' theory of dreams."

14. *Philosophical Investigations*, §§93–96. In the Early Investigations, these paragraphs form a single section.

that thought and language picture the world very seriously, they were so detached from the rest of his life that they had no practical implications at all:

> A simile belongs to our edifice; but we can't infer anything from it; it doesn't lead us beyond itself; rather, it must stay as a simile. —We can't draw any consequences from it. As when we compare a sentence to a picture (in which case, of course, what we understand by "picture" must have already been established in us), or compare the application of propositions, operating with propositions, with the application of a calculus, e.g., multiplying.[15]

In his post-*Tractatus* writing, Wittgenstein gave up the picture theory for the view that philosophy should not provide a theory of meaning at all: one should look at how words are actually used and explained, rather than construct elaborate fictions about how they must work. While his new strategy leads him to stress the how words are used when he discusses attempts to give a general theory of what words mean, he never offered a "use" theory to replace the picture theory. At one point in the *Philosophical Investigations*, he sums up his later response to questions about what the meaning of a word consists in with the following remark: "'The meaning of the word is what is explained by the explanation of the meaning.' I.e.: if you want to understand the use of the word 'meaning,' look for what are called 'explanations of meaning.'"[16] This is not an "explanation theory of meaning," but rather one of Wittgenstein's many ways of directing his readers' attention to how words are explained and taught in order to get us to see the uselessness of wholly general philosophical theories.

Throughout his later writing, he returns to the question of how specific philosophical theories he opposes might be put to use in our lives or the lives of an imaginary group of people, precisely so that we are forced to recognize that the theory in question has no substantive implications. In the midst of a discussion of such examples in a manuscript written in 1948, he asks himself "Am I doing child psychology?" and replies "I am making a connection between the concept of teaching and the concept of meaning." Those words are followed by a pointed example of what he has in mind:

> One man is a convinced realist, another a convinced idealist and teaches his children accordingly. In such an important matter as the existence and non-existence of the external world they don't want to teach their children anything wrong.
>
> What will the children be taught? To include in what they say: "There are physical objects" or the opposite?
>
> If someone does not believe in fairies, he does not need to teach his children "There are no fairies": he can omit to teach them the word "fairy." On what occasion are they to say: "There are . . ." or "There are no . . ."? Only when they meet people of the contrary belief.
>
> But the idealist will teach his children the word "chair" after all, for of course he wants to teach them to do this and that, e.g. to fetch a chair. Then where will be

---

15. Early Investigations, §102 (104), first paragraph; not included in the final draft of the book. Cf. MS 110, pp. 216–217; Big Typescript, §89, p. 418.

16. *Philosophical Investigations*, §560.

the difference between what the idealist-educated children say and the realist ones? Won't the difference only be one of the battle cry?[17]

Wittgenstein was well aware that convinced realists or idealists will regard such strategies as irrelevant, for they do not take their words to have any practical significance. Rather than simply dismissing philosophical theories as meaningless, as he had in the *Tractatus*, he recognized the need for a more sympathetic treatment of their origins, with the goal of identifying the apparently innocent steps that lead up to the formulation of a philosophical problem. Wittgenstein's later investigation and criticism of philosophical problems does not aim to solve them by giving a new answer as to how knowledge is possible or impossible, but rather by dissolving the presuppositions that generate the traditional problems, so that an answer is no longer needed:

> But is it an adequate answer to the scepticism of the idealist, or the assurances of the realist, to say that "There are physical objects" is nonsense? For them after all it is not nonsense. It would, however, be an answer to say: this assertion, or its opposite is a misfiring attempt to express what can't be expressed like that. And that it does misfire can be shown; but that isn't the end of the matter. We need to realise that what presents itself to us as the first expression of a difficulty, or of its solution, may as yet not be correctly expressed at all. Just as one who has a just censure of a picture to make will often at first offer the censure where it does not belong, and an *investigation* is needed in order to find the right point of attack for the critic.[18]

The analogy in the last sentence indicates the fundamental reversal that had taken place in Wittgenstein's conception of philosophy: instead of taking literal pictures as a guide to the nature of meaning, he now thinks of philosophical theories as akin to expressing an aesthetic preference for a certain style of representation. The change in Wittgenstein's conception of the pictorial has to do with the decline of the picture theory and the emergence of the notion of a "philosophical picture," his term for the pictures and models that lead us into fanciful philosophical theories, such as the picture theory of meaning.

Just what Wittgenstein meant by the term is best understood by looking at his discussion of specific instances of philosophical pictures. Obviously, the picture theory is a quite specific philosophical theory, while the idea that philosophers are seduced by pictures is a much more general diagnosis of the hubris of philosophical theorizing. But one of the reasons for the decline of the picture theory was his recognition that it depended on precisely those errors that were characteristic of a "philosophical picture," and his choice of *this* term has to be seen in the light of that response to his earlier conception of a picture as a sure guide to the nature of language. The picture theory of the proposition had maintained that a proposition's function can be understood by comparing it to a picture. The theory treats pictures as a model that makes clear the philosophically salient features of propositions. Later, when Wittgenstein came to distance himself from the *Tractatus*, he recognized that he had emphasized certain similarities between propositions and pictures and had mistak-

---

17. *Remarks on the Philosophy of Psychology*, II §§338–339; *Zettel*, §§413–414. Cf. *Philosophical Investigations*, §402.

18. *On Certainty*, §37. Cf. *Remarks on the Philosophy of Psychology*, II §§336 ff.; *Tractatus* 6.51.

enly convinced himself that he had found the essence of the proposition. The picture theory provides an account of how language and world have a common structure. The idea that language and the world share a certain structure is itself a result of tacitly accepting that projective simile.

In the *Philosophical Investigations*, Wittgenstein described the predicament in the following terms: "We predicate of the thing what lies in the method of representing it. Impressed by the possibility of a comparison, we think we are perceiving a state of affairs of the highest generality."[19] Wittgenstein's later response to the picture theory takes the idea that the analogy points to an inexpressible truth about how language represents the world and turns it around. Instead, the conviction that the analogy points to an inexpressible truth is itself a product of the analogy's unrecognized hold over the philosopher. As Wittgenstein puts it in the *Investigations*: "A picture held us captive. And we could not get outside it, for it lay in our language and language seemed to repeat it to us inexorably."[20] In seeing how that came about, one also sees how the analogy concealed itself. Wittgenstein's changing conception of the relationship between propositions and pictures is a central part of his reorientation. In the *Tractatus*, the analogy between propositions and pictures led him to the picture theory of meaning. In 1929, he used the picture theory as the basis for his account of the nature of intentionality and experience. Only later did he recognize the weakness of his reliance on the pictorial analogy: it had allowed a philosophical prejudice in favour of a certain kind of representation to masquerade as an unbiassed presentation of the facts. To see how that came about, we need to consider Wittgenstein's earlier conception of logic and the rules of language.

2.2 The Limits of Language

Before he developed the picture theory, Wittgenstein's work with Russell had concentrated on the analysis of logic and mathematics. Logical and mathematical truths are true no matter what may happen to be the case; one of Wittgenstein's main concerns had been to explain how that can be so. He had arrived at an account on which the truth of logical propositions arises out of certain very general aspects of the way they are constructed—their formal structure. The business of a factual assertion is to make a definite claim about the state of the world, and so its truth or falsity depends on whether the world is as it says it is. As an example of such a proposition, consider "It rained in Vienna on the first day of 1901." It makes a definite claim—it is true if it did rain there then, and false if it didn't. Let us suppose that it did not rain in Vienna on the first day of the twentieth century, in which case the proposition is false. But things could have turned out otherwise—it could have rained—and then it would have been true. Logical truths, on the other hand, are constructed in such a way that they rule nothing out and so are compatible with whatever is the case. For instance, consider "Either it rained in Vienna on New Year's Day 1901 or it didn't." There is no need to check the records to tell whether that proposition is true, for no conceiv-

19. *Philosophical Investigations*, §104. Early Investigations, §110 (112).
20. *Philosophical Investigations*, §115.

able state of affairs can falsify a logical truth. Just as a logical truth rules nothing out, a logical falsehood rules everything out. For instance, "It rained in Vienna and it didn't rain in Vienna," provided we construe it literally, is incompatible with any state of affairs whatsoever.

Part of the attraction of the picture theory was that it suggested a principled way of extending such an approach to the structure of logical propositions to the case of factual assertion. For an empirical proposition has a logical structure, too, and that is what enables it to say "this is how things stand" and in so doing rule out any state of affairs where things are otherwise. Just as the logical structure of a truth of logic guarantees its truth, so the logical structure of a contingent proposition ensures that it is either true or false, depending on whether or not the world is as it says it is.

To accept the picture theory is to hold that language is essentially representational, that language has one central function: to talk about contingent states of affairs. For the Wittgenstein of the *Tractatus*, if a proposition has a sense, it must show how things stand if it is true: "To understand a proposition means to know what is the case if it is true."[21] Only declarative propositions have a sense.[22] Paradoxically, this leads to problems explaining how we understand the rules of logic, the principles that govern how a proposition is constructed. Because any proposition belonging to a propositional system must conform to the system's constitutive rules, any statement in which one tried to express those rules would be logically true. In that case, however, it would not describe a contingent state of affairs and so, strictly speaking, it would be senseless. Therefore, understanding a logical rule cannot be a matter of grasping its sense. How then can we account for our grasp of the rules of logic?

Wittgenstein touches on the difficulty in one of the opening paragraphs of the *Philosophical Remarks*, where he tries to explain why the point of "grammatical conventions," the rules that reflect the logic of our language, can't be stated:

> If I could describe the point of grammatical conventions by saying they are made necessary by certain properties of the colours (say), then that would make the conventions superfluous, since in that case I would be able to say precisely that which the conventions exclude my saying. Conversely, if the conventions were necessary, i.e. if certain combinations of words had to be excluded as nonsensical, then for that very reason I cannot cite a property of colours that makes the conventions necessary, since it would then be conceivable that the colours should not have this property, and I could only express that by violating the conventions.[23]

Grammatical conventions are supposed to tell us which combinations of words are well-formed and which are not. In the case of colour propositions, they tell us that

21. *Tractatus*, 4.024.

22. While it is sometimes said that the recognition that assertion is only one of many uses of language is central to Wittgenstein's later philosophy, this point is actually quite compatible with a development of the picture theory along these lines. Questions can be construed as asking whether a particular state of affairs is true, commands as ordering that some proposition be made true. An early draft of *Philosophical Investigations*, §12, which compares language to the variety of different handles in a locomotive, all looking alike at first, but with very different modes of operation and effects, can be found in the *Philosophical Remarks*, §13. But there it is in the context of a discussion of how "if you think of sentences as instructions for making models, their pictorial nature becomes even clearer" (§10.) Cf. A. Kenny, *Wittgenstein*, pp. 120–123.

23. *Philosophical Remarks*, §4.

"reddish blue" is well-formed and "reddish green" is not, for instance. Wittgenstein holds that we cannot give a rationale for speaking this way, for if anything *could* be said that would justify it, then the conventions would be superfluous, for "in that case I would be able to say precisely that which the conventions exclude my saying." Any justification would have to base itself on an appeal to certain properties of the colours. As it is always conceivable that the colours lack those properties, the convention would not, after all, state a grammatical rule. His argument depends on the presupposition that if a thing has a property it must be possible that it lack that property, that there are no essential properties. Because we can only use language to state contingencies, we cannot say anything in justification of an apparent necessity: instead, the necessity expresses itself in a linguistic rule that certain combinations of words are admissable and all others are inadmissable: "Language can express one method of projection as opposed to another. It cannot express what cannot be otherwise. . . . What is essential to the world cannot be said *about* the world; for then it could be otherwise, as any proposition can be negated."[24] To say that we can talk about possibilities, but not what is essential, that which cannot be otherwise, is to restate the problem we began with, not to solve it.

Wittgenstein returned to the problem of justifying rules again and again in his lectures in the 1930–1931 academic year, a time when he was still working within a broadly Tractarian conception of logic. At one point, he discussed what he meant by saying that "all grammatical rules are arbitrary."[25] He first said that it is impossible to "justify" any grammatical rule and that this amounts to saying that one can't "give reasons" for a grammatical rule, reasons for following one rule rather than another. In explaining his point, he "laid very great stress" on an argument that began from the following premises:

<1> Any reason "would have to be a description of reality"
<2> "Any description of reality must be capable of truth and falsehood"[26]

The next step is to argue that

[3] "if it were false, it would have to be said in a language not using this grammar."[27]

No such language is possible, for to fail to conform to the rules of grammar is to fail to say anything at all: "the rules of grammar distinguish sense and nonsense and if I use the forbidden combinations I talk nonsense."[28]

In other words, if we were to try to justify a grammatical rule, we would have to make use of a proposition that stated a fact. However, in principle, it must be possible for any such proposition to be either true or false. For a proposition that justified a grammatical rule to be false, it would have to place itself outside the grammatical rules and describe a state of affairs where they no longer applied. But there

24. *Wittgenstein's Lectures, Cambridge, 1930–32*, p. 34, 1930.
25. Moore, "Wittgenstein's Lectures in 1930–33," p. 277.
26. Moore, "Wittgenstein's Lectures in 1930–33," pp. 277–278.
27. Moore, "Wittgenstein's Lectures in 1930–33," p. 278. All three quotations are Moore's transcriptions of Wittgenstein's words.
28. *Wittgenstein's Lectures, Cambridge, 1930–32*, p. 47. Lent Term, 1931.

is no such place beyond the rules: if we break the constitutive rules of language, we do not start to speak a new language, but nonsense—nothing at all.

In his introduction to the *Tractatus*, Russell suggested that Wittgenstein's problem only arises for someone who tries to give a representation of the rules of a given language in that very language, and that it could be avoided by moving to a new language, a language with a different structure.[29] Russell thought that, for any given language, one could always construct a metalanguage, a language about the first language, in such a way that the original language and the metalanguage would have different logics. Because the rules of the original language would not be rules of the metalanguage, they would have a sense when they were discussed in the new context. Wittgenstein refused to accept Russell's proffered solution. His reply was that Russell had failed to see the depth of the problem: it concerns the deep structure of all languages, not those peculiarities of a given language that might be avoided by moving to another. Because the rules in question are the rules for any meaningful language, they will apply to whatever metalanguage one constructs in just the same way that they apply to whatever language one started with.[30] It follows that *logical form cannot be the subject of a declarative proposition in any language.*

How then, are we to arrive at a proper understanding of logical form? One might think that one could accommodate Wittgenstein's point by adopting the following strategy. Our everyday assertions concern the objects that make up the everyday world; as grammatical rules cannot refer to that world, but are clearly not simply nonsense, we can infer that they must refer to a separate domain composed of what one could call "logical objects." These objects correspond to the logical operators in a fully analysed language—connectives such as "and" and "not," or whatever their replacements may be in the final analysis. But such ontological generosity has all the advantages of theft over honest toil: while it seems to provide what we desired—an account of what logical rules are about—it does not give us any *explanation* of the conceptual abilities that were the original cause of our puzzlement. The theory as it stands has nothing to say as to why my grasping a specific logical object enables me to understand the form of a proposition in which it occurs. The original question just gets pushed back one step: How do the newly postulated entities, the "logical objects," enable us to understand the structure of our language? Russell's original way out of the problem amounted to invoking a new language that would enable us to explain how our present language works; the new way out invokes new objects, but neither gets us any closer to understanding the role of the rules of language. In other words, the logical platonist response I have just sketched is no more than an ontologically phrased reformulation of Russell's linguistically formulated solution.

Wittgenstein's rejection of Russell's way out amounts to denying that one can ever formulate propositions-with-a-sense (*sinnvolle Sätze*) about the logic of our language. But even though these rules do not enjoy the sense-endowing relations with the world characteristic of declarative propositions, they remain significant and, in some sense, meaningful. They may lack a sense (be *Sinnlos*, senseless) but they are hardly nonsense (*Unsinn*). True nonsense, such as "The bandersnatch was frumious"

29. *Tractatus*, p. xxii.
30. See *Philosophical Remarks*, §7.

or "cat mat the the on" breaks linguistic rules by introducing meaningless words or illegitimate constructions. Even though a statement expressing a rule is unlike an ordinary proposition, because it does not make any factual claim, it is unlike nonsense in that it does not break the rule: it actually exemplifies it. How, then, are we to understand our grasp of the logical forms that the linguistic rules capture, if it is not a matter of grasping their sense? The same problem arises in the case of factual propositions. Our grasp of their senses, of which states of affairs they rule in, and which states of affairs they rule out, obtains in virtue of our grasp of their logical structure. We are as much in need of a philosophical understanding of this phenomenon as we were in the analogous case of logical propositions. Until we have an answer to these questions about logical form and the rules of our language, we will be unable to form a clear idea of the early Wittgenstein's conception of philosophy as the elucidation of the logical form of the proposition.

Wittgenstein's denial that we can refer to logical form or state the rules of our language is based on the premise that our grasp of logical form is quite unlike our acquaintance with objects. He described the thesis that we cannot talk about logic in terms of referring to objects as *the* fundamental idea behind the *Tractatus*: "My fundamental idea is that the logical constants are not representatives; that there can be no representatives of the *logic* of facts."[31] The Russellian and logical platonist approaches amount to attempts to get around the problem and reinstate reference to logical form by a back route.[32] To speak in the same way of our understanding of logic and our understanding of contingent propositions would be to assimilate two fundamentally different capacities. What Wittgenstein needed was an account of our grasp of logical form that reflects the fact that understanding the grammar of one's language is not a matter of referring to objects, regardless of how one construes the nature of the referential relation or the objects referred to.[33] In fact, Wittgenstein concluded the difference is so radical that it cannot even be captured by a categorial distinction. Rather than continuing the search for a way of specifying the difference between logic and factual assertion, Wittgenstein came to think that it reflected a distinction between what can and cannot be *said* at all: we can say what is and what is not the case, but we cannot, strictly speaking, say anything about logic at all.

2.3 Showing and Saying

The logic of our language cannot be referred to by any of the terms in our language; neither can it be spoken of in some further language, nor can it be explained in terms of the existence of a domain of logical objects. The upshot of Wittgenstein's anatomy

---

31. *Tractatus*, 4.0312. Cf. *Notebooks 1914–1916*, p. 37, 25–29 December 1914.

32. My formulation of Wittgenstein's objections is indebted to Pears' exposition of the central role that Wittgenstein's critique of Russell played in the formation of the central logical doctrines of the *Tractatus* in David Pears, *Bertrand Russell and the British Tradition in Philosophy*, and Peter Hylton, "The Nature of the Proposition and the Revolt Against Idealism."

33. Cf. Wittgenstein's letter to Russell in July 1913: "I am very sorry to hear that my objection to your theory of judgment paralyses you. I think it can only be removed by a correct theory of propositions" *Letters to Russell, Keynes and Moore*, p. 24.

of the nature of the proposition is that *nothing* he wanted to say about the essence of the world, or meaning, can be said, for one can only *say* factual assertions that picture contingent states of affairs. If logic is not a thing, and cannot be described, it is not nothing either: it is an essential aspect of language.

Wittgenstein's way out of the impasse was to hold that we can grasp logical form in another way: although it cannot be *said*, it can be *shown*. In fact, that was the true significance of the discovery of the picture theory, as we can see if we look back at his original notebook entry. Immediately after the entry in his notebooks where he refers to the Paris law court's use of models, he writes: "This must yield the nature of truth straight away (if I were not blind.)"[34] Understanding the logic of our language is simply a matter of *seeing* the logical relations that obtain between the terms we use in formulating our sentences. It follows that there is no need for a philosophical theory of meaning, because what we want to know is something that can be shown to us if only we look carefully enough at our everyday language. But in that case, as Wittgenstein asked himself, "Why is philosophy so *complicated*? It ought, after all, to be completely simple."[35] Wittgenstein's answer, an answer he accepted throughout his life, depended on distinguishing between the complex results of philosophical theorizing, and his own philosophy, whose complexity arose from the need to anatomize and undo those theories:

> Philosophy unties the knots in our thinking, which we have tangled up in an absurd way; but to do that, it must make movements which are just as complicated as the knots. Although the *result* of philosophy is simple, its methods for arriving there cannot be so.
> The complexity of philosophy is not in its matter, but in our tangled understanding.[36]

In the *Tractatus* Wittgenstein proceeds on the assumption that if only we had an untangled language that clearly mirrored the structure of the world, we would have no philosophical problems. Instead, we would just *see* their common structure. But because our language emerged in response to the pragmatic need to communicate about and to control our environment, the precise nature of its relationship to the simple objects must be left an open-ended question. As ordinary language conceals its form, giving a full analysis of even part of our language is an extremely complex task. Wittgenstein leaves that task undone in the *Tractatus*, covering his path with the following remarks about the relationship between the tacit conventions of everyday language and its underlying logic, revealed in the form of thought:

> Everyday language is a part of the human organism and is no less complicated than it.
> It is not humanly possible to gather immediately from it what the logic of language is.
> Language disguises thought. So much so, that from the outward form of the clothing it is impossible to infer the form of the thought beneath it, because the

34. *Notebooks 1914–1916*, p. 7, 29 September 1914.
35. *Philosophical Remarks*, §2.
36. *Philosophical Remarks*, §2. Cf. Big Typescript, §89, p. 420; *Zettel*, §452.

outward form of the clothing is not designed to reveal the form of the body, but for entirely different purposes.

The tacit conventions on which the understanding of everyday language depends are enormously complicated.[37]

Although Wittgenstein held that any attempt to state philosophical truths is doomed to failure, he still believed that there was a sense in which his philosophical outlook was true and others false, for the underlying structure of language showed its truth. The distinction between saying and showing arises out of the conviction that there is a fundamental difference between the information that can be communicated in language and those aspects of language that make communication possible. The difference runs so deep that the latter category cannot be spoken of but can only be conveyed indirectly, if at all. Whatever makes it possible for a proposition to be a representation, or for a tautology to be unconditionally true, cannot be described in language but is shown by the forms of words in question.

The notion of showing is primarily applied to propositions: an assertoric proposition shows its sense—that is, it shows how things stand if it is true; a tautology, a contradiction or a mathematical equation shows that it has no sense, that it says nothing.[38] Because logical and mathematical propositions are independent of how things stand, their truth or falsity is entirely a function of their logical structure. Thus factual propositions bring out the way showing is tied up with representational relations between language and world, while logical and mathematical propositions display the internal structure of language and world.

Wittgenstein held that philosophical analysis will show us the rules we tacitly accept, the underlying structure of our language, and so enable us to avoid the misunderstandings that had generated traditional philosophical controversies. He thought one could do so by specifying rules for translating from our ordinary language into a new symbolism that would clearly display the rules governing the underlying structure of ordinary language.[39] Thus, while the concept of a rule is not given much explicit attention in the *Tractatus*, it plays an essential role in Wittgenstein's early conception of the task of philosophy. For instance, Wittgenstein maintains that we can see what all truth-functional notations have in common, once we see that a notation that uses "not p" and "p or q" can be substituted for any other truth-functional notation; the sense of the symbols is mirrored in the rule for the use of the signs.[40] Likewise, he holds that the rules governing a proposition's underlying structure, its "logical syntax," also govern its representational relation to the world, if any. For instance, a musician both in reading a symphony from a score and in playing a recording makes use of these "laws of projection," or "rules of translation," as we all do whenever we think or talk.[41]

Thus Wittgenstein's proposals as to how to analyse logical propositions, math-

37. *Tractatus*, 4.002.
38. *Tractatus*, 4.022, 4.461.
39. *Tractatus*, 3.343–3.344. Cf. 4.241: "A definition is a rule dealing with signs." On the Tractarian conception of analysis, see 3.2 ff., 3.25, 4.113 ff., 4.221 ff.
40. *Tractatus*, 3.3441, 5.514; see also 5.5511–5.5512.
41. *Tractatus*, 4.014–4.0141.

ematical equations, and factual assertions all depend on defining the rules governing the signs in question.[42] But questions about the nature of the "laws of projection," the rules connecting a representation and what it represents, or the nature of rules in general, are not a topic for further investigation in the *Tractatus*. In part, that is because all explanation must come to an end at some point, and in the *Tractatus* the end point consists in the "fact" that the world consists of the objects that it does and their logical form, the ways they can combine with one another. The rules governing the combination of objects constitute not only the very nature of these objects but also the nature of logic itself, and the rules of our language simply reflect these constitutive rules.[43] One consequence of his view is that all these rules can only be shown by a well-constructed sign language and cannot be explicitly stated. That, of course, is the other reason why these rules cannot be a matter for discussion. Instead, "the rules of logical syntax must go without saying, once we know how each sign signifies."[44]

The *Tractatus* offers the following schematic illustration of how our understanding of how signs signify will illuminate their form:

> [O]ne proposition "*fa*" shows that the object a occurs in its sense, two propositions "*fa*" and "*ga*" show that the same object is mentioned in both of them.
> If two propositions contradict one another, then their structure shows it; the same is true if one of them follows from the other. And so on.[45]

In the case of contradictory propositions, Wittgenstein gives a precise account of how their structure shows that they are contradictory. He gives us a new notation, one that represents each of the elementary propositions making up the contradictory proposition as having two "poles" attached to it (see Figures 2.1 and 2.2). Thus an elementary proposition, ordinarily signified by a single letter, say "p," is instead given the sign "TpF." The letters "T" and "F," Wittgenstein's "poles," represent the two possible values each elementary proposition can have—namely, truth or falsity. "Not p" is given the sign "F-TpF-T"; the left-hand side shows us that if "p" is true, "not p" is false, while the right-hand side shows us that if "p" is false, "not p" is true. In a similar way, one can represent the logical relations between propositions by drawing lines connecting each of the poles of each proposition and writing a T or an F next to each of those lines where the compound proposition is true or false, respectively. Thus p&q is written as Figure 2.1 and ~(p & ~q) as Figure 2.2.

Finally, by substituting "p" for "q" in Figure 2.2, one will see that there is no combination of possible truth values that is correlated with the falsity of the whole proposition.[46] That is what Wittgenstein had in mind when he wrote that "if two propositions contradict one another, then their structure shows it; the same is true if one of

---

42. The analyses of logical, mathematical, and factual propositions are not the only contexts in which Wittgenstein makes use of rules in the *Tractatus*, however. Because he treats "law" and "rule" as virtually interchangeable (see 3.031 and 4.0141), a comprehensive discussion would also need to take into account his treatment of the laws of physics, geometry, and least action at 3.03 ff. and 6.3 ff.
43. *Tractatus*, 5.55 ff. and especially 5.552; cf. 6.44.
44. *Tractatus*, 3.334.
45. *Tractatus*, 4.1211.
46. *Tractatus*, 6.1203.

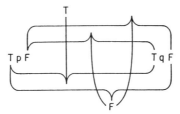

Figure 2.1

them follows from the other. And so on." We can take "p & ~p" and put it into a surveyable notation that clearly shows the structure of the proposition. Wittgenstein holds that is *all* there is to philosophical analysis: in following out the programme of analysis hinted at by his "and so on," the task of philosophy will have been completed, for one will have clarified everything that can be said. Philosophy "must set limits to what cannot be thought by working outwards through what can be thought."[47] If the logical form of all propositions is clarified, by means of the production of appropriate forms of expression, then the problems of philosophy will have been dispelled. The philosopher's task is to make it clear to us what they show, so that we are not misled into trying to say what cannot be said. And so what is shown enables us to resolve our philosophical perplexities.

Because we have Wittgenstein's examples of how logical propositions show their form, it is a relatively straightforward matter to set out his conception of what is shown by a logical proposition composed of elementary propositions linked by truth-functional connectives. But he also talks of showing in a number of other contexts, where we do not have such clear and concrete examples to guide us. As we consider contexts with fewer affinities to formal logic, we will see that it becomes increasingly difficult to see how the notion of showing is meant to do its work.

We can start by considering the case of mathematics, because it closely resembles formal logic and originally provided one of the main motivations for Wittgenstein's work on logic. Perhaps the main obstacle here is the widespread belief that Wittgenstein, as a student of Russell, must have been working on the Russellian programme of reducing mathematics to logic, by showing that the propositions of mathematics can be reduced to tautologies. But that is a myth. First, the *Tractatus* rejects the very idea of reducing either logic or mathematics to a small number of supposedly self-evident axioms, from which all other propositions can be proved: Wittgenstein holds that mathematics, like logic, is self-justifying: proof is simply a matter of clearly displaying a proposition's form.[48] Thus he held that Russell's use of the identity sign, to show that two signs stand for the same object, in a proposition such as "a = b," was both illegitimate and unnecessary. Instead, what it intended to say would be shown in a logically perspicuous language by only using one sign for each object.[49] Second, the *Tractatus* recognizes a fundamental difference between tautologies and equations. A "tautology" is a proposition consisting of elementary propositions linked

47. *Tractatus*, 4.114.
48. *Tractatus*, 6.2 ff.
49. *Tractatus*, 5.53 ff.

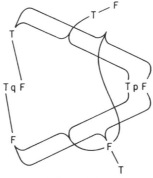

Figure 2.2

by truth-functional connectives, whose logical form guarantees its truth.[50] An "equation," on the other hand, shows that the expressions on either side of the identity sign can be substituted for one another.[51] Calculation in mathematics consists in substituting expressions in one equation by appealing to a second equation.[52] One important consequence of his treatment of mathematics is that it leaves no room for intuition or any other mental process in mathematics, for a perspicuous notation determines its own application:

> The question whether intuition is needed for the solution of mathematical problems must be given the answer that in this case language itself provides the necessary intuition.
>
> The process of *calculating* serves to bring about that intuition.[53]

While Wittgenstein's cryptic remarks do provide some indication as to how he thought the notion of showing should be applied to the analysis of mathematical propositions, its application to factual propositions depends on how one understands his extremely sketchy account of their analysis in the *Tractatus*. We are told that factual propositions conceal their true logical form, but there are no worked out examples of such an analysis and very few clues as to how it might proceed. Still, the basic idea is clear: factual propositions, like logical ones, have a structure of some kind, and it must be possible to show that form by using an appropriate notation. We now turn to how this idea was articulated in the *Tractatus*.

50. *Tractatus*, 6.126–6.127.
51. *Tractatus*, 6.23–6.2323.
52. *Tractatus*, 6.24.
53. *Tractatus*, 6.233–6.2331.

3

Subject and Object

3.1 Logical Atomism

While the *Tractatus* ends by saying that anyone who understands its propositions will finally see them as nonsensical, that one must transcend them in order to see the world aright, and that what we cannot speak about we must pass over in silence,[1] it begins with a series of ontological doctrines. Wittgenstein's opening remarks set out both an intricate philosophical system and an abstract vision of the nature of language and world. The world Wittgenstein describes is the world demanded by the picture theory: it is a world of facts. As we can represent the world in language, world and language must be constructed in such a way that this is possible. Facts, states of affairs, just are the subject matter of propositions:

> The world is all that is the case.
>
> The world is the totality of facts, not of things.[2]

Wittgenstein is not denying here that there are things in the world; rather, he is insisting that we have to think of the world as composed of facts, the correlate in the world of the true propositions that we express in language. In turn the facts are arrangements of things, but these objects must be understood in terms of their contribution to the facts they make up. Some facts are complex—that is, they are composed of a number of simpler facts, linked by logical operators. If we analyse complex facts into their constituents we must eventually arrive at atomic facts. Atomic facts, which are not further decomposable into component facts, are concatenations of simple objects. These objects are a little like subatomic particles: the everyday facts about the world around us are the product of the way the objects are combined.

The structure of the world is mirrored, or pictured, by the structure of language: all meaningful language is analysable into "elementary propositions," logical atoms. The names that make up an elementary proposition are related to each other in a determinate manner, and "fit into one another like the links in a chain."[3] An elementary proposition is true if the objects that it refers to are arranged in the same way as the names in the proposition; otherwise, it is false. Each such proposition is logically

---

1. Tractatus, 6.54–7.
2. *Tractatus*, 1–1.1.
3. *Tractatus*, 2.03.

independent of all other elementary propositions—the truth or falsity of each atomic proposition is independent of the truth or falsity of any other atomic proposition. An atomic proposition is composed of names, and each name refers to one of the simple objects out of which the world is composed. On this view, the meaning of every significant utterance is the logical product of the combination of these subatomic particles into the molecules of ordinary speech.

In both the *Blue Book* and *Philosophical Investigations*, Wittgenstein suggested that the picture theory and the simple objects of the *Tractatus* had been motivated by the aim of providing a systematic explanation of what must be the case in order for true and false statements to be possible, where that is understood as a matter of picturing states of affairs. As examples of the kind of move he had in mind, he would cite certain passages from Plato, especially the *Theaetetus*.[4] In 1944, when he was putting the first part of the *Philosophical Investigations* into its final form, he wrote to a friend that he was reading Plato's *Theaetetus*: "'Plato in this dialogue is occupied with the same problems that I am writing about.'"[5] He quotes from the following passage from the *Theaetetus* in both the *Philosophical Grammar* and *Philosophical Investigations*:

> Socrates to Theaetetus: And if you imagine mustn't you imagine *something*? —Theaetetus: Necessarily. —Socrates: And if you imagine something, mustn't it be something real? —Theaetetus: It seems so.
> Socrates: So if someone imagines what is not, he has an idea of nothing? — Theaetetus: It seems so. Socrates: But surely if he has an idea of nothing, then he hasn't any idea at all? —Theaetetus: That seems plain.[6]

How can we think both about what is and what is not? Socrates and Theaetetus take it for granted that if I imagine something, then there is some *thing* I imagine. But what is that thing? It can't just be my idea of what I imagine, for I can also imagine things that are real. But then what are we to say about the case where I imagine something that doesn't exist?

In outline, the Tractarian answer is that when one imagines something that does not exist, one does so not by imagining a nonexistent object, but rather by imagining that certain simpler objects are arranged one way when they are actually arranged differently. In order to avoid a regress, one is forced to conclude that there must be

---

4. Wittgenstein owned a five-volume German translation of Plato by Preisendanz, and was well acquainted with the *Theaetetus* and *Cratylus*. He referred to passages in Plato quite frequently. There are references to the *Theaetetus* in the *Blue Book*, p. 20, the *Philosophical Investigations*, §§46, 48, 518, and the *Philosophical Grammar*, §§76 ff., 90, 114, p. 208. Wittgenstein refers to the *Sophist* and *Philebus* in the *Philosophical Grammar*, §§19, 93, to the *Charmides* in *Zettel*, §454, and to the *Cratylus* in the Big Typescript, §10, p. 40.

5. M. O'C. Drury "Conversations with Wittgenstein," p. 163. Shortly afterward, Wittgenstein sent a copy of a translation of the *Theaetetus* to Drury.

6. Plato, *Theaetetus*, 189. Wittgenstein quotes both paragraphs in TS 228 (*Bermerkungen I*), a typescript drawn up as a source for the final arrangement of Part I of the *Philosophical Investigations*. The translations of Wittgenstein's quotations from Plato are from the German translation Wittgenstein used (Preisendanz), not the original Greek. The first paragraph is also quoted in *Philosophical Investigations*, §518; the second, in *Philosophical Grammar*, §90; Source: MS 114, p. 134. In *Zettel*, §69, Geach erroneously inserted the first passage, to precede a copy of Wittgenstein's discussion of the second passage. Cf. *Philosophical Grammar*, §114, and *Blue Book*, pp. 36–39, especially p. 38.

some simple terms that refer to things that must exist. The meanings of these directly referring terms just are the objects to which they refer. For Russell, these terms were demonstratives that picked out the contents of immediate experience; for the early Wittgenstein, they were the names that referred to simple objects. These simples cannot come into existence or cease to be, for they are the unchanging ground that makes change possible. Thus, in the *Tractatus*, Wittgenstein writes:

> The object is simple.
>
> Only if there are objects can there be a fixed form of the world.
>
> The fixed, the existent and the object are one.
>
> The simple signs employed in propositions are called names.
>
> Objects can only be *named*.[7]

The Tractarian "solution" amounts to conceding that we can't really talk about nonexistent objects: when we say something doesn't exist, we are to be construed as talking about certain existent objects and denying that they are arranged in a specific way.

In the *Philosophical Investigations*, Wittgenstein asks himself, "What lies behind the idea that names really signify simples?", and replies by quoting what Socrates says in the *Theaetetus*:

> "If I make no mistake, I have heard some people say this: there is no definition of the primary elements—so to speak—out of which we and everything else are composed; for everything that exists in its own right can only be *named*, no other determination is possible, neither that it *is* nor that it is *not*. . . . But what exists in and for itself has to be . . . named without any other determination. In consequence it is impossible to give an account of any primary element; for it, nothing is possible but the bare name; its name is all it has. But just as what consists of these primary elements is itself complex, so the names of the elements become descriptive language by being compounded together. For the essence of speech is the composition of names."
>
>   Both Russell's "individuals" and my "objects" (*Tractatus Logico-Philosophicus*) were such primary elements.[8]

Here Wittgenstein retrospectively acknowledges the central role of these Socratic concerns about the composition of language and the possibility of referring to objects in his postulation in the *Tractatus* of simple objects which could only be named and had to exist. But the conception of objects and facts I have just sketched is extremely abstract, so abstract that there are any number of ways of developing a plausible specification of the notions of an object and a fact on the basis of what one can find in the *Tractatus*. To understand why Wittgenstein begins with the words that he does, we need to look at his reasons for beginnning the *Tractatus* with a skeletal outline of his ontology and conception of analysis, rather than the full-blooded doctrines that most expositors have tried to read into it.

At the heart of the Tractarian system is an argument for the necessary existence

---

7. *Tractatus*, 2.02, 2.026, 2.027, 3.202, 3.221.

8. *Philosophical Investigations*, §46, 1936 or earlier. Cf. *Philosophical Grammar*, p. 208 ff. The standard pagination for Socrates' dream is 201d–202c.

of simple objects. That argument begins from the observation that I speak and understand language, and leads to the conclusion that language must be analysable into
elementary propositions, "logical atoms." The argument is very general, for it turns
on establishing that it is only possible for a language to have parts at all if it is ultimately composed of simples. As a result, Wittgenstein concluded that every significant statement must be composed of logical atoms, yet was unable to give any examples. As we shall see, the ontology of the *Tractatus* is best understood, not as the
foundation on which it is built, but rather as the consequence of Wittgenstein's conception of logic and representation.

In its barest outline, Wittgenstein's argument for the necessary existence of simple
objects depends on arguing that it is only possible for language to be composite if
there are simples out of which it is composed. At this level of generality, Wittgenstein's
argument for the existence of logical atoms runs parallel to Leibniz' argument for
the existence of monads in the opening sections of the *Monadology*:

> The monad, which we shall discuss here, is nothing but a simple substance that
> enters into composites—simple, that is, without parts.
>
> And there must be simple substances, since there are composites; for the com-
> posite is nothing more than a collection, or *aggregate*, of simples.
>
> But where there are no parts, neither extension, nor shape, nor divisibility is
> possible. These monads are the true atoms of nature and, in brief, the elements of
> things.[9]

But by the time the *Tractatus* was arranged in its final form, only a few traces were
left of any such train of argument. Three of the remarks attached to proposition 2.02,
"Objects are simple," are perhaps the best place to start:

> Objects make up the substance of the world. That is why they cannot be com-
> posite.
>
> If the world had no substance, then whether a proposition had sense would
> depend on whether another proposition was true.
>
> In that case we could not sketch any picture of the world (true or false.)[10]

The first remark states Wittgenstein's desired conclusion: objects, the elements
we reach at the end of analysis, cannot themselves be composed of smaller parts.
The central role of Wittgenstein's notion of analysis is made clear in the passage
immediately before this one, which asserts that every statement about complexes can
be analyzed into a statement about their constituents together with the propositions
that completely describe the complexes.[11] Wittgenstein's conception of analysis here
is extremely abstract, but at the very least we can say that it is the activity of clarifying the sense of ordinary propositions by replacing them with propositions about their
constituents by means of rules that preserve the sense of the original proposition.

The second remark sketches an argument by *reductio ad absurdum*: we are to
assume for the sake of argument that the world has no substance—that is, we are to
assume it cannot be analysed into indivisible simples, and then look for an absurd

9. G. W. Leibniz, *Philosophical Essays*, p. 213.
10. *Tractatus*, 2.021–2.0212.
11. *Tractatus*, 2.0201.

consequence of that assumption. If the absurd consequence is unacceptable, then we will have to reject our initial assumption and conclude that the world can be analysed into indivisible simples.

The third remark states the absurd conclusion that is supposed to follow from the assumption that there are no simples: we would not be able to picture the world. In other words, if there were no simple objects, language would be impossible. But as we do speak a language, there must be simple objects. Therefore, the world's consisting of simple objects is a necessary condition for our propositions making sense.

To see how the argument is supposed to work, we need to look more closely at the premise that is the basis for the *reductio*. What Wittgenstein asks us to imagine is that there is no final level of analysis, that any analysis of a proposition into simpler components will be provisional, always capable of being supplanted by a yet more exhaustive analysis. But in that case, he states, a given proposition's sense would depend on whether another proposition was true. He does not explicitly say what the other proposition would be, but the most plausible candidate is a proposition concerning the as-yet-unanalysed constituents of a proposition that expresses a provisional analysis.[12] If the analysis concerning those constituents were not true, then the proposition in question would not have a sense; the sense of any complex proposition is, in this way, always vulnerable to any falsehoods that may be discovered in the subordinate propositions that go to make up its analysis. If analysis never terminates, then no proposition has a self-contained sense; the sense of any proposition will presuppose the truth of yet further propositions that make up its analysis.

Suppose the proposition we want to analyse is called "p," and it is about the complex fact p. A provisional analysis might lead us to analyse it into a conjunction of three simpler propositions, q1, q2, and q3; we can call this analysis "q." But if there is no final level of analysis, it will be possible to give a further analysis of q, perhaps into a conjunction of six more propositions, r1, r2 . . . r6, which we can call "r." Of course, this is only an illustration of one way we might proceed from one level of analysis of the next. If we assume that there is no final level of analysis, then we are assuming that the process of analysis can go on indefinitely, without any ultimate terminus.

But why shouldn't we accept these conclusions and be content with a conception of analysis that is relativized to our current ability to carry it out? Why can't we say that q is our current analysis of p, and leave it at that? We can see why Wittgenstein rejected such a solution if we consider the logical relations between p and its analyses. In this case, q is a logical consequence of p, and r is a logical consequence of q. But then the sense of p depends on the truth of q, and r, too: each of these propositions further specifies what one understands when one understands p. And if the process of analysis can go on forever, then the sense of p will never stop expanding, either. The sense of the proposition would be indeterminate, always open to revision in the light of further analysis. To sum up: if there is no final level of analysis, then

---

12. Strictly speaking, there are a number of other candidates that could have filled this role, such as the proposition that the form of "p" exists, or the even more general proposition that something exists. For a careful consideration of these alternatives, see David Pears, "The Logical Independence of Elementary Propositions."

each new level of analysis will modify the sense, and possibly even the truth-value, of the proposition to be analyzed, and so it will not have a determinate sense.

At this point in the argument we confront Wittgenstein's suppressed premise: he maintains that every significant proposition has a determinate sense, for an indeterminate sense is no sense at all. In the *Tractatus* the premise is hardly mentioned, let alone defended; nevertheless, it is evident that its author was convinced that every meaningful proposition must have a clear-cut meaning. For there is an extended discussion of the thesis that sense must be determinate in the 1914–1916 notebooks, where it is closely linked with the requirement that every meaningful proposition must refer to simple objects, summarized in the following unequivocal dictum: "The demand for simple things *is* the demand for determinacy of sense."[13] The remark provides the basis for the one explicit remark on the topic to be found in the *Tractatus*, where the point has been rephrased in terms of names, the simple signs in a fully analysed proposition that stand for simple things: "The requirement that simple signs be possible is the requirement that sense be determinate."[14]

In the *Prototractatus*, an arrangement of the material in his notebooks that provided the basis for the final text of the *Tractatus*, Wittgenstein included a couple of other remarks that provide some further explanation of the requirement:

> The analysis of signs must come to an end at some point, because if signs are to express anything at all, meaning must belong to them in a way that is once and for all complete.

> The requirement of determinateness could also be formulated in the following way: if a proposition is to have sense, the syntactical employment of each of its parts must have been established in advance. For example, it cannot occur to one only subsequently that a certain proposition follows from it. Before a proposition can have a sense, it must be completely settled what propositions follow from it.[15]

In this passage we can see a compressed form of the argument just given in defence of simple objects—if analysis did not come to an end, signs would not have a determinate meaning, and then they would not express anything at all. For a proposition to have a determinate sense is just a matter of establishing which propositions follow from it, and that is only possible if analysis comes to an end.

Wittgenstein's thesis of determinacy of sense is sometimes described as a bold generalization of Frege's thesis that piecemeal and partial definitions of concepts are illegitimate and that a concept's application must be completely determined when it is introduced.[16] While Wittgenstein was in sympathy with Frege, he certainly did not regard the determinacy thesis as simply a generalization of Frege's thesis, any more than he saw the picture theory as an extension of the work of Hertz and Boltzmann. As in the case of the picture theory, it appears that Wittgenstein arrived at the thesis

---

13. *Notebooks 1914–1916*, p. 63, 18 June 1915.

14. *Tractatus*, 3.23.

15. *Prototractatus*, 3.20102–3.20103. *Tractatus* 3.23 immediately precedes these remarks and has the number 3.20101.

16. Cf. *Prototractatus* 3.20103, cited earlier, and based on *Notebooks 1914–1916*, p. 64, 18 June 1915. See Gottlob Frege, *Grundgesetze der Arithmetik*, Vol. 2, §§56 ff., and *Translations from the Philosophical Writings of Gottlob Frege*, p. 159 ff. Cf. Hacker, *Insight and Illusion*, 1st ed., p. 16.

that the sense of a proposition must be determinate by considering a very limited range of examples he found intuitively convincing and treated his results as a demonstration of the nature of any significant proposition. In his notebook entries for June 1915, Wittgenstein treats the determinacy thesis as a corollary of the picture theory, for he conceived of a picture as a completely specifying how the world must be if it is to be true:

> Every proposition that has a sense has a COMPLETE sense, and it is a picture of reality in such a way that what is not yet said in it simply cannot belong to its sense.
>
> If the proposition "this watch is shiny" has a sense, it must be explicable HOW THIS proposition has THIS sense.
>
> If a proposition tells us something, then it must be a picture of reality just as it is, and a complete picture at that. —There will, of course, also be something that it does *not* say—but what it does say it says completely and it must be susceptible of SHARP definition.[17]

A few days later, he discusses determinacy of sense as though it were a truism—if we are to mean anything at all by our words, what we mean must be quite definite:

> When I say "The book is lying on the table," does this really have a completely clear sense? (An EXTREMELY important question.)
>
> But the sense must be clear, for after all we mean *something* by the proposition, and as much as we *certainly* mean must surely be clear.[18]
>
> It seems clear that what we MEAN must always be sharp.[19]

To sum up: the argument for the existence of *Tractatus* objects begins with the observation that if there were no ultimate level of analysis, then the sense of a proposition would not be determinate. It then appeals to the additional premise that sense must be determinate in order to arrive at the conclusion that there must be an ultimate level of analysis where we reach simple names that stand for simple objects. While the argument is clearly stated in Wittgenstein's pre-*Tractatus* writing, the slender textual basis we have found for it within the text of the *Tractatus* raises the question whether it is really appropriate to read the *Tractatus* as arguing for the existence of simple objects at all. Instead, we might well see it as presenting us with certain commitments and exploring their implications.[20] However, proposition 3.23—"The requirement that simple signs be possible is the requirement that sense be determinate"—makes it clear that Wittgenstein had not given up the train of thought we have examined when he assembled the *Tractatus*. It certainly led him to some of the central doctrines in that book, and even if he chose not to emphasize it in the final arrangement he gave to his early work, it does provide a valuable clue as to the nature of the system he was proposing, for it strongly suggests that the objects of the *Tractatus* are a postulate of reason, a "logical necessity demanded by theory,"[21] as Russell put

17. *Notebooks 1914–1916*, p. 61, 16 June 1915. Small capitals correspond to double underlining in the original.

18. *Notebooks 1914–1916*, p. 67, 20 June 1915.

19. *Notebooks 1914–1916*, p. 68, 20 June 1915.

20. This reading is advocated by Robert Fogelin in *Wittgenstein*, 1st ed., pp. 12–15; 2nd ed., pp. 14–17.

21. *Tractatus*, Ogden edition, p. 12; Pears and McGuinness edition, p. xiii.

it. The following passage from the pre-*Tractatus* notebooks strongly supports such a reading:

> It seems that the idea of the SIMPLE is already to be found contained in that of the complex and in the idea of analysis, and in such a way that we come to this idea quite apart from any examples of simple objects, or of propositions which mention them, and we realize the existence of the simple object—*a priori*—as a logical necessity.[22]

Once we recognize that Wittgenstein arrived at the idea of simple objects on the basis of an abstract argument about the nature of complexes and of analysis, "quite apart from any examples of simple objects," it is easy to see the need for caution in attributing any characteristics to the objects over and above those demanded by Wittgenstein's logicolinguistic commitments. The *Tractatus* is an abstract metaphysical framework, an attempt at a systematic resolution of a number of key issues in the philosophy of logic and language that Wittgenstein took from Frege and Russell. While the book does begin with a series of ontological doctrines, in the end these doctrines must be seen as a shadow cast by Wittgenstein's conception of reason and representation. Unfortunately, most expositors of the *Tractatus* have gone much further: they have given substance to these shadows by supplementing them with additional metaphysical and epistemological theses about the nature of propositions, facts, and objects, and our knowledge of them. While there is a long and honourable tradition of interpreting the work of others in the light of one's own philosophical commitments, the wealth of competing interpretations of the *Tractatus* has made it almost impossible for its readers to separate the controversies engendered by such reconstructions from the more limited project of exegesis. Of course, exegesis and interpretation are intimately linked, and it would be pointless to insist that they be sharply separated. Nevertheless, the extremely abstract character of the system presented in the *Tractatus* has not merely tempted generations of philosophers to read their own commitments back into the text; it has also prevented them from realizing that they have done so. We shall see that Wittgenstein experimented with a variety of different ways of specifying his shadowy ontology before arriving at the austere exposition of the *Tractatus*, and he himself was the first interpreter unable to rest content with such austerity.[23]

3.2 Analysis in the *Tractatus*

One of the earliest of Wittgenstein's surviving notebook entries already hints at the considerations that ultimately led him to the highly abstract conception of the nature of language and world he set out in the *Tractatus*. "Logic must take care of itself," the remark that begins the published edition of the first of Wittgenstein's wartime notebooks is, among other things, a rejection of Russell's idea that the logician must take care of logic by giving it an axiomatic formulation. That had been the goal of *Principia Mathematica*: to show how logic and mathematics can be built up on the

22. *Notebooks 1914–1916*, p. 60, 14 June 1915.
23. See chapter 5, section 1.

basis of a few simple rules of inference and fundamental assumptions. Instead, Wittgenstein thought of each logical and mathematical proposition as showing its own structure, without any need for further validation. "Logic must take care of itself" is also an anticipation of the conception of logic set out here in chapter 2, section 2: the rules of logic cannot be explicitly stated, but rather are shown by the structure of our language. More generally, the saying also sums up Wittgenstein's insistence on a sharp separation between logic and empirical facts: logic cannot depend on any contingent truths.

A few paragraphs down the page, Wittgenstein asks himself: "How is it reconcilable with the task of philosophy, that logic should take care of itself?"[24] By "the task of philosophy," Wittgenstein means the analysis of our language: questions about the nature of language and world are supposed to be resolved by systematically reformulating problematic sentences so that they yield a rationally compelling insight into their underlying structure. His problem is that if logic takes care of itself, is a self-contained, self-validating system that needs no assistance from us, so that every meaningful sentence is already in order as it is, how are we to tell when we have arrived at a full analysis, a proposition that clearly displays its complete logical structure? And which structures will such analyses employ? The surface grammar of everyday English and German employs relatively few forms, principally subject-predicate and relational, but that is surely not a reliable guide to their analysis. In that case, Wittgenstein asks, how are we to answer the question

> whether, "A is good" is a subject-predicate proposition; or whether "A is brighter than B" is a relational proposition? *How can such a question be settled at all?* What sort of evidence can satisfy me that—*for example*—the first question must be answered in the affirmative? (This is an extremely important question.)[25]

The final parenthetical remark is something of an understatement, for the question how such questions can be settled at all is a way of asking a basic epistemological question: how do we know what we know? After offhandedly dismissing Cartesian (and Russellian) appeals to self-evidence, Wittgenstein then turns to a question about the nature of experience that he describes as closely related but also "simpler and more fundamental":

> Is a point in our visual field a *simple object*, a *thing*? Up to now I have always regarded such questions as the real philosophical ones: and so for sure they are in some sense—but once more what evidence could settle a question of this sort at all? Is there not a mistake in formulation here, for it looks as if *nothing at all* were self-evident to me on this question; it looks as if I could say definitively that these questions could never be settled at all.[26]

Wittgenstein takes it for granted that while logic does not depend on acquaintance with facts of a given form, such acquaintance may be necessary for empirical knowledge. As the last sentence of the quotation suggests, he must have considered the possibility that analysis of specific propositions depends on knowledge of the form of the facts in question and so lies beyond the task of philosophy proper, or that they

24. *Notebooks 1914–1916*, p. 2, 3 September 1914.
25. *Notebooks 1914–1916*, p. 3, 3 September 1914.
26. *Notebooks 1914–1916*, p. 3, 3 September 1914.

are simply irresoluble. In any case, it must have been tempting to conclude that these further analyses were not part of the task of philosophy. As he wrote the next day, "If logic can be completed without answering certain questions, it *must* be completed *without* them."[27] A few days later, Wittgenstein recorded the insights into the nature of the picture theory discussed in the previous chapter. We can now see that they also pointed the way to a programmatic answer to his questions about the form of propositions about goodness or simple objects: insofar as answers to such questions are possible, they cannot be stated, but can only be shown.

In the pages that follow, Wittgenstein considers a variety of possible candidates for the role of "simple objects," notably both the smallest discernible parts of the visual field, and physical points:

> As examples of the simple I always think of points in the visual field (just as parts of the visual field always come before my mind as typical composite objects.)[28]

> The division of the body into *material points*, as we have it in physics, is nothing more than analysis into *simple components*.[29]

> It always looks as if there were complex objects functioning as simples, and then also *really* simple ones, like the material points of physics, etc.[30]

These illustrations of objects in terms of points in the visual field and physical points have provided support for conflicting interpretations of the nature of *Tractatus* objects: sense data and physicalistic construals, respectively. While these construals involve radically different epistemological positions—physicalism, unlike classical sense-data theory, involves not only a commitment to the existence of the external world, but also to the thesis that all meaningful language can be analysed into physicalistic propositions—they are both realistic, in the sense that they maintain that it is possible to specify a domain, independent of language, to which the language of the *Tractatus* is to be applied. They are also reductive and revisionary, in that they would analyse our everyday discourse into a language about special philosophical objects—whether they be components of the visual field or physical points. Another possibility Wittgenstein considers is a nonreductive realism, on which the objects we ordinarily name in our current language are the simple objects.[31]

On the other hand, the antirealistic interpretation of *Tractatus* objects holds that objects are not to be identified with any independently specifiable things, for they can only be identified in terms of their role within propositional contexts. The reading lays great stress on Wittgenstein's Fregean dictum that "Only the proposition has sense; only in the context of a proposition does a name have meaning."[32] On this interpretation, the notion of names as independently referring to objects does no real

27. *Notebooks 1914–1916*, p. 3, 4 September 1914.
28. *Notebooks 1914–1916*, p. 45, 6 May 1915. Cf. p. 64, where Wittgenstein says that it is "perfectly possible that patches in our visual field are simple objects, in that we do not perceive any single point of the patch separately." The case for treating the objects of the *Tractatus* as objects of acquaintance is set out in M. B. Hintikka and J. Hintikka, *Investigating Wittgenstein*, ch. 3.
29. *Notebooks 1914–1916*, p. 67, 20 June 1915. For an interpretation of *Tractatus* objects as physical point masses, see J. Griffin, *Wittgenstein's Logical Atomism*.
30. *Notebooks 1914–1916*, p. 69, 21 June 1915.
31. *Notebooks 1914–1916*, p. 60, 16 June 1915.
32. *Tractatus*, 3.3.

work: the meaning of a name just is its role in its language.[33] Alternatively, one can read Wittgenstein as holding that we do not need to reach an ultimate level of analysis, but can stop with whatever we find to be simple:

> The simple thing for us IS: the simplest thing we are acquainted with. —The simplest thing which our analysis can attain—it need appear only as a prototype, as a variable in our propositions—*that* is the simple thing that we mean and look for.[34]

Of course, this is only the barest sketch of a number of leading alternatives in a controversy that has given rise to a huge literature. But all of these positions—whether realistic, antirealistic, or analysis-relative—depend on the assumption that Wittgenstein must have arrived at a specific conception of the nature of objects when he wrote the *Tractatus*. We have already seen that the schematic nature of Wittgenstein's argument for the existence of simple objects and elementary propositions does not yield such a conception. I really see no reason to doubt or ingeniously interpret Norman Malcolm's report that Wittgenstein later told him he had been unable to give any examples of objects when he wrote the *Tractatus*:

> I asked Wittgenstein whether, when he wrote the *Tractatus*, he had ever decided upon anything as an *example* of a "simple object." His reply was that at the time his thought had been that he was a *logician*; and that it was not his business, as a logician, to try to decide whether this thing or that was a simple matter or a complex thing, that being a purely *empirical* matter![35]

Commentators have taken the *Tractatus* to be setting out a bewildering variety of highly specific views about the nature of objects, but the truth is that the book is so programmatic that it can be elaborated in any number of ways. It is highly implausible that Wittgenstein would have avoided a clear resolution of the issue in the *Tractatus* if he had known how to do so. But as he did not reach the ultimate level of analysis, he was unable to say what a *Tractatus* object is, other than to say that it is whatever satisfies the specified conditions: it is logically simple; it has logical form and logical structure; its arrangement with other objects gives rise to elementary propositions that are logically independent of one another; and so forth. Further questions about the ontological status of those objects are left unanswered.

As a result, Wittgenstein's Tractarian conception of the ultimate level of analysis, a notation that clearly presents the structure of the facts, is quite extraordinarily abstract. An analysis is whatever results at the end of an exhaustive specification of a proposition's constituents, thus laying bare the full implications of the proposition to be analysed. What an ordinary sentence conceals by means of enormously complex tacit conventions, a fully analysed sentence will reveal for all to see. The *Tractatus*

33. See Hide Ishiguro, "Use and Reference of Names," and Brian McGuinness, "The So-Called Realism of the *Tractatus*."

34. *Notebooks 1914–1916*, p. 47, 11 May 1915. Cf. "This object is *simple* for *me*!", p. 70, 22 June 1915. For an interpretation of the *Tractatus* treatment of subject and object along these lines, see Hans Sluga "Subjectivity in the *Tractatus*."

35. Malcolm, *Ludwig Wittgenstein: A Memoir*, p. 70. For an excellent example of such an ingenious but implausible reinterpretation of this passage, see Hintikka and Hintikka, *Investigating Wittgenstein*, pp. 73, 79–80.

makes it clear that the process is something like the one we find in Russell's theory of descriptions, Wittgenstein's paradigm of analysis: "It was Russell who performed the service of showing that the apparent logical form of a proposition need not be its real one."[36] But while Wittgenstein seized on Russell's insight that the underlying form may be radically different from the surface form, he neither endorsed Russell's theory of descriptions as the tool to guide an analysis of ordinary language nor offered a clearly defined alternative. Yet again, Wittgenstein had drawn on a convincing example—in this case Russell's theory of descriptions—to underwrite a quite general philosophical programme he had not carried out in any detail. In a lecture given in 1932, Wittgenstein reflected on these problems, saying that both he and Russell

> were at fault for giving no examples of atomic propositions or individuals. We both in different ways pushed the question of examples aside. We should not have said "We can't give them because analysis has not gone far enough, but we'll get there in time." Atomic propositions are not the result of an analysis which has yet to be made.[37]

Four years later, he brought together many of his objections to his own earlier conception of logical atomism in a passage in which he explicitly admits that, though he had expected that a complete analysis would be possible, he had only the most programmatic conception of what it would yield. He begins by contrasting a minimal conception of an elementary proposition, which he still finds acceptable—any ordinary sentence whose truth or falsity is not determined by the truth or falsity of simpler sentences—with his older, much more ambitious conception, which aimed at a complete analysis:

> If you want to use the appellation "elementary proposition" as I did in the *Tractatus*, and as Russell used "atomic proposition," you may call the sentence "Here there is a red rose" an elementary proposition. That is to say, it doesn't contain a truth-function and it isn't defined by an expression which contains one. But if we're to say that a proposition isn't an elementary proposition unless its complete logical analysis shows that it isn't built out of other propositions by truth-functions, we are presupposing that we have an idea of what such an "analysis" would be. Formerly, I myself spoke of a "complete analysis," and I used to believe that philosophy had to give a definitive dissection of propositions so as to set out clearly all their connections and remove all possibilities of misunderstanding. I spoke as if there was a calculus in which such a dissection would be possible. I vaguely had in mind something like the definition that Russell had given for the definite article, and I used to think that in a similar way one would be able to use visual impressions etc. to define the concept say of a sphere, and thus exhibit once for all the connections between the concepts and lay bare the source of all misunderstandings, etc. At the root of all this was a false and idealized picture of the use of language.[38]

36. *Tractatus*, 4.0031.
37. *Wittgenstein's Lectures, Cambridge, 1932–1935*, p. 11.
38. *Philosophical Grammar*, p. 211. "Probably written in summer 1936." MS 116, p. 80; cf. *Wittgenstein's Lectures, Cambridge, 1932–1935*, p. 11.

Because Wittgenstein did not carry through the project of analyzing ordinary propositions in the *Tractatus*, his conception of analysis and atomic propositions was left untested. The explanation for this shortcoming was that the complex conventions that govern the use of our language conceal its true form. When he wrote the *Tractatus*, Wittgenstein took it for granted that the true form of all logical relations between propositions is truth-functional. But truth-functional logic deals with the logical relations between propositions that are logically independent of one another—in other words, cases where the truth or falsity of any one proposition is not affected by the truth or falsity of any other proposition. As a result, Wittgenstein held that all atomic propositions, the propositions that are reached at the final stage of analysis, are logically independent. As there are no logical connections between atomic propositions, one atomic proposition cannot be deduced from another.[39] Any logically complex proposition must be analysable into a set of atomic propositions, linked by truth-functional connectives. Here, at least, Wittgenstein thought he had anticipated the overall form of any analysis, regardless of whatever might later be discovered.

In the *Tractatus*, Wittgenstein simply put apparent counterexamples—such as propositions about the relationship between different shades of a colour, or different possible positions in space—to one side, expecting these anomalies would yield to further analysis. Thus, while he states in the *Tractatus* that the simultaneous presence of two colours at the same place in the visual field is logically impossible, "ruled out by the logical structure of colour,"[40] he gave no principled explanation of how that could be so. Instead, he said that the contradiction is roughly like the impossibility in physics of a particle's having two velocities at the same time—"i.e. it can't be in two places at the same time, i.e. particles in different places at the same time can't be identical."[41] But the comparison only presents us with an additional problem; it does not solve either of them. *Both* of them call for further analysis, analyses that Wittgenstein does not, and cannot, give. Instead, he parenthetically reminds his reader that "(It is clear that the logical product of two elementary propositions can neither be a tautology nor a contradiction. The statement that a point in the visual field has two different colours at the same time is a contradiction.)"[42] The reader is left to draw the conclusion that statements about points in the visual field are not elementary propositions and therefore we do not need to worry about the problem any further. But that is no solution to the problem he began with, a problem he put to one side until his return to full-time philosophical work in 1929.

3.3 The Application of Language

Like Kant, Wittgenstein held that the resolution of philosophical problems about the nature of representation depends on an understanding of the nature of the limits of mind and world. In a famous letter to Marcus Herz, Kant says that the question of

39. *Tractatus*, 5.134. Cf. 2.062, 4.211, and 5.135.
40. *Tractatus*, 6.3751. Cf. the more tentative expression of this train of thought on 16 August 1916, in *Notebooks 1914–1916*, p. 81.
41. *Tractatus*, 6.3751.
42. *Tractatus*, 6.3751.

the ground of the relation of representation to its object "constitutes the key to the whole secret of hitherto still obscure metaphysics."[43] The obscure metaphysical question that occupied Kant was the problem of understanding how knowledge is possible. If mind and world are separate, how can we know that the mind represents the world correctly? In response to the conflict between rationalism, which dogmatically asserts that we must have knowledge of the world, and empiricism, which leads to scepticism, Kant insisted that we must first understand the nature of the mind. Kant's "Copernican revolution" consisted in the insight that representation is a rule-governed activity and that the rules which constitute the mind also constitute the world. Mind and world are so interrelated that they can only be understood together, by examining their common structure. Despite the many differences of detail, each philosopher appeals to certain logical principles that constitute the common structure of representation and that which is represented. In Kant's critical philosophy, the structure is provided by the forms of judgment; in Wittgenstein's, by the notion of logical form. In a note written in 1931, Wittgenstein referred to the Kantian connection in the following terms:

> The limit of language shows itself in the impossibility of describing the fact which corresponds to a sentence (is its translation) without repeating that very sentence.
> (What we are dealing with here is the Kantian solution to the problem of philosophy.)[44]

What corresponds to a true sentence is itself a fact, a linguistically structured state of affairs. On this conception of what there is, the world ("all that is the case") has the same structure as language, so that the very idea of stepping outside our language to check whether it fits the facts, whether it describes the world correctly, or to give a further characterization of the representational relation between language and the world, is incoherent. The insight plays a central role in Wittgenstein's rejection of any semantic theory throughout his philosophical work; nevertheless, the Tractarian doctrine of showing enabled him to retain a sublimated semantic theory—one that supposedly can only be shown—while simultaneously denying that anything can be *said* about the relation between language and the world.

Thus, while the Wittgenstein of the *Tractatus* was convinced that language pictures the world and so the underlying structure of a sentence must be equivalent to the structure of the facts it represents, the problem of setting out, in any detail, *how* a given proposition does so was left untouched. Nonetheless, he had no doubt that everyday language is in order as it is and that it does mirror the structure of the world:

> If we know on purely logical grounds that there must be elementary propositions, then everyone who understands propositions in their unanalysed form must know it.

43. Letter to Marcus Herz, February 21, 1772. Immanuel Kant, *Kant—Philosophical Correspondence 1759–99*, pp. 71–72. See L. W. Beck, "Kant's Letter to Marcus Herz." Kant's letter to Herz is the starting point for David Stern, "'What is the ground of the relationship of that in us which we call "representation" to the object?' Reflections on the Kantian Legacy in the Philosophy of Mind."
44. *Culture and Value*, p. 10. Source: MS 110, p. 61, 1931.

In fact, all the propositions of our everyday language, just as they stand, are in perfect logical order.[45]

Of course, the signs from which our propositions are constructed—the words of everyday language, and the corresponding psychical constituents that make up our thoughts—do not clearly display the underlying structure that Wittgenstein had deduced.[46] However, he believed that any meaningful proposition of ordinary language must have an analysis that clearly displays its underlying structure, a truth-functionally related set of atomic propositions whose surface structure is identical with the structure of the facts it represents.

While the inscriptions we see on the page or the acoustical vibrations we produce when we speak do not clearly display their structure, that structure is supposed to be shown by the use we make of them, by their *application*. In the *Tractatus*, Wittgenstein draws a corresponding distinction between a propositional sign and a propositional symbol (*Zeichen* and *Symbol*). The sign is the perceptible part of a proposition, such as the inscriptions or vibrations, while the symbol is the perceptible sign plus its application, its imperceptible projective relation to the world: "A sign is what can be perceived of a symbol. So one and the same sign (written, spoken, etc.) can be common to two different symbols—in which case they will signify in different ways. . . . [T]he sign, of course, is arbitrary."[47] The relationship between sign and symbol is summed up as follows: "What does not get expressed in the sign is shown by its application. What signs conceal, their application expresses."[48] That remark replaces a longer and much more specific passage in the *Prototractatus* contrasting the complex application of our ordinary signs and the application of a fully analysed language:

> Although every word has meaning via its definitions, this only means that these definitions are necessary in order to present in our sign-language the full linguistic depiction of the thought to whose expression the word contributes. But the definitions can be left tacit and the word does not then lose its meaning, since it still stands in the same relation to the objects which are depicted by means of the definitions—only we do not specifically depict that relation. Naturally this often simplifies the sign-language and makes the understanding of it more and more difficult, because the decisive factor now lies outside the signs in something that is not expressed—their relation to their objects.[49]

Characteristically, Wittgenstein even thought this elucidatory proposition could itself be left out of the published *Tractatus*. But there is no reason to think he had rejected the train of thought he sets out here—namely, the contrast between ordinary language, consisting of relatively simple signs that stand in a very complex representational relationship with the world, and a fully analysed language, consisting of a much more complex arrangement of signs in a very simple representational relationship with the world.

45. *Tractatus*, 5.5562–5.5563.
46. See *Tractatus*, 4.002; quoted in chapter 2, pp. 48–49.
47. *Tractatus*, 3.32, 3.322.
48. *Tractatus*, 3.262. Cf. 3.31, 3.32.
49. *Prototractatus*, 3.202111. This remark, which does not occur in the *Tractatus*, follows 3.20211 (= *Tractatus* 3.261) and is followed by 3.2012 (= *Tractatus* 3.263).

Given Wittgenstein's definition of a sign, no sign, taken by itself, can be considered intrinsically meaningful: one always has to see how a sign is to be applied, to grasp the way it represents. As a result, he distinguishes two ways of conceiving of a picture, corresponding to his distinction between sign and symbol: as a fact, a determinate arrangement of objects, and that fact together with the representational relation which makes it into a picture.[50]

The ability to apply language, to see signs as symbols, as intrinsically related to their objects, is not itself a further fact in the world, but is a matter of our establishing a projective relationship between certain facts. The projective relation, the sign's meaning, cannot itself be a fact, for all facts are logically independent of one another, and there is a logical connection between a picture qua symbol and what it pictures. Thus the connection cannot itself be stated, for only facts can be stated. But it can be shown by the structure of our language, much as the projective connection between two depictions of the same thing in different perspectives can be shown. Any combination of signs is only meaningful due to our applying them in a certain way; everyday language depends on the existence of extremely complex conventions connecting the words we use with the objects they stand for. Similarly, even the signs of a fully analysed language would have to be explained before we could understand them. Like the signs that make up the propositions we presently speak and think, they would be conventionally meaningful: their meaning would be a product of linguistic conventions, just as the meaning of the words we presently use is conventional. In both cases, we would also have to know how to use the words in question, how to apply them. Not all signs can be given a meaning in this way, however: some must be nonconventionally meaningful and so not susceptible to being either interpreted or misinterpreted. In the *Tractatus*, "thoughts" play this role: a thought is an *applied* propositional sign, a picture together with the method of projection that gives it its significance:[51]

> In a proposition a thought finds an expression that can be perceived by the senses.
>
> We use the perceptible sign of a proposition (spoken or written, etc.) as a projection of a possible situation.
> The method of projection is to think the sense of the proposition.[52]

A Tractarian thought is not simply an inner monologue or image, for these are facts on a par with physical facts composed of words and pictures. Indeed, Wittgenstein explicitly told Russell that a thought consists of "psychical constituents that have the same sort of relation to reality as words. What those constituents are I don't know."[53] On the Tractarian use of the term, a thought is not just a concatenation of signs, but the signs together with their application, the act of thinking the projective relation that gives them their life.

In *Tractatus* number 3.5, Wittgenstein defines a thought as an "applied, thought out, propositional sign," and in the next proposition, number 4, he equates it with a

50. *Tractatus*, 2.14, 2.1513.
51. *Tractatus*, 3.5; see 3 ff. and 4.
52. *Tractatus*, 3.1–3.11.
53. *Letters to Russell, Keynes and Moore*, p. 72, 19 August 1919.

proposition with a sense. Unlike the signs in a merely physical language, thoughts are essentially meaningful. They comprise not only the mental signs that correspond to the signs we use in written and spoken language, but also the act of thinking those signs. The mental entity or process, whatever it may be, that animates our use of language is what distinguishes the merely mechanical process of simply manipulating signs and behaving in the appropriate way from genuine understanding. Thus a thought, in the *Tractatus* sense of the term, is intrinsically related to its object—there is a logical connection between the two—a connection that could only be established by the mental activity of applying language to the world.[54] These mysterious and shadowy mental processes give public language its significance. On this view, our language is like paper currency in an economy on the gold standard, only meaningful insofar as it is backed up by gold in the bank—that is, intrinsically representational processes. The account of the sense of a sentence as consisting in a special mental process depends almost entirely on the metaphor of the "projective relationship" between signs and what they stand for, yet, because Wittgenstein maintains the application of language cannot be described in language, he never really develops the theory he intimates. The views about the application of language set out in the previous section are only sketched in the *Tractatus*, protected from further formulation by the Tractarian doctrine that the relation between language and world cannot be stated, but can only be "shown." While the picture of the relationship between language, experience, and world that I have just set out is hinted at in the *Tractatus*, in the central role Wittgenstein gives to thought in his account of propositions, in his sympathy for solipsism and his identification of the world with life, it only emerges clearly in his subsequent work.[55] It was only in the late 1920s, when Wittgenstein realized that the *Tractatus*' dogmatism would not do, that he returned to grappling with the problems raised by his essentialism about meaning and the need for an account of the relationship between language and experience.

3.4 The Subjects of the *Tractatus*

While most of the *Tractatus* is devoted to developing the account of logic and language that enables Wittgenstein to draw the limits of language "from within," there is a sense in which all this is only an elaboration of some of the implications of the distinction between showing and saying. Wittgenstein began his reply to Russell's preliminary questions about the book by insisting on this very point:

> —Now I'm afraid you haven't really got hold of my main contention, to which the whole business of logical propositions is only a corollary. The main point is the theory of what can be said by propositions—i.e. by language—(and, which

54. This view of the irreducibly mental and intentional character of meaning was diametrically opposed to Russell's Humean view of meaning, on which it is nothing more than a feeling which accompanies certain mental processes. See Bertrand Russell "On Propositions: What They Are and How They Mean"; Richard McDonough, *The Argument of the* Tractatus, ch. VI.1; and S. S. Hilmy, *The Later Wittgenstein*, p. 109 ff.

55. See *Tractatus* 3–3.12; 5.6–5.641; 6.431–6.4311. The further development of these ideas in 1929 and the years immediately afterward is one of the main topics of chapters 4 and 5 in this volume.

comes to the same thing, what can be *thought*) and what cannot be said by proposi-tions, but only shown; which, I believe, is the cardinal problem of philosophy.—[56]

The "cardinal problem of philosophy" is the question of the limits and nature of lan-guage, the question of what, in general, can be said, and what can only be shown. In the preface to the *Tractatus*, Wittgenstein expressed his belief that he had arrived at the definitive "final solution" to the problems of philosophy. That confidence was based on his conviction that the book makes clear the limits of language by sharply demarcating what can be said—namely, factual assertion—and placing all philosophi-cal theses about such matters as the nature of self and world, aesthetics, morality, or religion on the other side of the limit. The demarcation depends on a conception of language and logic that is not so much defended as presented in the text of the *Tractatus*, where Wittgenstein aims at an insight that lies beyond assertion, argu-ment, or theory formation. For that reason, my exposition of the *Tractatus* began with a discussion of the crucial role of insight in the picture theory. As the very use of the term "picture *theory*" suggests, however, Wittgenstein's insistence that all philo-sophical theories are nonsense was subverted by his own dependence on a distinc-tion between plain nonsense, which can be dismissed, and important nonsense, which points to philosophical insights that cannot be put into words. The concept of show-ing is supposed to bridge the gap: while any attempt to state the picture theory as though it were an empirical fact must lead to nonsense, the truth of the theory can be shown by drawing the reader's attention to the structure of certain sentences. As we have seen, the notion of showing is central to Wittgenstein's account of the nature of logical propositions and factual assertion. Simple logical propositions are Wittgen-stein's exemplars of how language shows what it cannot say, and the account is then extended, by means of the picture theory, so that it applies to factual propositions.

These uses of the concept of showing—where an insight into the structure of a certain form of words leads to a specific insight into the structure in question—are only part of the task assigned to showing in Wittgenstein's early philosophy. He believed he had safeguarded what really mattered, the ethical point of his book, as he put it in his letter to Ludwig von Ficker,[57] precisely by placing it beyond the limits of language altogether. These crucial insights into the nature of the subject, ethics, and religion are not supposed to be shown by logical analysis; instead, they "show themselves" in philosophy's running up against the limits of language and so attempt-ing to say the unsayable. A number of crucial doctrines that can neither be said nor shown are accommodated within the Tractarian system in this way. Thus, the limits of empirical reality, what the solipsist means, whether two expressions are inter-substitutible, that there are laws of nature, and the meaning of life are all said to "show themselves."[58]

Leading examples of important nonsense that arises when Wittgenstein attempts to talk about the inexpressible are such theses as *The limits of my language* mean

56. *Letters to Russell, Keynes and Moore*, p. 71, 19 August 1919.
57. See chapter 1, p. 8.
58. *Tractatus*, 5.5561, 5.62, 6.23, 6.36, 6.52–6.522. The nature of internal properties (4.122), the nature of logical constants (5.4), and that "p v ~p" says nothing (5.513) are also said to "show them-selves." The notion is obscured by the 1961 translation, where *"sich zeigen"* is translated as "makes itself manifest."

[handwritten top margin: "Q, there a difference between the problem of actually showing something and that of something showing itself?"]

the limits of my world . . . I am my world";[59] "The sense of the world must lie outside the world";[60] "ethics cannot be put into words";[61] "God does not reveal himself
in the world."[62] Nevertheless, the inexpressible and mystical "shows itself":

> We feel that even when all *possible* scientific questions have been answered,
> the problems of life remain completely untouched. Of course there are then no ques-
> tions left, and this itself is the answer.

> There is indeed the inexpressible. This *shows* itself; it is the mystical.[63]

Wittgenstein did connect his mysticism with a sense of wonder at the existence of
the world, an amazement that there is something rather than nothing, and also with
"feeling the world as a limited whole," experiences that involve an awareness of the
world as a whole and its mystical nature that cannot be literally stated.[64] In the 1929
"Lecture on Ethics," a short talk written for a Cambridge club, he tried to convey his
ethical and religious convictions by offering some vivid examples of experiences of
his own. One of them he sums up in the phrase "I wonder at the existence of the world,"
by which he means wondering, marvelling, at the fact that anything at all should exist.
Another is the experience of feeling absolutely safe, the feeling that nothing whatsoever can harm one. But then he goes on to argue that neither of these expressions
makes sense, for to talk of absolute safety, or to wonder at the existence of the world,
is to use words that have come adrift from the specific contexts where they have
meaning. That leads him to reflect on the limitations of the similes he had been using
in attempting to convey the insights that he connected with these experiences:

> [I]n ethical and religious language we seem constantly to be using similes. But a
> simile must be the simile for *something*. And if I can describe a fact by means of
> a simile I must also be able to drop the simile and to describe the facts without it.
> Now in our case as soon as we try to drop the simile and simply to state the facts
> which stand behind it, we find that there are no such facts. And so, what at first
> appeared to be a simile now seems to be mere nonsense.[65]

[handwritten margin note: "+ metaphors?"]

While a great deal depends on the notion of showing in the *Tractatus*, it is entirely consistent with Wittgenstein's ideas about the limits of language that the book
has so little to say about how certain matters "show theselves," for it is a direct consequence of the central role of the picture theory that Wittgenstein is unable to articulate a positive conception of his ethical and religious views. According to the
Tractatus, the philosopher's task is to make clear what propositions show so that we
do not fall prey to saying what we cannot say, to help us avoid misunderstanding
and in so doing, "see the world aright." Consequently, the crucial aspects of Wittgenstein's ethical and religious outlook cannot be stated, only seen.

Although Wittgenstein's reliance on the notion of matters that "show themselves"
is integral to his conception of the ultimately ethical aim of the *Tractatus*, most read-

59. *Tractatus*, 5.6–5.63.
60. *Tractatus*, 6.41.
61. *Tractatus*, 6.421.
62. *Tractatus*, 6.432.
63. *Tractatus*, 6.52, 6.522.
64. "A Lecture on Ethics," p. 8 ff.; *Tractatus*, 6.45.
65. "Lecture on Ethics," p. 10.

ers have found it hard to see what connects the ethical dimension of the book with its account of logical form, other than Wittgenstein's need to find some way of expressing his views about self, religion, and morality within the constraints imposed by the Tractarian system. To put the same point in slightly different terms, it is extremely difficult to see precisely *how* the logic and ontology of the *Tractatus*, the ostensible subject matter of most of the book, are connected with the transcendent insights that Wittgenstein regarded as its real point. While the book is supposedly restricted to mapping the limits of language from within, it is absolutely essential that these further insights cannot be expressed in language. In his wartime notebooks, Wittgenstein did consider the possibility that some other medium, such as music, might be the answer:

> But is *language*: the *only* language?
> Why should there not be a mode of expression through which I can talk *about* language in such a way that it can appear to me in co-ordination with something else?
>
> Suppose that music were such a mode of expression: then it is at any rate characteristic of *science* that *no* musical themes can occur in it.[66]

At the same time, he was well aware of the incoherence of any such train of thought. A few days earlier, he had placed another formulation of his question about an alternative means of expression in quotation marks, indicating an interlocutory voice, and then gave his own reply:

> "But might there not be something which cannot be expressed by a *proposition* (and which is also not an object)?" In that case, this could not be expressed by means of *language*; and it is also impossible for us to *ask* about it. . . .
>
> What cannot be expressed we do not express——. And how try to *ask* whether THAT can be expressed which cannot be EXPRESSED?[67]

While Wittgenstein rejected the idea of something lying beyond the facts as incoherent, he nevertheless found it deeply tempting. Thus the seemingly unequivocal passage I have just quoted is immediately followed by an emphatic reiteration of the original interlocutory question (the italics are in the original): *"Is there no domain outside the facts?"*

The manifest tension between what his theory of language allows him to say and what it leaves him wanting to say is particularly apparent in his discussion of the self in the *Notebooks* and *Tractatus*. For it is here that the positivistic doctrines of the *Tractatus* and the antipositivistic subtext collide most directly. On the one hand, the conclusion that the self as subject of experience, the self conceived of as a simple thing that is related to the many different things that pass through experience, cannot be a part of the Tractarian world is a direct consequence of the conception of the nature of facts, objects, and representation we have already encountered. Because both picturing fact and pictured fact are equally complex, there is no room in such a world of facts for a simple self that represents its world: "here we have no co-ordination of a fact and an object [the fact thought about and the self that does the think-

66. *Notebooks 1914–1916*, p. 52, 29 May 1915.
67. *Notebooks 1914–1916*, pp. 51, 52, 27 May 1915. Cf. *Tractatus* 6.522, cited on p. 71.

ing], but a co-ordination of facts by means of a co-ordination of their objects."[68] On the other hand, there is still a sense in which the existence of the self must nevertheless be admitted, if one reflects on the "the world as I find it," both because its *structure* implies the existence of a self, even though no self can be found within it—in Wittgenstein's cryptic summary, "the world is *my* world"—and because of the ethical need for a bearer of moral value. All these lines of inquiry converge on the issue of the nature of the self, with the result that it only came to seem even less comprehensible: "The I, the I is what is deeply mysterious!"[69]

From the secondary level, one can identify human bodies and experiences as the bodies and experiences of particular human subjects, but these subjects are only complex constructs that allow us to organize certain kinds of information in convenient ways. From the primary level, one cannot identify a self, a thing that has the experiences that make up the primary world, but if one looks at that world in the right way, it supposedly shows the sense in which there is a "philosophical self"[70]—precisely what one cannot say. In this way, the *Tractatus* simultaneously excludes subjectivity from the world and recognizes that it cannot be altogether excluded.

The central negative point in the *Tractatus* treatment of the self is the denial that there is a self to be found *within* immediate experience by means of introspection, a "thinking, representing subject"[71] that both possesses my experiences and is itself experienced. Two complementary lines of argument are offered for this Humean conclusion. The first turns on the point that everything to be found within experience is just another content of experience that could have been otherwise, not something that *has* all of those experiences. Experience contains a certain ensemble of facts—namely, all that is the case within what Wittgenstein calls "the world," "my world," "life," "the microcosm," and "the world as I found it," but no self:

The world and life are one.

I am my world. (The microcosm.)

There is no such thing as the subject that thinks or entertains ideas.

If I wrote a book called *The world as I found it*, I should have to include a report on my body, and should have to say which parts were subordinate to my will, and which were not, etc., this being a method of isolating the subject, or rather of showing that in an important sense there is no subject; for it alone could *not* be mentioned in that book.—[72]

68. *Tractatus*, 5.542. Cf. 5.5421: "This shows that there is no such thing as the soul—the subject, etc.—as it is conceived in the superficial psychology of the present day."

69. *Notebooks 1914–1916*, p. 80, 5 August 1916.

70. *Tractatus*, 5.64.

71. *Tractatus*, 5.631.

72. *Tractatus*, 5.621–5.631. In the "Lecture on Ethics," p. 6, Wittgenstein made a parallel point about the impossibility of inferring anything about what is ethically right or wrong from such a description of what is the case:

Suppose one of you were an omniscient person and therefore knew all the movements of all the bodies in the world dead or alive and that he also knew all the states of mind of all human beings that ever lived, and suppose this man wrote all he knew in a big book, then this book would contain the whole description of the world; and what I want to say is, that this book would contain nothing that we would call an *ethical* judgment or anything that would logi-

The observation that we do not have an experience of a self over and above the contents of experience is reiterated in the *Philosophical Remarks* and Big Typescript:

> The experience of feeling pain is not that a person "I" has something.
> I distinguish an intensity, a location, etc. in the pain, but not an owner.[73]

Wittgenstein also argues that the very idea of a subject of experience, a thing within experience that is its owner, is ruled out by the nature of representation. Assume for the sake of argument that there were a psychological subject, a thing that had each of one's experiences, that was itself experienced. That thing would necessarily be related to every other experience. But such necessary connections are not to be found within experience, for it consists of facts that are logically independent of one another. In the *Philosophical Remarks*, Wittgenstein put the point in the following terms: "The essential thing is that the representation of visual space is the representation of an object and contains no suggestion of a subject."[74]

Wittgenstein does not simply deny the existence of the self of introspective psychology, a self that might provide the solipsist with a starting point from which to draw a distinction between "my world" and "the world." He also affirms the existence of a "metaphysical subject, the limit of the world."[75] The first mention of such a conception of the subject in the *Notebooks* occurs in June 1916, where, after a month during which he recorded nothing at all, Wittgenstein asks, "What do I know about God and the purpose of life?", and responds with a list of answers that amount to a summary statement of his conception of the nature of self, world, and God when seen from a moral standpoint:

> I know that this world exists.
> That I am placed in it like my eye in its visual field.
> That something about it is problematic, which we call its meaning.
> That this meaning does not lie in it but outside it.
> That life is the world.
> That my will penetrates the world.
> That my will is good and evil.
> Therefore that good and evil are somehow connected with the meaning of the
> world.
> The meaning of life, i.e. the meaning of the world, we can call God.
> And connect it with the comparison of God to a father.
> To pray is to think about the meaning of life.
> I cannot bend the happenings of the world to my will: I am completely power
> less.

---

cally imply such a judgment. It would of course contain all relative judgments of value and all true scientific propositions and in fact all true propositions that can be made. But all the facts described would, as it were, stand on the same level and in the same way all propositions stand on the same level. There are no propositions which, in any absolute sense, are sublime, important, or trivial.

73. *Philosophical Remarks*, §65; Big Typescript, §104, p. 506.
74. *Philosophical Remarks*, §71.
75. *Tractatus*, 5.641.

I can only make myself independent of the world—and so in a certain sense master it—by renouncing any influence on happenings.[76]

Wittgenstein's elaboration of his conception of the metaphysical subject in the *Tractatus* turns on the analogy mentioned in the second item in his catechism: the analogy between the relation between the eye and the visual field and the relation between metaphysical subject and the world. Just as one cannot find an "I" by introspection, one cannot find the eye by looking in the visual field: all one can find are the contents of visual experience, not the place from which they are seen.

The outer limits of the visual field are like the outer limits of the physical world; in neither case does it make sense to think of going beyond those limits. While there is empty unseen physical space beyond the physical walls of my room, there is no unseen visual space behind the walls in my visual image, the walls that are the present limit of my visual field. If I were to turn toward the window, I would be able to see beyond the space I now see, if we talk in physical terms. But nothing I could do could ever count as seeing beyond the limits of my visual field, for whatever I come to see will itself be part of that field.

Visual space and physical space have different geometries: visual space has an outer limit which we cannot see past and an inner limit which we cannot see, while a room only has an outer limit which we can see past. In the Big Typescript and *Blue Book*, Wittgenstein explores these geometries by looking in greater detail at how we talk about visual and physical space. Thus he writes, in a section of the Big Typescript on "The Seeing Subject and Visual Space," that "the term 'visual space' of course only refers to a geometry, I mean to a portion of the grammar of our language."[77] Here, he denies that it makes sense to think of visual space as a part of physical space, or as a screen on which the current visual picture occurs. After warning of the dangers of identifying the contents of visual space with the contents of physical space, he elaborates a parallel moral about the seeing subject:

> It is now important, that the proposition "I cannot immediately see the eye with which I see" is either a surreptitious grammatical proposition or nonsense. Actually, the expression "nearer to (or, further from) the seeing eye" has another grammar than "nearer to the blue object which I see." The visual appearance which corresponds to the description "A puts on the glasses" is fundamentally different from that which I describe with the words: "I put on the glasses." I could now say: "my visual space is similar to a cone," but then it must be understood that here I am thinking of the cone as a space, as representative of a geometry, not as part of a space (room).[78]

In the *Blue Book*, Wittgenstein spells out this distinction between the physical eye, the biological mechanism we usually use to see, and the geometrical eye, the place from which visual space is seen, which is determined by my pointing at it.[79] While physical eyes and geometrical eyes usually coincide, it is conceivable that I might start to see from the tip of my nose or from a point outside my body altogether.

76. *Notebooks, 1914–1916* p. 73, 11 June 1916.
77. Big Typescript, §97, p. 463. [German in appendix.]
78. Big Typescript, §97, pp. 463–464. [German in appendix.]
79. *Blue Book*, pp. 63–64.

Within physical space it is perfectly possible to identify someone's geometric eye: it is the place a person points to when asked to point to the place from which he or she sees. But that place is not a part of the person's visual field, and so from within the context of the visual field it cannot be identified—it lies at its inner limit.

However, the aspect of the analogy that Wittgenstein explicitly develops in the *Tractatus* concerns the case of the inner limit of visual space—the eye:

> Where *in* the world is a metaphysical subject to be found?
> You will say that this is exactly like the case of the eye and the visual field.
> But really you do *not* see the eye.
> And nothing *in the visual field* allows you to infer that it is seen by the eye.
>
> For the form of the visual field is surely not like this:[80]

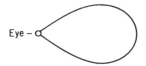

Wittgenstein replies to the rhetorical question at the beginning of this passage by acknowledging that someone who thinks there really is a metaphysical subject in my world, over and above all of the things that I find in it, will turn his analogy against him: "You will say that this is exactly like the case of the eye and the visual field." At first sight, there is an apparently straightforward rebuttal to the view that the self is not a part of experience: one can reply that although the eye is not part of the field of vision, it is an independent object with a definite location, one that can be inferred from what one does see within one's visual field. Wittgenstein's cryptic response turns on the idea that if we are to take the analogy seriously, then we must treat the visual field as analogous to the world as a whole, in which case it would be illegitimate to appeal to anything outside the visual field in attempting to identify the eye: "you do *not* really see the eye."[81] To understand this move, it is crucial to see that he is not talking about the physical relation between the objects I look at and the physiological organ I use to see, for in that sense, one *can* see one's eye in a mirror. What "you do *not* really see" is the geometrical relation between the contents of your present visual experience and the perspectival point from which it is seen, the inner vanishing point constructed by extrapolating from the structure of the contents of experience. Wittgenstein is not interested in the empirical eye, or the empirical subject, physical objects with a history and a location, but a transcendental standpoint that makes the world possible yet is not a part of it, a subject that vanishes if it is correctly understood:

> The I of solipsism shrinks to an extensionless point and what remains is the reality co-ordinated with it.
>
> What has history to do with me? Mine is the first and only world.[82]

80. *Tractatus*, 5.633–5.6331.
81. *Tractatus*, 5.633.
82. *Notebooks, 1914–1916*, p. 82, 2 September 1916. Cf. *Tractatus*, 5.64.

In other words, by "the eye" in these passages Wittgenstein means the inner limit of the visual field, the point from which the contents of the visual field are seen. For instance, when I look at myself in the mirror I can see a visual image of my physical eye in the mirror, but I cannot see the inner limit of my visual field, the point from which it is projected.

The train of thought I have just set out is closely connected with the Tractarian dictum that the subject does not belong to the world but is its limit.[83] The limit of the world cannot be a boundary or border of the normal kind, separating two different regions, for the world is all there can be, and so there can be nothing beyond it.[84] Instead, Wittgenstein identifies the metaphysical subject with the logical structure of my world when it is seen in a certain way. Any experience must satisfy whatever constraints that structure imposes, and these limits are also expressed by the grammar of the language we use to talk about the phenomena. Just as a geometrical space has a structure that determines what figures can and cannot occur, so grammar determines what propositions can be said. Like the closed space of Riemannian geometry, the space of the *Tractatus* curves in on itself, so that it makes no sense to ask whether there is something that lies beyond those limits. Wittgenstein's view about the status of the subject is summed up in the thesis that "The subject does not belong to the world; rather, it is a limit of the world."[85] The *Tractatus* discussion of solipsism concludes with the following amplification of the positive part of that message:

> [T]here is really a sense in which, in philosophy, there is a non-psychological issue about the self.
> What brings the self into philosophy is the fact that "the world is my world."
> The philosophical self is not the human being, not the human body, or the human soul, with which psychology deals, but rather the metaphysical subject, the limit of the world—not a part of it.[86]

While what the solipsist means to say about the metaphysical subject cannot be spoken of coherently, Wittgenstein's positive pronouncement is that what the solipsist means to say "shows itself."[87] If the exoteric doctrine of the *Tractatus* is that there is no such thing as the subject of experience, the esoteric doctrine is that there is.

Wittgenstein's early critique of solipsism arises out of a deep sympathy for what the solipsist wants to say. Thus, he writes in the *Tractatus* that "what the solipsist *means* is quite correct."[88] Yet whenever he attempted to articulate these ideas more fully, he ran up against the limits of language, for "what belongs to the essence of the world cannot be expressed by language."[89] As a result, we have no systematic exposition of his conception of the relationship between primary and secondary sys-

---

83. *Tractatus*, 5.632.
84. Cf. *Tractatus*, 3.03 ff.
85. *Tractatus*, 5.632.
86. *Tractatus*, 5.641.
87. *Tractatus*, 5.62.
88. *Tractatus*, 5.62.
89. *Philosophical Remarks*, §54; Big Typescript, §91, p. 427.

tems, only occasional fragmentary remarks and a number of later criticisms. One of Ramsey's notes from the 1920s is quite unequivocal on the question whether Wittgenstein was ever a solipsist, identifying "the world is my world" of the *Tractatus* with a view on which all one can really talk about is what is given in experience. On the construal of Wittgenstein set out in that note, talk of such things as my body, your body, your mind, is only a logical construction, a matter of what Wittgenstein termed "hypothesis." Ramsey's note has the telegraphic character of a note summarizing a discussion. Whether or not it is accurate in every detail, the general character of his description of Wittgenstein's characteristic combination of solipsism and behaviourism at this point in his career is quite unmistakable:

> W[ittgenstein] says [it's] nonsense to believe in anything not given in experience not merely [anything] different in kind. For to be mine, to be given in experience is [a] formal property [for anything] to be a genuine entity. Other people's s[ense] d[ata] and my s[ense] d[ata] i.e. those attached to my body as other people's to their bodies are logical constructions. For all we know does not involve them; they simplify general laws but are not required by them any more than m[aterial] o[bject]s. Take the criterion of "he sees" to be the meaning of "he sees." Similar[ly, take the criterion of] "I see" [to be the meaning of] "I see." Then "I see" is also connected with reality (visual appearance) other than how his seeing is, and this is that the world is my world.[90]

On this view, to be real, to be a "genuine entity," as Ramsey puts it, is to be given in my experience, and it is nonsensical to say that anything else is real. Reality is equated with what I see. Like Wittgenstein, Ramsey begins by talking about experience and then shifts to visual appearance, taking it for granted that it will stand in for all the senses: the world is nothing more than what I experience, although it may be convenient to augment our language with some inessential hypotheses. This view about the nature of knowledge is presented as a corollary of a verificationist theory of meaning: the meaning of a proposition is equated with the procedure which connects that proposition with some aspect of my experience. Talk of anything that is not given in my immediate experience—whether it is a physical object, someone else's experience, or even experiences one once had but can no longer remember—is merely an hypothesis, a "logical construction." It is convenient to make use of such constructions, but nonsense to believe that they refer to anything. In short, a proposition has meaning in virtue of its relation to the contents of experience, and reality is equated with what is given in experience.

In the Big Typescript, Wittgenstein summarizes the contrast between the secondary level of talk about physical objects, where talk of a self is a convenient hypothesis, and the primary level of experiential description, where no self is to be found, in the following terms:

> The subject-object form refers to the body and the things around it which affect it.

90. Ramsey, unpublished manuscript, Pittsburgh catalogue number 004-21-02. The square brackets contain my interpolations; the final parentheses are Ramsey's.

In the non-hypothetical description of the seen, heard—these words designate grammatical forms here—the I does not enter, there is no talk of subject and object here.

Solipsism would be refuted by the fact that the word "I" has no central position in grammar, but rather is a word like any other.

As in visual space, there is no metaphysical subject in language either.

/ The difficulty, which speaking about visual space without a subject, and about "*my* and *his* toothaches" causes us, is that of straightening out language so that it fits the facts correctly./[91]

The third and fifth paragraphs allude to a technique that he developed in his post-*Tractatus* work as a way of expounding his rejection of the notion that a self is to be found within experience: proposing that we consider a language that dispenses with the word "I" altogether. In the *Philosophical Remarks*, Wittgenstein writes that use of the word "I" in talk about immediate experience is "one of the most misleading representational techniques in our language."[92] He maintains that the subject-predicate grammar of our everyday language has such a firm grip on us that we are usually quite unaware of its influence. Because the grammar of ordinary language has been shaped by the need to successfully manipulate our environment, and because we use the same language to describe our immediate experience, we fail to see that they are fundamentally different. As a result, we usually understand experience in subject-predicate terms: we say such things as "I have a headache" and take it for granted that the term "I" refers to a subject, the self.

Wittgenstein's response to these difficulties is to suggest that we imagine talking about one's experience without using the word "I." As we shall see, there is a sense in which his new language is equivalent to our present one, in that one can drop the use of "I" along these lines without introducing any new ambiguities. But the real point of the proposal is that it is supposed to let us see what is essential to any form of expression[93] by providing an impartial way of describing the phenomena in question:

> We could adopt the following way of representing matters. If I, L.W., have toothache, then that is expressed by means of the proposition "There is toothache." But if that is so, what we now express by the proposition "A has toothache" is put as follows: "A is behaving as L.W. does when there is toothache." Similarly we shall say "It is thinking" and "A is behaving as L.W. does when it is thinking."[94]

What Wittgenstein is suggesting is that we imagine giving up using "I" in talking about one's own experience; instead of saying "I have a toothache," one says "there is toothache." More generally, in talking about one's experience, one dispenses with

91. Big Typescript, §104, pp. 508–509. [German in appendix.]

92. *Philosophical Remarks*, §57. Wittgenstein's suspicion of talk about a self and its states is just one instance of his general mistrust of the subject-predicate grammar of everyday language as a guide to a philosophical analysis. See the discussion of phenomenology and Wittgenstein's use of the analogy of the two planes on pp. 129–131.

93. *Philosophical Remarks*, §58. Cf. Big Typescript §104, p. 512.

94. *Philosophical Remarks*, §58. Source: MS 108, p. 8, December 1929.

the first-person pronoun and simply states that the experience in question has occurred. The point of the imagined reconstrual is that the new sentences now have a
dummy subject and so conform to the subject-predicate conventions of our language,
but do not have a logical subject. We are to think of the "there is" in "there is toothache" as like the "it is" in "it is snowing": in both cases something is going on, but
there is no subject. Wittgenstein also proposes that talk about someone else's experience be based on talk about their behaviour. Obviously, we can construct such a
language around any person we choose:

> If I spoke this language, I should say, "Wittgenstein has toothache. But Waismann
> is behaving as Wittgenstein does when he has toothache." In the language whose
> centre you are it would be expressed just the other way round, "Waismann has
> toothache, Wittgenstein is behaving like Waismann when he has toothache."[95]

Wittgenstein did acknowledge that his proposed way of looking at things sharply
separates propositions concerning one's own pain from those about everyone else's,
but he maintained that was entirely appropriate, for feeling pain and seeing someone
else in pain are very different:

> We simply want to separate two different regions of experience; as when we sepa-
> rate the taste experience and visual experience of a body. And nothing can be more
> different than the experience of pain and the experience of seeing a human body
> squirm, hearing cries uttered, etc. And, indeed, here there is no difference between
> my body and that of the other, for there is also the experience of seeing the move-
> ment of one's own body and hearing the cries it utters.[96]

In this passage, Wittgenstein is appealing to what Ernst Tugendhat has called the
condition of "epistemic asymmetry": my reasons for ascribing an experience to myself
are quite different from my reasons for ascribing experience to others.[97] To put the
point more bluntly than Wittgenstein's proposed language permits, we can say that
each of us is directly aware of a stream of experiential phenomena, but one's awareness of the experience of others is always indirect, based on observing a physical
object or objects—usually the body of the person in question. So "I have pain" is
directly related to my pain experience, while "he has pain" is only indirectly related
to the other's pain. Rather than say such things explicitly, Wittgenstein prefers to let
specific examples do the work for him: "'How a proposition is to be verified—it says
that': and now consider the propositions: "I have pain,' 'N has pain.'"[98]

On the other hand, Wittgenstein maintains that for any given first-person self-
ascription, there is always a third-person proposition with the same truth-conditions.
For instance, the proposition that there is toothache can be translated into the proposition that the person in question is behaving as L.W. does when he has toothache.
Tugendhat calls this aspect of the relationship between the first person and the third
person, the principle of "veritative symmetry": my self-ascription of an experience
and your ascription of that experience to me share the same truth-conditions. Either

95. *Wittgenstein and the Vienna Circle*, p. 49, 22 December 1929.
96. Big Typescript, §104, p. 514. [German in appendix.]
97. Ernst Tugendhat, *Self-Consciousness and Self-Determination*, p. 75.
98. Big Typescript, §104, p. 512. [German in appendix.]

both propositions are true or neither of them are. In effect, Wittgenstein's reconstrual of our language divides it into two domains and makes one principle sovereign in each: the principle of veritative symmetry governs physicalistic language; the principle of epistemological asymmetry governs phenomenological language.

The principle of veritative symmetry yields the requirement that every realization of Wittgenstein's language schema, whoever it is centred on, must be equivalent. Anything I say about my experience in the phenomenological language can also be said in the physical language. At this point, it may seem as though both languages are too impartial and impersonal, however. The phenomenological language represents my experience as just happening, impersonally, while the physicalistic language treats the experience of others as a matter of mere behaviour. In other words, the new languages talk about the "human being . . . the human body, or the human soul with which psychology deals,"[99] but not a subject of experience. Neither language will let me say that it's *my* experience, that *I* have it. How, then, am I to express the differences between myself and others?[100] The price of recognizing the veritative symmetry between the phenomenological and physicalistic languages appears to be the denial of the epistemological asymmetry for me between my phenomenological language and all other languages.

Wittgenstein's response to such objections was that they were motivated by the mistaken desire to talk about the application of both languages, a matter that is supposedly shown by the very language he proposes. Thus, in 1929–1930, he described the self-centred phenomenological language as "particularly adequate" and said it had a "special position."[101] But he immediately went on to say that the advantage cannot be put into words:

> For, if I do it in the language with me as its centre, then the exceptional status of the description of this language in its own terms is nothing very remarkable, and in the terms of another language my language occupies no privileged status whatever.[102]

On this view, the "fact" that my language is about my world cannot be literally stated; instead, it is meant to show itself in the application of language, the projective relation between language and the world, not on anything one can speak about within the world.[103]

Similarly, at the end of his discussion of the "I"-less languages in the *Philosophical Remarks*, Wittgenstein wrote:

> Only their application really differentiates languages; but if we disregard this, all languages are equivalent. All these languages represent only a single incomparable and *cannot* represent anything else. (Both these approaches must lead to the

99. *Tractatus*, 5.641.
100. Strictly speaking, the difference can also be drawn in my own case: here it amounts to the distinction between myself as subject of experience and as a person.
101. *Philosophical Remarks*, §58. Source: MS 108, p. 9, December 1929. The paragraph is conspicuously absent from the closely related treatment in §104 of the Big Typescript, entitled "*Having Pain*." See pp. 84–85 this volume.
102. *Philosophical Remarks*, §58.
103. See pp. 67–69 on the application of language.

same result: first, that what is represented is not one thing among others, that it is not capable of being contrasted with anything; second, that I cannot express the advantage of *my* language.")[104]

Wittgenstein's normal term for representation is *vorstellen*. But "represent" in the passage above translates *darstellen*: it points to an unsayable transcendent relation between language as a whole on the one hand and something else, beyond language, on the other. Here, as before, Wittgenstein is being drawn in two directions at once. On the one hand, he insists that Cartesian talk of the subject of experience as a *res cogitans* must be rejected, explained away as a delusory shadow cast by surface grammar. On the other hand, he regards the Cartesian conception as embodying a partial insight as to how subjectivity and the subject are to be understood by the philosopher: as products of the form of our experience. The philosophical subject is like a focal point whose construction is demanded by the logical form of every proposition within logical space yet lies outside that space. The substance of the insight is not something that can be said, but if one gets a clear view of one's language, it shows itself. For this reason, the subjectless language centred on me is said to be "particularly appropriate."

The shadowy and elusive conception of the self that I have just outlined is far from being an eccentric or idiosyncratic doctrine superimposed on the basic outlook of the *Tractatus*; it would be closer to the truth to regard it as a natural consequence of the Tractarian conception of a world made up of facts, a world where there is no room for a subject of experience. We can see this more clearly if we consider a parallel argument for a strikingly similar conception of subjectivity in the work of Thomas Nagel. In a well-known paper on physicalism, Nagel offered an argument about what can be said in a language that lacked indexicals—words such as "I," "here," or "now"—that he regarded as giving one "strong reasons for rejecting any view which identifies the subject of psychological states with a substance and construes the states as attributes of that substance."[105] He first asks the reader to consider everything that can be said while dispensing with indexicals. Like Wittgenstein, his scheme enables him to describe "the entire world and everything that is happening in it—and this will include a description of Thomas Nagel and what he is thinking and feeling."[106] But then, like Wittgenstein's interlocutor, he notices that one fact cannot be stated in such a description: the fact that the description of Thomas Nagel is a description of *him*, that *he* is the subject of those experiences, that *he* is TN. Therefore, not only is he not a body, he is also not a mental substance, either, thus reaching the paradoxical conclusion that the true psychological subject—like Wittgenstein's transcendental ego—has a subjectivity that cannot be expressed in factual language. Nagel sets out this train of thought with great force:

---

104. *Philosophical Remarks*, §58. In speaking of a "single incomparable" in the second sentence of this passage, Wittgenstein was careful to avoid talking of a *thing* that these languages represent: "*Alle diese Sprache stellen nur ein Einziges, Unvergleichliches dar, und können nichts anders darstellen.*" Strangely, the published translation adds the very word that is conspicuously absent from the German: "All these languages only describe one single incomparable thing and *cannot* represent anything else."

105. Thomas Nagel, "Physicalism," p. 354.

106. Nagel, "Physicalism," p. 355.

Now it follows from this not only that a sensation's being mine cannot consist simply in its being an attribute of a particular body; it follows also that it cannot consist in the sensation's being an attribute of a particular soul which is joined to that body; for nothing in the specification of that soul will determine that *it* is mine, that I am *that* person. So long as we construe psychological states as attributes of a substance, no matter what substance we pick, it can be thrown, along with the body, into the "objective" world; its states and its relation to a particular body can be described completely without touching upon the fact that I am that person.[107] It turns out therefore that, given the requirements which led us to reject physicalism, the quest for the self, for a substance which *is* me and whose possession of a psychological attribute will *be* its being mine, is a quest for something which could not exist. The only possible conclusion is that the self is not a substance, and that the special kind of possession which characterises the relation between me and my psychological states cannot be represented as the possession of certain attributes by a subject, no matter what that subject may be. The subjectivity of the true psychological subject is of a different kind from that of the mere subject of attributes.[108]

But the real reason for Nagel's conclusion that one cannot conceive of the psychological subject as a substance is the impoverished means of representation he allowed himself in setting up the problem: his indexical-less language. The seemingly "physicalistic" language he restricts himself to is, of course, identical in all essential respects with Wittgenstein's phenomenological language. And, as we have seen, such a language *cannot* incorporate the logical resources which would enable one to individuate subjects. By restricting himself to such a language, Nagel commits himself to concluding that that the soul *cannot* be a substance. The true moral of Nagel's story is that we need to use indexicals in order to be able to think of the subject as being in the world. Once indexicals are readmitted, one can conceive of one's own experiences as being the experiences of this person here and another person's experiences as being the experiences of that person over there—because thoughts can be located, we can individuate subjects. It is ironical that the very statements Nagel thinks of as expressing the facts that show we cannot conceive of the psychological subject in physicalistic terms—for example, "I am TN"—are the statements containing the indexicals that are essential in specifying one's location in the first person.[109]

We can now see that Wittgenstein's "subjectless" language actually articulates a conceptual scheme whose domain is limited to the experience of a single person. No one would ordinarily use "there is a toothache" as a way of saying "I have toothache," for the simple reason that his or her hearers wouldn't know *whose* toothache was under discussion. Wittgenstein only gets around the difficulty by adopting the convention that when I say "there is a toothache" it is understood that I mean that *I* have a toothache. Once inside my phenomenological language, there is only one subject of experience to be taken into consideration, and so all the experiences that can be spoken of must be ascribed to its centre. It follows that words such as "I" or

107. Here Nagel gives a footnote that refers to *Tractatus*, 5.64.
108. Nagel, "Physicalism," p. 355.
109. See John Perry, "The Problem of the Essential Indexical."

"my," whose function is that of marking the distinction between that which is mine and that which is not, can do no useful work within this conception—it will be sufficient, in talking of my experiences, to simply state that they have occurred. In the phenomenological language, where everything that can be said is, of necessity, "centred" on the philosophical subject, it makes no sense to speak of the subject *having* the experiences which are reported in that language. Talk of "having" only makes sense when "not having" is also a possibility. And that pair of concepts only makes sense in the physical language:

> In the sense of the phrase "sense data" in which it is inconceivable that some-
> one else should have them, it cannot, for this very reason, be said that someone
> else does not have them. And by the same token, it's senseless to say that *I*, as
> opposed to someone else, *have* them.[110]

> There isn't an eye belonging to me and eyes belonging to others in visual space.
> Only the space itself is asymmetrical, the objects in it are on a par. In the space of
> physics however this presents itself in such a way that one of the eyes which are
> on a par is singled out and called *my* eye.[111]

It is because a language designed for the sole function of expressing everything that a subject might experience has no need for a term designating that subject that one cannot refer to a subject of experience from within the phenomenological language. In that case, it will be impossible to represent another's experience, as that person experiences it, from within a given phenomenological language. In short, the phenomenological language is "subjectless" because it is a language in which one can do nothing but talk about what a single subject might experience. To say that is already to step outside the limits of phenomenological language, however. From within, one cannot individuate a subject at all. The metaphysical subject is not an object of experience, but a way of indicating the overall structure of experience. As a result, Wittgenstein has to treat the thesis that others have experience as an empty hypothesis—one that can neither be verified nor falsified by any experience:

> The two hypotheses that other people have toothache and that they behave just
> as I do but don't have toothache, possibly have identical senses. That is, if I had,
> for example, learnt the second form of expression, I would talk in a pitying tone of
> voice about people who don't have toothache, but are behaving as I do when I
> have.[112]

> The two hypotheses, that others have pain, and that they don't and merely be-
> have as I do when I have, must have identical senses if every *possible* experience
> confirming the one confirms the other as well. In other words, if a decision be-
> tween them on the basis of experience is inconceivable.[113]

The grammar of the phenomenological language ensures that all statements about experience are expressed in the same—ownerless—way. As long as one only uses a

110. *Philosophical Remarks*, §61; Big Typescript, §104, p. 510.
111. *Philosophical Remarks*, §73.
112. *Philosophical Remarks*, §64.
113. *Philosophical Remarks*, §65; Big Typescript, §104, p. 506.

realization of the phenomenological language-schema to represent one's own experiences, it imposes no restriction. When one tries to use it to represent another subject's experiences, however, its limitations become apparent: one cannot use it to represent someone else's experiences as being that person's experiences. Consequently, Wittgenstein maintains:

> If I use language to get another to understand me, then this must be a matter of understanding in the behaviouristic sense. That he has understood me is a hypothesis, as is that I have understood him.

> "For whom would I describe my immediate experience? Not for myself, for I just have it; and not for someone else, for that person could never get it from the description?" —He can get it just as much and just as little from the description as from a painted picture. The agreements about language are of course arranged with the help of painted pictures (or what amounts to the same thing). And, according to our usual means of expression he does, of course, get something from a painted picture.[114]

The nearest surrogate that Wittgenstein can offer is for me to conceive of myself as having the experiences in question, in the way in which the other person would have them (for example, as centred on that person's body). Thus he writes:

> When I feel sorry for someone with toothache, I put myself in his place. But I put *myself* in his place.[115]

> When I am sorry for someone else because he's in pain, I do of course imagine the pain, but I imagine that *I* have it.[116]

In these passages, Wittgenstein is trying to account for sympathetic imagination: my imagining what it is like for you, on the basis of projective imagination; my imagining what it would be like for me. Characteristically, he can be read in two ways on this point: either as denying that there is such a phenomenon as sympathetic imagination, or as maintaining that sympathetic imagination is really only projective imagination. In either case, his proposal amounts to turning imagining *someone else's* pain into imagining *my* having a pain. The *Philosophical Investigations* wryly point to some of the difficulties with such an approach:

> If one has to imagine someone else's pain on the model of one's own, this is none too easy a thing to do: for I have to imagine pain which I *do not feel* on the model of the pain which I *do feel*. That is, what I have to do is not simply to make a transition in imagination from one place of pain to another. As, from pain in the hand to pain in the arm. For I am not to imagine that I feel pain in some region of his body. (Which would also be possible).[117]

114. Big Typescript, §101, p. 493. [German in appendix.] For further discussion of §101, see pp. 143–145, 155, 158–159, 172–174.

115. *Philosophical Remarks*, §63; Big Typescript, §104, p. 504.

116. *Philosophical Remarks*, §65; Big Typescript §104, p. 506. Compare the following passage from the "Paralogisms of Pure Reason": "It is obvious that if I wish to represent to myself a thinking being, I must put myself in his place, and thus substitute, as it were, my own subject for the object I am seeking to consider" (Kant, *Critique of Pure Reason*, A353–354).

117. *Philosophical Investigations*, §302.

Wittgenstein's point in this passage is that to imagine the occurrence of experience located in another person's body on the model of one's own experience is not to imagine the other person's experience, but to imagine *my* having the experience. Projectively imagining my experience taking place in a variety of locations does not amount to conceiving of an experience that is had by someone else.

While Wittgenstein's reliance on the use of analogies is explicitly emphasized in his later work, the analogies and models that motivate his early philosophy presented themselves as incontestable facts. The project of articulating the analyses that had simply been taken for granted in the *Tractatus* ultimately led Wittgenstein far from his point of departure. To see how that occurred, we must look more closely at his early conception of the visual world and his critique of that conception in the 1930s. In effect, Wittgenstein came to see that his earlier philosophy had given an unjustified priority to disengaged contemplation and a private experiential world, and had led to an oversimplified conception of language and experience.

In the *Philosophical Investigations*, Wittgenstein wrote that "philosophical problems arise when language *goes on holiday*."[118] By this, he meant that philosophical problems do not arise in the ordinary course of life, but only once we have taken language out of its everyday setting, in such a way that it can do no useful work. In the *Investigations*, Wittgenstein offers the example of the conception of naming as a mysterious connection between word and object which, he says, arises if one tries to grasp the nature of naming by staring at the object in front of one and repeats a name or the word "this" to oneself. In an unpublished notebook entry written in December 1937, he discussed how vision, too, had gone "on holiday" when he had philosophized in the past:

> One can say: if we philosophize, it isn't only our language that goes on holiday, so does our vision. For, while I light the stove I see it differently from when I stare at it philosophizing, don't think about the "visual stove," the sense datum, etc.
>
> A philosopher who, when philosophizing, always closes an eye, may be captivated by different intuitions than one who always looks with two.[119]

The final sentence is an elliptical reference to the text of the *Tractatus*. There, he had dismissed a conception of visual experience that makes the eye itself a part of what

---

118. *Philosophical Investigations*, §38. As there is no known manuscript source, the passage probably originated in MS 142, written during the last two months of 1936, where Wittgenstein first assembled sections 1–188 of the *Philosophical Investigations*. The manuscript has since been lost.

119. MS 120, pp. 87–88, 12 December 1937; also in MS 116, pp. 225–226. [German in appendix.] MS 120 is a notebook containing a large number of remarks on solipsism, some of which found their way into the *Philosophical Investigations*; Wittgenstein made a preliminary selection from MS 120 in MS 116. The next remark in MS 116, taken from MS 120, p. 89, reads as follows:

> The person who says one cannot step twice into the same river can only feel that way under very special circumstances; i.e., only tempted to say it under these circumstances. // can only feel that way under *special* circumstances; i.e., only tempted to say this in quite determinate circumstances. [German in appendix.]

In chapter 6, I argue that one of the principal intuitions that captivated Wittgenstein was the idea that experience is constantly in flux, flowing away on time's river, summed up in the words "one cannot step twice into the same river."

is experienced by drawing a diagram of an elliptical field of vision with a point representing an eye at one end and pointing out that visual experience is not like that: the point from which one sees is not part of the field of vision.[120] In his retrospective remark, Wittgenstein notes that the perspective he had adopted in the *Tractatus* had led him to overlook, or regard as irrelevant, the fact that we ordinarily see with two eyes, not just one. The point is put more explicitly in a related remark in the Big Typescript:

/It is odd that I wrote, the visual field does not have the form

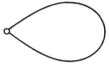

and not, it would not have the form

and that I wrote the first one, is very significant/.[121]

The traditional philosophical way of looking at things gives priority to disengaged contemplation as a source of knowledge about the true nature of things, a contemplation in which such matters as the fact that we are usually actively involved in our world, that our ability to discriminate and locate objects is dependent on seeing with two eyes and not just one, and so forth, can seem irrelevant. But that philosophical conception of the world, he now argues, is not primary: it is only what we see when we let our eyes wander in a particular way. The intuitions that had captivated Wittgenstein when philosophizing "with one eye closed" had led him to a worldview that he could no longer accept. Instead, he turned his attention to the ways of looking that had generated that worldview.

Ultimately, Wittgenstein came to regard the whole notion of a fundamental distinction between inner and outer, primary and secondary language, as due to misunderstanding the grammar of our language. The notions of the metaphysical self and the visual world only arise when our language and our vision "go on holiday": when we are misled into giving up our ordinary ways of talking and looking. He had transmuted the difference between the first-person and third-person modes of speech into differences between two worlds and then had tried to put them back together again.

120. *Tractatus*, 5.6331, cited on p. 76.
121. MS 112, pp. 54–55, 14 October 1931. Also in Big Typescript, §98, p. 467, but with blank spaces for the diagrams; as they were added to TS 212, the source for the Big Typescript, the blank spaces were probably due to an oversight. [German in appendix.]

II

WITTGENSTEIN'S
LATER PHILOSOPHY

4

From Logical Atomism
to Practical Holism

4.1 Wittgenstein's Later Writing

After the war, Wittgenstein insisted on giving away his substantial inheritance to his brothers and sisters and spent a year training to be a schoolteacher. From 1920 to 1926 he taught in several small villages in the Viennese Alps. One of the first readers of the *Tractatus* was Frank Ramsey, who composed the first English translation of the book while he was still a teenager.[1] Ramsey also helped prepare the translation, which was published under C. K. Ogden's name in 1922, and wrote a penetrating review of the *Tractatus* for *Mind*, still one of the best introductions to that book.[2] In 1923, Wittgenstein, who was the only teacher in Puchberg am Schneeberg, a small village in the mountains near Vienna, received Ogden's translation; when he learned from Ogden that Ramsey would be visiting Austria, he wrote Ramsey a letter.[3] That letter led Ramsey to stay with Wittgenstein for a couple of weeks that September and discuss the *Tractatus* with him in detail. Thus began the close friendship between Ramsey and Wittgenstein. Ramsey returned to Vienna in spring and summer 1924 and visited Wittgenstein from time to time. Later that year, Ramsey was made a fellow of King's College, Cambridge.[4]

In 1926, after a period of indecision, Wittgenstein became preoccupied with designing and building a house for his sister in Vienna, a project he completed in 1928. During these years he occasionally met with Moritz Schlick, Friedrich Waismann, Rudolf Carnap and other members of the Vienna Circle. In January 1929, Wittgenstein visited Cambridge, at John Maynard Keynes' invitation, and decided to stay there for a while to engage in some philosophical research. He was readmitted to Trinity College, as an advanced student, on January 18, 1929. By the middle of February, Wittgenstein's plans were firm enough for him to write to Schlick that

1. *Letters to C. K. Ogden*, p. 8.
2. Frank Ramsey, "Critical Notice of the *Tractatus.*"
3. *Letters to C. K. Ogden*, p. 77. The appendix contains letters Ramsey wrote to Wittgenstein in 1923–1924 and some background information.
4. Little is known about the extent of their correspondence between Ramsey's visit to Vienna in 1924 and the beginning of 1929, when Wittgenstein took up academic residence in Cambridge again. Wittgenstein's only visit to Cambridge during this period was in summer 1925. The only correspondence that has been published is part of a letter of Wittgenstein's to Ramsey on identity, dated June 1927. The letter is in *Ludwig Wittgenstein and the Vienna Circle*, pp. 189–191.

he had decided "to stay on in Cambridge for a couple of terms and work on visual space and other things."[5] Within a few months of his arrival in Cambridge, Wittgenstein had rejected some of the central tenets of the *Tractatus* and had begun work on new projects. Wittgenstein and Ramsey met frequently during 1929, when Wittgenstein regularly gave Ramsey copies of his writing for safekeeping. In the preface to the *Philosophical Investigations*, Wittgenstein said that Ramsey had helped him realize the mistakes in the *Tractatus* to a degree that he was "hardly able to estimate."[6] Within a year of Wittgenstein's return, however, Ramsey died, at the age of 26. Ramsey had drafted a substantial study of Wittgenstein's logic, metaphysics, and philosophy of mind, beginning with a summary of Wittgenstein's philosophical outlook in 1929.[7] As Wittgenstein had already satisfied the statutory residence requirements, he was entitled to submit the *Tractatus* as his dissertation; in June 1929, Moore and Russell administered his oral examination and duly awarded him the Ph.D. About this time, the Council of Trinity College had to decide whether or not to give Wittgenstein a research grant, and so Moore asked Ramsey to write a supporting letter. In it, he said that Wittgenstein seemed to "have made remarkable progress. He began with certain questions in the analysis of propositions which have now led him to problems about infinity which lie at the root of current controversies on the foundations of Mathematics."[8] The college gave Wittgenstein a grant for the second half of 1929, which was renewed in December. He began giving lectures in January 1930, and was regularly on the university's lecture lists in the years that followed.[9]

5. *Wittgenstein and the Vienna Circle*, p. 17. Presumably he had in mind the work on the structure of colour and visual space in the early pages of MS 105, known to Wittgenstein as *"Band I"* (Volume I), the first manuscript volume he wrote after his return to Cambridge. The material at the beginning of MS 105 is the basis for chapters 20–21 of the *Philosophical Remarks* and the "Phenomenology" chapter of the Big Typescript. For instance, a passage in MS 105, pp. 29–41, is the source for TS 208, pp. 3–4, itself the source for a continuous stretch of *Philosophical Remarks*, §§206–207. In lectures given in 1930, Wittgenstein discussed the problem of distinguishing the logical relations between primary and nonprimary colours at length. See Moore, "Wittgenstein's Lectures in 1930–33," pp. 317–318.

6. *Philosophical Investigations*, p. viii.

7. The study itself is missing, but a four-page manuscript of a synoptic table of contents has been preserved. The manuscript is arranged in three columns, which give a brief summary of the contents of each section, the page on which the section begins, and the section number. While the first page of the synopsis is an outline of the overall nature of Wittgenstein's work, the last three are a critical study of his philosophy of logic. Surprisingly, the main thesis Ramsey argues for is that the logical constants *do* refer. The manuscript, which is in the hands of Michael Nedo, who has worked on the Wittgenstein papers at Trinity College, Cambridge, is not on the microfilm of the unpublished Ramsey papers in the Wren Library, Cambridge. I was only able to look at it briefly and have not been able to obtain a copy for further study.

8. Moore, "Wittgenstein's Lectures in 1930–33," p. 254. Wittgenstein did a great deal of work on the philosophy of mathematics in this period, and this work is intimately related to his work in metaphysics and epistemology. In particular, his rejection of the notion of the completed infinite and the idea that the Russellian analysis of generality in terms of universal quantification is unsuitable for propositions concerning objects of acquaintance are closely connected with his new interest in the nature of immediate experience. Much of this early material can be found in the *Philosophical Remarks*, chapter 10 ff.

9. A number of detailed reports, based on notes taken at the time, covering nearly all the lectures he gave during the period from 1930 to 1936, have since been published: *Wittgenstein's Lectures, Cambridge, 1930–32*, from John King and Desmond Lee's notes; *Wittgenstein's Lectures, Cambridge,*

On February 2, 1929, Wittgenstein began writing in a bound manuscript volume, the first of a series of numbered volumes, which he continued for many years. Concentrating his attention on a limited number of topics at any one time, he would write short remarks, sometimes a single paragraph in length, sometimes a few pages long. These underwent successive stages of revision and rearrangement, first in rough notebooks, then in the manuscript volumes. The manuscript volumes filled up rapidly: by September he had written more than 400 pages and was making the first entries in volume III.

Wittgenstein usually returned to Vienna to be with his family during the lengthy Cambridge vacations. There he had frequent meetings with Waismann, Schlick, and other members of the Vienna Circle; Waismann's shorthand record of many of these talks and discussions has been published as *Wittgenstein and the Vienna Circle*. By the end of 1929, Wittgenstein and Waismann had decided to collaborate on a systematic exposition of the *Tractatus*; this project was advertised in the first volume of *Erkenntnis*, the official journal of the Vienna Circle.[10]

During the 1930 Easter vacation, Wittgenstein dictated selected passages from volumes I to IV, roughly half of the material he had written, as Russell had to write a report on Wittgenstein's new work. The dictation yielded two copies of a 144-page typescript. He cut up the carbon copy into slips, rearranged them, and pasted them up in a bound volume, since published as the *Philosophical Remarks*.[11] Shortly afterward, Wittgenstein gave the typescript to Moore. It was lost after Moore gave it to the trustees of Wittgenstein's estate, but copies of the original exist, and are available in Cambridge and Bergen. There were few revisions and lacunae, probably because it was hastily assembled and afterward put to one side. Rush Rhees, the editor, gave it a more orderly appearance: he chose the title, divided it into chapters, and added a synoptic table of contents. In addition, some paragraphs that had been crossed out were left unpublished.

After he spent several days talking to Wittgenstein about the *Philosophical Remarks*, Russell reported to the Council of Trinity College that he had only read about a third, describing it as rough notes which "would have been very difficult to understand without the help of the conversations."[12] Wittgenstein's grant was extended until December of that year, when he was given a research fellowship which was to support him for the next six years. By June 1932, Wittgenstein had filled nearly 2,500 pages with his drafts. During 1932–1933, he selected, revised, and rearranged remarks from his manuscript volumes, resulting in the production of an untitled 760-page book

---

1932–1935; from Alice Ambrose and Margaret Macdonald's notes; Moore, "Wittgenstein's Lectures in 1930–33," from G. E. Moore's notes; and Rush Rhees, "The Language of Sense Data and Private Experience," from Rhees' notes, taken in 1935–1936.

10. See Gordon Baker, "*Verehrung* und *Verkehrung*: Waismann and Wittgenstein," p. 249.

11. The *Philosophical Remarks* is based on TS 209, which is a rearrangement of nearly everything in TS 208, the source typescript. TS 208 is roughly half the length of the underlying manuscripts, but still in chronological order; in the *Philosophical Remarks* Wittgenstein was clearly aiming at a topical sequence, although the chapters, section numbers, and table of contents in the published book are an editorial contribution.

12. *The Autobiography of Bertrand Russell*, Vol. 2, pp. 196–200. Quoted in the "Editor's Note" to the *Philosophical Remarks*, p. 347.

draft that has since become known as the "Big Typescript." He began the process by reading selected passages from his manuscripts to a typist, producing a typescript that provided a basis for further revision and rearrangement. Actually, Wittgenstein had three typescripts to draw on at this point: a copy of the typescript based on volumes I, II, III and the first part of volume IV that had been used as the basis for the *Philosophical Remarks* in spring 1930; a typescript based on the second part of volume IV, also dating from 1930; and the new typescript, based on volumes V to X.[13] These typescripts were cut into slips and rearranged into sections and chapters, yielding the material listed in the catalogue of the Wittgenstein papers as Typescript (TS) 212. The resulting arrangement was once again typed up, and it is this stage in the process of rewriting, Typescript 213, that is known as the Big Typescript.

At first sight, the Big Typescript is the best organized item in the *Nachlass*. Unlike the rest of Wittgenstein's writing, the Big Typescript is organized into conventionally titled and numbered chapters and sections. It is divided into nineteen chapters, which are, in turn, subdivided into 140 sections. An eight-page analytical table of contents indicates the topic of each section by a brief phrase or sentence. Despite the elaborate structure, the Big Typescript was far from being a finished work. Wittgenstein soon began to revise it, and the first half is heavily annotated. In addition, there are three successive drafts of detailed plans for revising most of the material on the philosophy of mind and language. Wittgenstein's ideas were changing and developing rapidly; he never completed these revisions.

Rhees made use of the first and second of these plans in producing the text which he published as Part I of the *Philosophical Grammar*, giving it a new table of contents and chapter divisions. The chapters on mathematics (chapters 9–10 and 15–19), which Wittgenstein left unrevised, were incorporated in the *Philosophical Grammar* as Part II; the table of contents and section titles are Wittgenstein's. However, three crucial chapters, which Wittgenstein had also left unrevised, with the titles "Philosophy," "Phenomenology," and "Idealism, etc.," (chapters 12–14), were not included in the text of the *Philosophical Grammar*. Unfortunately, these decisions are neither stated nor explained in the editor's introduction.[14] The chapter entitled "Philosophy," which recently appeared in print, both illuminates Wittgenstein's exposition of his philosophical method in the *Philosophical Investigations* and makes clear how much of it was drafted in the early 1930s.[15] But the "Phenomenology" chapter—on such topics as visual space, minima visibilia, and colour—and the chapter on "Idealism, etc."—on the dangers in attempting to describe immediate experience, the ascription of pain, solipsism, and memory time—remain unpublished.

Between 1933 and 1936 Wittgenstein continued to work on both revising his planned book and writing fresh material for it; he also experimented with working in

13. These are listed in von Wright's catalogue as TS 208, 97 pp. long, based on MSS 105–107 and the first half of MS 108; TS 210, 87 pp. long, based on the second half of MS 108; and TS 211, 771 pp. long, based on MSS 109–113 and the beginning of MS 114.

14. For further discussion of the place of the Big Typescript in the Wittgenstein oeuvre,7 see A. Kenny, "From the Big Typescript to the *Philosophical Grammar*," and Hilmy, *The Later Wittgenstein*, pp. 25–39.

15. *Philosophical Occasions: 1912–1951*, pp. 160–199. As the book shows the pagination in the Big Typescript, and provides both Wittgenstein's German and an English translation, I have not given page references to the book for each quotation from the "Philosophy" chapter (§§86–93).

English, and during the 1933–1934 and 1934–1935 academic years, he regularly dictated in English, to a group of students, yielding transcripts that have since been published as the *Blue Book* and the *Brown Book*.[16]

Wittgenstein experienced a number of crises in 1936. In 1935, he had been granted a one-year extension to his five-year research fellowship at Trinity so that it continued to the end of the 1935–1936 academic year. At the beginning of the year, he still planned to collaborate with Waismann on an exposition of his philosophy, although their relationship was not nearly as close as it had been a few years earlier. But in May 1936, Wittgenstein took offence at an article of Waismann's which he regarded as plagiarism. Schlick, by now Wittgenstein's closest link with the Vienna Circle, might have smoothed things over again, were it not for the fact that he was murdered by one of his students in early June. During summer 1936, Waismann set in motion plans for publication of the manuscript he had been working on under his own name. Wittgenstein had been learning Russian and was thinking of moving to the USSR— Keynes had spoken to the Soviet ambassador in London on his behalf. Fania Pascal, Wittgenstein's Russian tutor, remembers him as being under particularly intense pressure at the time.

Wittgenstein set off for his isolated cabin near the Norwegian village of Skjolden, which he had built while on a lengthy retreat there shortly before the war. The cabin was in an impressive location, with a panoramic view of the far end of the longest fjord in Norway. At first, he worked on a German translation of the *Brown Book*, but gave up three-quarters of the way through and devoted himself to a new arrangement of his thoughts. The fresh start resulted in construction of a manuscript which can be regarded as a first draft of the first 188 sections of the *Philosophical Investigations* during November and December 1936. Although some passages in the final version are not to be found in the early version, and some passages in the early version were cut in the process of revision, the differences between the two are relatively small. As many sections draw on earlier drafts, including a substantial number of passages based on the material in the Big Typescript and the *Brown Book*, there is considerable overlap in content between the Early Investigations and the work he had done in previous years. But the structure and arrangement are quite distinct from anything he had attempted before. Although the manuscript he wrote at the end of 1936 has since been lost, a typescript dating from 1937 or 1938 that is based on it has survived.[17] In a letter from this period, Wittgenstein referred to it as the "first volume" of a work in progress. The "second volume," on the philosophy of mathematics, was mostly drafted in manuscript notebooks written in the autumn of 1937; it was assembled into a typescript in 1938.[18] Originally intended as a sequel to the early draft of Part I the *Investigations*, it was Wittgenstein's last relatively finished

16. While this material was published under the title of *Preliminary Studies for the "Philosophical Investigations" Generally Known as "The Blue and Brown Books,"* the Blue Book certainly belongs to an earlier phase of Wittgenstein's work, and the title suggests a much closer relationship between these dictations and the *Investigations* than is warranted.

17. MS 142 and TS 220.

18. TS 221; the principal manuscript sources are MSS 117–120, composed in 1937–1938 (volumes 8–18). Some material in MS 162a, dating from January 1939, was incorporated at the end of TS 221.

piece of work on the philosophy of mathematics. It was published in 1956 as Part I of the *Remarks on the Foundations of Mathematics*.[19]

During the 1970s and early 1980s, von Wright, assisted by Heikki Nyman and André Maury, investigated the connections between the *Philosophical Investigations* and its sources in the Wittgenstein papers. Their work on a number of carefully edited typescripts of successive versions of the *Philosophical Investigations* is outlined in the preface to von Wright's book on Wittgenstein.[20] Von Wright calls the three principal stages in the composition of the book that he has reconstructed the "early," "intermediate," and "final" versions. The early version, constructed circa 1936–1939, is based on the typescripts described in the preceding paragraph.

In 1942–1943 Wittgenstein revised and partially reorganized the early version of Part I, producing what von Wright calls the intermediate version. The typescript consisted of a slight revision and rearrangement of the first part of the Early Investigations, followed by roughly half the material in *Philosophical Investigations*, Part I, sections 189–425. While it has not survived as a single document, it proved possible to reconstruct it—partly from surviving pages that were not used in subsequent revisions and partly by identifying pages of that typescript that were incorporated into later typescripts.

Early in 1945, Wittgenstein added more than 100 new remarks to the revisions of 1942–1943; later in the the year he added another 400 remarks, mostly drawn from a typescript known as *Bemerkungen I*,[21] which was, in turn, composed of remarks from manuscripts dating from 1929 to 1945. These revisions yielded a typescript that was the basis for the published Part I of the *Philosophical Investigations*. As the typescripts of Parts I and II that were actually used in the publication of the book have since been lost, von Wright's final version is actually based on the only surviving copy of the typescript. Part II of the published book was based primarily on material written in a series of manuscript volumes written between 1946 and 1949.[22] Several typescripts consisting of selections from these volumes, used in the construction of Part II, have been published as *Remarks on the Philosophy of Psychology*, volumes I and II.

In the preface to the *Philosophical Investigations*, dated January 1945, Wittgenstein said that he would have liked to have produced a good book, but that although he had not done so, the time had gone in which he could have improved it. One reason for his inability to write the book he had envisaged was the difficulty he had in

---

19. Although Wittgenstein wrote extensively on the philosophy of mathematics in the late 1930s and early 1940s, this later material on mathematics was not typed up or further revised. Selections from these manuscripts have been published as Parts 2–7 of the *Remarks on the Foundations of Mathematics*.

20. G. H. von Wright, *Wittgenstein*, pp. 6–10. Von Wright's pathbreaking work in publicizing the extent and character of the mass of papers Wittgenstein left behind him began in the late 1960s with his guide to the *Nachlass* and his study of the origin of the *Tractatus*. That material was later amended and extended in his *Wittgenstein*, which also contains important essays on the origin and composition of the *Tractatus* and *Philosophical Investigations*. These essays are an invaluable resource, providing a systematic catalogue and preliminary chronology for the Wittgenstein papers as a whole, together with an indication of some of the main interconnections between the different strata of revision and rearrangement.

21. TS 228.

22. MSS 130–138.

bringing his various ideas together in a single typescript. That preface also makes it clear that he was far from satisfied with the final arrangement of his remarks that he had produced, despite the fact that he devoted an enormous amount of time and energy to considering alternative arrangements:

> I have written down all these thoughts as *remarks*, short paragraphs, of which there is sometimes a fairly long chain about the same subject, while I sometimes make a sudden change, jumping from one topic to another. —It was my intention at first to bring all this together in a book whose form I pictured differently at different times. But the essential thing was that the thoughts should proceed from one subject to another in a natural order and without breaks.
>
> After several unsuccessful attempts to weld my results together into such a whole, I realized that I should never succeed. The best that I could write would never be more than philosophical remarks; my thoughts were soon crippled if I tried to force them on in any single direction against their natural inclination.[23]

Wittgenstein's insistence that he was unable to write a book which would be a whole, proceeding in an orderly way from topic to topic, has rarely been heeded. Considered as an isolated text, it can seem self-contained. But the text of the *Philosophical Investigations* is only one of a number of possible arrangements of those remarks that Wittgenstein proposed, many of which extend, amplify, or cast light on the remarks in the book as published. Wittgenstein's inner dialogue often took the form of a lengthy struggle between conflicting intuitions, with the final result a telegraphic recapitulation of his train of thought. For instance, his discussion of solipsism, a central thread throughout the development of his later philosophy, takes up only a few extremely compressed remarks, beginning with section 398 of the *Philosophical Investigations*.

The way of writing and thinking that Wittgenstein describes in his preface led him to continually rewrite and rearrange his work, so that it can be extremely difficult to separate one piece of writing from another. The *Philosophical Investigations* is itself an excellent example of the problem. His editors state in their introductory note to the book that, had Wittgenstein published his work himself, he would have replaced many of the last 200 remarks in Part I with a revised version of Part II. More recently, von Wright has suggested that Wittgenstein had planned to use *Zettel* as a way of "'bridging the gap' between the present Part I and Part II of the *Investigations*."[24] But the final preface, dated January 1945, was written before any of the postwar material was drafted. Gordon Baker and Peter Hacker reject the view that Wittgenstein considered the later material to be part of the *Philosophical Investigations*, pointing out that "there is no published evidence, nor any indication in the *Nachlass*, that Part II was conceived as either a continuation of Part I or as material to be worked into it."[25] While Wittgenstein's editors may well have described and published the *Philosophical Investigations* as he would have wanted, the fact remains that the published Part II is a selection from material that Wittgenstein had once intended to work

---

23. *Philosophical Investigations*, p. ix.
24. Von Wright, *Wittgenstein*, p. 136.
25. G. Baker and P. Hacker, *Wittgenstein: Understanding and Meaning*, p. 19. For von Wright's most recent thoughts on the topic, see "The Troubled History of Part II of the *Investigations*."

into the end of Part I, not an autonomous sequel, and needs to be understood in that context.

Even if we restrict our attention to Part I, it is clear that the published text of sections 189–693 is only one of a number of ways of adding to sections 1–188—which were originally Part I of the Early Investigations—that Wittgenstein explored. As we have seen, sections 189 ff. of subsequent versions of the *Investigations* effectively supplanted Part II of the Early Investigations. Baker and Hacker call them "two fruits upon one tree"[26] and show that as late as 1949 Wittgenstein referred to his work on mathematics as the second part of his book. While Baker and Hacker carefully discuss the stages leading up to the construction of sections 189 ff., they do not give the same attention to Wittgenstein's later work on alternative arrangements of that material. Consider the case of Typescript 230, known as *Bemerkungen II*, which consists of 542 numbered remarks. Like *Philosophical Investigations* sections 189–693, it is a carefully constructed selection of material from *Bemerkungen I*, the source typescript Wittgenstein used to construct the final version of the *Investigations*. While it only contains approximately 50 remarks that are not included in the published version, the arrangement is markedly different. As a result, von Wright has proposed that it "may be regarded as an independent and final work by Wittgenstein."[27] Indeed, there may even be another such rearrangement in existence, for, according to Anscombe, "after completing *Philosophical Investigations* Part I, and without apparently any intention of superseding it, Wittgenstein spent many months making two quite different alternative arrangements, consisting for the most part of most of the *Investigations* material."[28] Typescript 235, described in von Wright's catalogue as "a table of contents to an unidentified work," a fascinating nine-page list of 161 numbered topics, most of them closely connected with remarks in the *Philosophical Investigations*, is probably connected with his work on these alternative arrangements.

While the available information about the connections between Wittgenstein's published and unpublished writings raises many more questions than can be answered at present, it does suggest there is much to be learned by looking at the process of revision that leads from the rejection of the leading ideas of the *Tractatus* to the development of Wittgenstein's later philosophy of mind and language. The remainder of this chapter provides a skeletal outline of the principal stages in this development, an outline that provides the basis for the more detailed exposition in the chapters that follow.

4.2 Logical Form and Logical Holism

In his 1929 manuscripts, Wittgenstein returned to the problems in the analysis of ordinary language that he had treated as inessential in the *Tractatus*. As we shall see, he soon came to the conclusion that there are logical relations between propositions that cannot be captured by the truth-functional logic of the *Tractatus*, and that there-

26. G. Baker and P. Hacker, *Wittgenstein: Rules, Grammar and Necessity*, p. 3 ff.
27. von Wright, *Wittgenstein*, p. 133.
28. Anscombe, "On the Form of Wittgenstein's Writing," p. 376.

fore the Tractarian conception of logic and elementary propositions was inadequate. Consequently, he gave up logical atomism, the thesis that all meaningful discourse can be analyzed into logically independent elementary propositions, for a view on which analysis leads to systems of logically related propositions, a position one can call "logical holism." On the new view, even the simplest propositions are not the independent atoms the *Tractatus* had postulated, but are logically related to others, and so form part of a larger whole.

At first, Wittgenstein retained the Tractarian conviction that language is grounded on reference to simple objects, which he now identified with the experientially given. The project of analysing the structure of experience that he envisaged is briefly set out in the paper, "Some remarks on logical form." When he wrote the paper, in the early months of 1929, he conceived of his aim as a matter of articulating a "phenomenological language," a language for the description of immediate experience. His conviction that philosophy ought to start with a canonical description of the structure of experience was motivated by his conception of immediate experience as "primary," the ground on which our ordinary "secondary" language is built.

The best introduction to the new direction in Wittgenstein's work is to look at his own informal presentation of his change of mind. In a conversation with Waismann and Schlick on Christmas Day, 1929, Wittgenstein summed up his new conception of the proposition in the following terms:

> Once, I wrote "A proposition is laid against reality like a measuring rod . . ." I now prefer to say that a *system of propositions* is laid against reality like a measuring rod. What I mean by this is the following. If I lay a measuring rod against a spatial object, I lay *all the graduating lines* against it at the same time. . . . If I know that the object extends to graduating line 10, I also know immediately that it does not extend to graduating lines 11, 12, and so forth. The statements describing for me the length of an object form a system, a system of propositions. Now it is such a system of propositions that is compared with reality, not a single proposition.[29]

Wittgenstein's first sentence is a reference to the *Tractatus*, where he had said that a picture reaches out to reality, is "laid against reality like a measuring rod. Only the end-points of the graduating lines actually *touch* the object that is to be measured."[30] But the new view was better suited to the simile than the old one, for it took account of the relationship between the different possible lengths represented by the series of graduating lines. On the new view, each elementary proposition belongs to a propositional system—in the present case, the set of statements about lengths—and is logically related to other members of that system. In addition to the case of propositions about measurement, Wittgenstein offered the example of colours:

> If, for instance, I say such and such a point in the visual field is *blue*, I not only know that, I also know that the point isn't green, isn't red, isn't yellow etc. I have simultaneously applied the whole colour scale. This is also the reason why a point

29. *Ludwig Wittgenstein and the Vienna Circle*, pp. 63–64, 25 December 1929.

30. *Tractatus*, 2.1512–2.15121. Cf. *Notebooks, 1914–1916*, p. 32, 24 November 1914 "Proposition and situation are related to one another like the measuring rod and the length to be measured."

cannot have different colours at the same time. . . . It's such a whole system which
is compared with reality, not a single proposition.[31]

"This is blue" expresses a proposition that is logically related to a whole family of
other colour propositions. Propositions about colour belong to a system of propositions that share a distinctive grammatical form, a system whose structure is given by
its grammar. Wittgenstein saw that he had to set out the characteristic logical structure, the "philosophical grammar" of each system of concepts, analysing the structure of each system of logically related concepts—numbers, colours, etc.—and so
clarifying their logical forms:

> When I was working on [the *Tractatus*] I was still unaware of all this and thought
> then that every inference depended on tautological form. I hadn't seen then that
> an inference can also have the form: A man is 6ft tall, therefore he isn't 7ft. This
> is bound up with my then believing that elementary propositions had to be inde-
> pendent of one another: from the fact that one state of affairs obtained you couldn't
> infer another did not. But if my present conception of a system of propositions is
> right, it's actually the rule that from the fact that one state of affairs obtains we can
> infer that all the others do not.[32]

In this passage, Wittgenstein admitted that when he wrote the *Tractatus*, he had mistakenly taken for granted that every logically valid inference could somehow be
analysed into truth-functionally valid inferences. Now he was forced to acknowledge the consequences of recognizing the limitations of truth-functional logic. For if
analysis leads to logically interrelated propositions, then logical atomism and the
Tractarian conception of logically independant elementary propositions must be given
up. That conclusion is drawn explicitly at the end of a closely related train of argument in the *Philosophical Remarks*, where Wittgenstein writes that "the concept of
an 'elementary proposition' now loses all of its earlier significance."[33]

In the conversation that followed Wittgenstein's exposition of his new conception of logic and analysis to the Vienna Circle, Schlick pressed Wittgenstein to explain
how he knew "that precisely these rules are valid and no others?"[34] In reply, Wittgenstein tried to characterize knowledge of grammatical rules by contrasting it with
empirical knowledge: it is not a matter of discovering new facts, but of finding a way
of expressing what we have known all along. "We can only do one thing—clearly
articulate the rule we have been applying unawares."[35] He offered the example of
measuring someone's height:

> If, then, I understand what the specification of a length means, I also know that if
> a man is 1.6m tall, he is not 2m tall. I know that a measurement determines only

---

31. *Ludwig Wittgenstein and the Vienna Circle*, p. 64, 25 December 1929; *Philosophical Remarks*,
Appendix 2, p. 317.

32. *Ludwig Wittgenstein and the Vienna Circle*, p. 64, 25 December 1929; *Philosophical Remarks*,
Appendix 2, p. 317.

33. *Philosophical Remarks*, §83. Some of the same ground is covered much more briefly in §28
of the Big Typescript, "Elementary Propositions" (published in *Philosophical Grammar* as Appendix
4A, pp. 210–211). Cf. the discussion of Appendix 4B of *Philosophical Grammar*, pp. 211–214, on
p. 64.

34. *Ludwig Wittgenstein and the Vienna Circle*, p. 78, 2 January 1930. See pp. 73–81.

35. *Ludwig Wittgenstein and the Vienna Circle*, p. 77, 2 January 1930.

one value on a scale and not several values. If you ask me, "how do I know that?" I shall simply answer, "because I understand the sense of the statement." It is impossible to understand the sense of such a statement without knowing the rule.[36]

Wittgenstein conceived of our grasp of the rule in question as quite unproblematic, just as he had taken our grasp of propositional logic for granted in the *Tractatus*: in both cases his answer is that the rules are presupposed by the language. Earlier in the same discussion, he had illustrated his conception of analysis by the example of using Cartesian coordinates to describe the distribution of coloured patches on a sheet of paper, parenthetically remarking that "this is not a mere analogy . . . it is really the same as this everywhere."[37] Wittgenstein treated the rules he was proposing for the description of visual experience like the rules of truth-functional logic: justification is simply a matter of clarifying the rules we have been following all along. He thus retained the Tractarian conviction that in speaking a language, any language, one tacitly commits oneself to certain rules, and that philosophy clarifies those rules by finding a way of speaking that unambiguously displays their structure, even as he rejected the specific conception of the proposition he had previously advocated.

In a subsequent conversation with Waismann, Wittgenstein put his rejection of the Tractarian conception of the elementary proposition in a broader context. The occasion was a discussion of Waismann's "Theses," an attempt at an exposition of Wittgenstein's thought that Waismann had been writing with Wittgenstein's assistance. Wittgenstein criticized the piece harshly for being too much like the *Tractatus*, which he now described as "arrogant" and "dogmatic."[38] He attacked the rationalistic character of his earlier work, saying that his programmatic dependence on abstract argumentation had led him to an oversimplified account of the nature of logic. He went on to say that what is "much more dangerous . . . is the conception that there are questions the answers to which will be found later on."[39] After describing the error as "pervading my whole book," he gave the following explanation of what he had in mind:

> It is held that, although a result is not known, there is a way of finding it. Thus I used to believe, for example, that it is the task of logical analysis to discover the elementary propositions. I wrote, We are unable to specify the form of elementary propositions, and that was quite correct too. . . . Yet I did think that the elementary propositions could be specified later on. Only in recent years have I broken away from that error. . . . In my book I still proceeded dogmatically. Such a procedure is legitimate only if it is a matter of capturing the features of the physiognomy, as it were, of what is only just discernible—and that is my excuse. I saw something from far away and in a very indefinite manner, and I wanted to elicit from it as much as possible.[40]

36. *Ludwig Wittgenstein and the Vienna Circle*, pp. 77–78, 2 January 1930.
37. *Ludwig Wittgenstein and the Vienna Circle*, p. 74, 2 January 1930.
38. A term with strongly Kantian overtones. In the second edition of the *Critique of Pure Reason*, Bxxxv, Kant characterizes dogmatism as "the presumption that it is possible to make progress with pure knowledge, according to principles, from concepts alone (those that are philosophical), as reason has long been in the habit of doing; and that it is possible to do this without having first investigated in what way and by what right reason has come into possession of these concepts."
39. *Ludwig Wittgenstein and the Vienna Circle*, p. 182, 9 December 1931.
40. *Wittgenstein and the Vienna Circle*, pp. 182, 184, 9 December 1931.

In the *Tractatus*, Wittgenstein had taken the thesis of determinacy of sense to entail that an analysis of our language must lead to logically independent elementary propositions. He now branded his earlier work as "dogmatic," precisely because he had placed so much weight on the claim that such an analysis was possible but had failed to carry it out. His belated recognition that elementary propositions could not be logically independent led to the realization that it had been a mistake to rely on such abstract arguments about the nature of language. The schematic program of analysis envisaged in the *Tractatus* had turned out, on closer examination, to be incoherent.

At first, the example of a measuring rod presented itself as a natural replacement for the picture as a paradigm in explaining the relationship between language and the world, enabling Wittgenstein to highlight the systematic improvements that the calculus conception had to offer. Later, he came to realize that the new model had its pitfalls, too, for our use of language is far less regimented than the model of a calculus or a system of measurement might suggest. But rather than simply rejecting the measuring rod analogy, he came to modify it in two crucial ways.

First, he no longer took the existence of a system of measurement for granted and came to place great emphasis on the fact that any system of measurement presupposes the existence of considerable prior agreement among those using it as to how it is to be used, agreement on what he called the "the framework on which the working of our language is based."[41] In the *Philosophical Investigations*, that leads his interlocutor to suggest that Wittgenstein has reduced truth and falsity to something that can be decided by human agreement. In response, Wittgenstein distinguishes between what is said in language, and the agreement that language presupposes, and explicitly appeals to the case of measurement as an example of what he has in mind:

> Disputes do not break out (among mathematicians, say) over the question whether a rule has been obeyed or not. People don't come to blows over it, for example. That is part of the framework on which the working of our language is based (for example, in giving descriptions.)
>
> "So you are saying that human agreement decides what is true and what is false?" —It is what human beings *say* that is true and false; and they agree in the *language* they use. That is not agreement in opinions but in form of life.
>
> If language is to be a means of communication, there must be agreement not only in definitions but also (queer as this may sound) in judgements. This seems to abolish logic, but does not do so. —It is one thing to describe methods of measurement, and another to obtain and state results of measurement. But what we call "measuring" is partly determined by a certain constancy in results of measurement.[42]

The role that human agreement plays in making not only measurement possible, but also mathematics and communication, appears to abolish the objectivity of logic by making it contingent on human institutions. Wittgenstein's reply here is to insist on drawing a clear distinction between agreement about particular truths and falsehoods on the one hand, and agreement in the language we use and in "forms of life" on the other. Later on, we shall return to the further details of his reply to this charge, which

41. *Philosophical Investigations*, §240.
42. *Philosophical Investigations*, §§240–242.

turn on showing that it is a misconception of objectivity that makes these observations about human agreement seem so threatening. For the present, however, we need to return to the way he modified the use of the example of measurement in his later work.

Second, as he came to distance himself from the calculus model of language, Wittgenstein modified his use of the example of measurement as an illustration of his conception of how language is applied to the world; he also used it to stress the point that any model or object of comparison will have its limitations. Whatever model we use, there will always be points where there are disanalogies with the phenomenon to be explained, and if we fail to recognize those disanalogies we will inevitably be misled. In the Early Investigations he writes:

> We can avoid ineptness or emptiness in our assertions only by presenting the prototype as what it is, as an object of comparison—as a measuring-rod, as it were; and not as the preconceived idea to which reality *must* correspond. (I am thinking of Spengler's way of looking at things.) Herein lies the dogmatism into which our philosophy can so easily fall.
>
> It is true: a unit of measurement is well chosen if it expresses many of the lengths that we want to measure with it in whole numbers. But dogmatism maintains that any length *must* be a whole multiple of our unit of measurement.[43]

In this way, the downfall of one of the central logical doctrines of the *Tractatus* led Wittgenstein to reject the aprioristic approach he had used there. But with what was he to replace it? If the logic of our language is not simply truth-functional logic, what is it? One can see much of his subsequent philosophical work as a series of answers to these questions, work that led him further and further away from the formal, systematic, and self-contained models of logic and mathematics and toward the model of a game, an activity embedded within a background of human practice. They were also to lead him to challenge his overreliance on certain key paradigms and metaphors in his early philosophy, such as the notions of language as a picture or a calculus. During the first half of the 1930s, Wittgenstein moved away from a conception of language as a formal system of rules and toward the view that mastery of rules depends on a background of shared practices. This transitional period ended in the mid-1930s with the first exposition of what has since become known as the "private language argument" and the construction of Part I of the Early Investigations. On his later view, the rules of our language are more like the rules of a game than a calculus, for they concern actions within a social context. It is that context—namely, our practices and forms of life, on the one hand, and the facts of nature on which those practices depend, on the other—that make up the background within which it is possible to give an explicit description of an action as a case of rule-following. Because an inherited background involves skills, habits, and customs, it cannot be spelled out in a theory. This emphasis on both the social and natural context of rule-following is characteristic of Wittgenstein's later conception of language as a practice.

In the *Blue Book*, Wittgenstein issued the following warning about the dangers of treating our language as though it were a calculus:

---

43. Early Investigations, §107 (109). [German in appendix.] Cf. *Philosophical Investigations*, §131; *Culture and Value*, p. 26. Source: MS 157b, pp. 30–31, 1937.

Remember that in general we don't use language according to strict rules—it hasn't been taught us by means of strict rules, either. *We*, in our discussions on the other hand, constantly compare language with a calculus proceeding according to exact rules.

This is a very one-sided way of looking at language. In practice we very rarely use language as such a calculus. For not only do we not think of the rules of usage—of definitions, etc.—while using language, but when we are asked to give such rules, in most cases we aren't able to do so. We are unable clearly to circumscribe the concepts we use; not because we don't know their real definition, but because there is no real "definition" to them. To suppose that there *must* be would be like supposing that whenever children play with a ball they play a game according to strict rules.[44]

In the *Philosophical Investigations*, Wittgenstein implies that his misunderstanding of the analogy between a calculus and ordinary language had been responsible for his conception of language as governed by a system of rules:

F. P. Ramsey once emphasized in conversation with me that logic was a "normative science." I do not know exactly what he had in mind, but it was doubtless closely related to what only dawned on me later: namely, that in philosophy we often *compare* the use of words with games and calculi which have fixed rules, but cannot say that someone who is using language *must* be playing such a game. . . .

All this can only appear in the right light when one has attained greater clarity about the concepts of understanding, meaning and thinking. For it will then also become clear what can lead us (and did lead me) to think that if anyone utters a sentence and *means* or *understands* it he is operating a calculus according to definite rules.[45]

At times, Wittgenstein ascribed the calculus conception of understanding to the *Tractatus*; in both the early and middle versions of the *Philosophical Investigations*, the parenthetical phrase "(and did lead me)" read "(and did lead me (*Tractatus*))." The calculus model only really came to prominence in the early 1930s, once Wittgenstein had given up logical atomism and began to insist on the variety of different ways that language can be used. While the *Tractatus* certainly treats meaning or understanding a sentence as though it were a matter of operating a calculus according to definite rules, there is none of the emphasis on the diversity of different calculi, each with its own rules, that one finds in his writings in the early 1930s. In addition, in the years preceding his full-blooded acceptance of the calculus model, he had been drawn to the idea that no system of signs, considered by itself, could ever *mean* anything: that meaning and understanding depend on an inner mental process that animates the otherwise lifeless signs that we use. Thus, in manuscripts written in the 1930s, Wittgenstein refers to his old view of meaning quite differently: as a "pneumatic" or "spiritual" (*pneumatisch*) conception. His use of the term suggests both a characterization of meaning as something ethereal, something that could only go on in the mind, while also connoting that he now regarded it as vacuous. In the *Philosophical Grammar*, Wittgenstein describes the train of thought that had misled him in the following terms:

44. *Blue Book*, p. 25.
45. *Philosophical Investigations*, §81.

I said that a proposition was laid against reality like a ruler. And a ruler—like all logical comparison for a proposition—is itself in a particular case a propositional sign. Now one would like to say: "Put the ruler against a body: it does not say that the body is of such-and-such a length. Rather it is in itself dead and achieves nothing of what thought achieves. It is as if we had imagined that the essential thing about a living being were the outward form. Then we made a lump of wood in that form, and were abashed to see the stupid block, which hasn't any similarity to life.[46]

In the opening pages of the *Blue Book*, Wittgenstein gave the following summary of the views about the nature of thought and language that had once tempted him, continually qualifying his description with the words "it seems" and "we are tempted to think that":

It seems that there are *certain definite* mental processes bound up with the working of language, processes through which alone language can function. I mean the processes of understanding and meaning. The signs of our language seem dead without these mental processes; and it might seem that the only function of the signs is to induce such processes, and that these are the only things we ought really to be interested in. . . . We are tempted to think that the action of language consists of two parts: an inorganic part, the handling of signs, and an organic part, which we may call understanding these signs, meaning them, interpreting them, thinking. These latter activities seem to take place in a queer kind of medium, the mind; and the mechanism of the mind, the nature of which, it seems, we don't quite understand, can bring about effects which no material mechanism could.[47]

A central example of this kind of misunderstanding of the mind follows immediately in the text, and is the subject of a critique that continues for most of the next forty pages: the conviction that only a thought or some other mental process can have a determinate sense, for any combination of signs, taken by itself, is always, in principle, open to any number of alternative interpretations.

But the *Blue Book*, unlike his more autobiographical manuscript notes, has relatively little to say about just how these temptations had affected his own earlier work. In 1931, he characterized the "false analogy" that was responsible for the errors he was continually inclined to make as lying "in the notion that the meaning of the word is an idea [*Vorstellung*] which accompanies the word." He connected this notion with the notion of consciousness [*Bewußt-Sein*] "which I always called 'the primary.'"[48] The idea he is alluding to here is not simply the crude conception, often attributed to

46. *Philosophical Grammar*, §85; cf. *Philosophical Investigations*, §430.
47. *Blue Book*, pp. 3–4.
48. MS 110, pp. 229–230, 1931. [German in appendix.] Cf. Big Typescript, §38, p. 154. The passage from which the quotations in the text are taken reads as follows: "It would be important to express generally the error that I am inclined to make in all these reflections. The false analogy from which it originates . . ." The next three paragraphs in the manuscript are some more general methodological reflections, the source for the passage from the Big Typescript, §87, p. 410, quoted in chapter 1, p. 27. MS 110 continues as follows:

I believe that that error lies in the notion that the meaning of the word is an idea that accompanies the word.
And this conception again has to do with /is connected with/ that of consciousness. That which I always called "the primary."

the British empiricists, on which the meaning of a word is identified with an occurent mental event present to consciousness—for instance, on which my understanding of the word "red" is explained in terms of my having a red image in mind—so much as the idea that there must be *something* going on in me that makes my otherwise potentially indeterminate words fully determinate. A few pages later, he expressed the point in the following terms:

> For the issue is precisely whether by the "meaning with which one uses a word" should be understood as a process that we experience while speaking or hearing the word.
>
> The source of the mistake seems to be the notion of *thoughts which accompany the sentence.* Or which precede its ~~symbolic~~ expression . . .[49]

For Wittgenstein, this remained a crucial misunderstanding of the nature of mind and meaning: in thinking that something in the mind must determine what we mean by our words, we commit ourselves to a theory of these mental processes. In the *Investigations*, he emphasized the importance of that "first step" in the following terms:

> How does the philosophical problem about mental processes and states and about behaviourism arise? —The first step is the one that altogether escapes notice. We talk of processes and states and leave their nature undecided. Sometime perhaps we shall know more about them—we think. But that is just what commits us to a particular way of looking at the matter. For we have a definite concept of what it means to know a process better. (The decisive movement in the conjuring trick has been made, and it was the very one we thought quite innocent).[50]

That first step leads us to think of experience as a "yet uncomprehended process in [a] yet unexplored medium."[51] Setting his face against the invitation to explore that domain, Wittgenstein responds to a question such as *"What goes on* if one understands, thinks, feels, pretends etc.?" by directing our attention to what such questions presuppose:

> In order to solve a philosophical problem, one must turn away from the way of putting the question which forces itself on us most strongly. This way of putting the question is what is problematic.[52]

In other words, Wittgenstein turned away from precisely the assumption that there must be something that goes on if one understands, thinks, feels, or pretends. In the passage that immediately follows his reference to the role he had once given to consciousness and "the primary," he responds to the train of thought he opposes not by offering any specific criticism of the notion that the meaning of a word consists in an accompanying idea, but by trying to bring out the utter implausibility of any such approach to our language:

---

49. MS 110, pp. 233-234, 1931. [German in appendix.] Cf. MS 114, pt. 2, pp. 26, 27; Big Typescript, §38, p. 155.

50. *Philosophical Investigations*, §308.

51. *Philosophical Investigations*, §308.

52. TS 235, §37; the quoted question is §36 in the same typescript. [German in appendix.] Cf. *Philosophical Investigations*, §154: "Try not to think of understanding as a 'mental process' at all."

Of course, if I talk about language—word, sentence, etc.—I must speak the language of everyday. —But is there then another one?

Is this language somehow too coarse, material, for what we want to say? And can there be another one? And how strange that we should be able to do anything at all with the one we have.

It surely is clear that any language can accomplish the same thing, must amount to the same thing. That thus our own ordinary language is no worse than any one.[53]

It was still tempting to think that the meaning of a sign must consist in *something* that goes in the mind of someone who understands it, and to think that if it was not something present to consciousness, then it could only consist in unconscious mental processes. In a much later retrospective remark, he connected his earlier search for the essence of language, his inability to actually provide such a general grammar, and his giving up the idea that meaning or understanding must consist in something "pneumatic" in the following way:

It became clear of course that I didn't *have* a general concept of a proposition and of language.

I had to recognize this and that as signs (Sraffa) and yet couldn't provide a grammar for them. Understanding and knowing the rules.

The pneumatic with respect to understanding completely vanished and with it the pneumatical in sense.

At first the strict rules seemed as something /still/ in the background, hidden in the /nebulous/ medium of the understanding; and one might say, "They *must* be there"—or "I see them, so to speak, through a thick medium, but I see them." They were thus *concrete*. I had used a metaphor (of the projection method, etc.) but through the grammatical illusion of a unitary concept it didn't seem to be a metaphor. The word "real."

The moment this illusion becomes obvious, the moment it becomes clearer that language is a family, the more clear it becomes that that was fictitious concreteness, an abstraction, a form, and that, if we pretend after all that they are present, our assertions become queer and senseless. Thus we no longer play logical tricks.

We see that we must cling to examples in order not to meander about aimlessly.

Our reflections though do not now lose their importance, but rather this shifts completely to the misunderstandings that mislead us.[54]

The parenthetical reference to Piero Sraffa, an Italian economist who was a friend of Wittgenstein's at Cambridge, is probably an allusion to a story Wittgenstein used to tell about how Sraffa had responded to Wittgenstein's picture theory by making an insulting Neapolitan gesture and challenging him to specify *its* logical form.[55] It

53. MS 110, pp. 230–231, 1931. [German in appendix.] The first two paragraphs are an early draft of *Philosophical Investigations*, §120; cf. MS 114, part 2, pp. 109–110; *Philosophical Grammar*, p. 121.

54. MS 157b, pp. 10–13, 1937. [German in appendix.] The fourth paragraph is an early draft of *Philosophical Investigations*, §102, and is immediately followed by drafts of *Philosophical Investigations*, §91–92.

55. See Malcolm, *Ludwig Wittgenstein: A Memoir*, pp. 57–58. In a footnote, Malcolm records that von Wright remembers that Wittgenstein "related this incident to him somewhat differently: the question at issue, according to Wittgenstein, was whether every proposition must have a 'grammar,' and Sraffa asked Wittgenstein what the 'grammar' of the gesture was. In describing the incident to von Wright, Wittgenstein did not mention the phrases 'logical form' or 'logical multiplicity'" (p. 58, n. 3).

must have been particularly clear that understanding Sraffa's gesture did not call for any particular occurrent mental process—the "pneumatic," as Wittgenstein called it—that gives a sign its meaning, nor did it involve the kind of calculus that Wittgenstein had regarded as paradigmatic in the early 1930s.

In response to the idea that meaning consists in something that goes on in the mind, Wittgenstein repeatedly insists on looking at how we actually go about explaining the use of words. Wittgenstein attacks the idea that there must be something behind what we actually say and think that gives it a determinate sense by means of a discussion of examples of how we actually use words—such as using a ruler, following a signpost, or giving a verbal instruction. His strategy is set out in the opening paragraphs of the *Blue Book*, which begins with the question "What is the meaning of a word?" Instead of giving a direct answer, Wittgenstein proposes attacking the question by asking, first, "What is an explanation of the meaning of a word?"[56] In the paragraphs that follow, he offers a preliminary justification of his approach to meaning by comparing it to questions about the nature of length: in each case, we need to look at how we make use of the term if we are to understand its significance and avoid the temptation of thinking that there is something that it consists in:

> The way this question helps us is analogous to the way the question "how do we measure a length?" helps us to understand the problem "what is length?"
> The questions "What is length?", "What is meaning?" "What is the number one?" etc., produce in us a mental cramp. We feel that we can't point to anything in reply to them and yet ought to point to something. (We are up against one of the great sources of philosophical bewilderment: a substantive makes us look for a thing that corresponds to it.)[57]

Similarly, in the opening paragraphs of a section of the Big Typescript entitled "The sense of a sentence, not a *soul*," Wittgenstein provides the following summary of his reply to the "pneumatic" conception of meaning:

> A method of measurement, e.g. spatial measurement, has exactly the same relation to a particular measurement as the sense of a sentence has to its truth or falsehood.
>
> The sense of a / the / sentence is not pneumatic; rather, it is what is given as an answer to a request for an explanation of the sense. And—or—one sense differs from another as the explanation of the one differs from the explanation of the other.
>
> The role the sentence plays in the calculus, that is its sense.
>
> The sense (therefore) doesn't stand *behind* it (as the psychic occurrence of ideas etc.).[58]

56. In *Philosophical Investigations* §560, he sums up his approach in the following terms: "'The meaning of the word is what is explained by the explanation of the meaning.' I.e.: if you want to understand the use of the word 'meaning,' look for what are called 'explanations of meaning.'"
57. *Blue Book*, p. 1.
58. Big Typescript, §20, p. 81. [German in appendix.] Based on MS 113, p. 82; revised in MS 114, II, p. 125, the source for *Philosophical Grammar*, §84; also in MS 116, pp. 65–66. Cf. Big Typescript, §9; *Philosophical Investigations*, §560; and the derogatory parenthetical reference in *Philosophical Investigations*, §109, to the "pneumatic conception of thought."

Here, he both prefaces and follows his negative remarks about the pneumatic conception of meaning with a positive characterization of his conception of the sense of a sentence at the time, its "role in the calculus": the sense of a sentence is comparable to a method of measurement, because both consist in a procedure for determining a certain result. To find out if a statement about the length of an object is true, one has to know how one goes about determining its length; similarly, to find out if a sentence is true or false, one has to know how one uses the words in question. In sharp contrast with the conceptions of verification discussed by the Vienna Circle, Wittgenstein did not think of the use of the sentence, its "role in the calculus," as a matter of identifying a specific operation that might verify or falsify the statement. Instead, he stressed that whatever explanations one offers will themselves be further linguistic signs and will presuppose the ability to understand language and make use of it.

In the *Philosophical Grammar*, he reiterates this point about the primacy of context, using the first paragraph in the preceding quotation. He argues that the meaning of two different sentences differs because we give different explanations of their meanings, and that fact has to be understood in the context of the overall system of signs, not the speaker's or hearer's thoughts. That paragraph is followed by the following material, further stressing the same point:

> The sense of a sentence is not pneumatic; rather, it is what is given as an answer to a request for an explanation of the sense. Or: one sense differs from another in the same way as the explanation of the one differs from the explanation of the other. So also: the sense of one proposition differs from the sense of another in the same way as the one proposition differs from another.
>
> The sense of a sentence is not a soul.
>
> It is only in a language that something is a sentence. To understand a sentence is to understand a language.
>
> A sentence is a sign in a system of signs. It is *one* combination of signs among a number of possibilities, and as opposed to other possibilities. As it were *one* position of an indicator as opposed to other possibilities.[59]

Wittgenstein turns his attention to the use of the sentence in language, to how one would actually go about explaining the meaning of the sentence in question to someone else, and, in the case of a factual assertion, what procedures one would use to determine whether it was true or false. Giving up any attempt at a mythology of mental processes amounts to accepting that one really cannot make use of language to get outside of language. There is a forceful statement of his position in a manuscript note written in 1930; the second paragraph is an early draft of *Philosophical Investigations,* section 504:

> What is expressible through language I call thought. Then it can be translated from this language into *another*. I want to say: all thought must then take place in signs.
>
> But if one says: "How am I supposed to know what he means, when I can see nothing but his signs," then I say: "How is *he* supposed to know what he means, when he has nothing but the signs either."

59. *Philosophical Grammar*, §84.

The question "How is that *meant*?" only makes sense when it amounts to "It is meant *thus*." This "thus" is a linguistic expression.[60]

4.3 Insight, Decision, and Practice

One of Wittgenstein's points of departure on his return to philosophy in 1929 was his dissatisfaction with the Tractarian thesis that our grasp of the concept of infinity can be accounted for in terms of our understanding a language with an infinite number of names. In the *Tractatus*, he had disposed of Russell's axiom of infinity, which postulates the existence of an infinite number of objects, as a pseudoproposition, while endorsing what Russell had wanted to say: "What the axiom of infinity intended to say would express itself in language through the existence of infinitely many names with different meanings."[61] Since then, he had come to see that his reply to Russell amounted to replacing a pseudoproposition by a pseudoexplanation, for a language with infinitely many names is an impossibility; our grasp of the infinite must rest on something we can do, not on something we can't:

> It isn't just impossible "for us men" to run through the natural numbers one by one; it's *impossible*, it means nothing.[62]

> If I were to say "If we were acquainted with an infinite extension, then it would be all right to talk of an actual infinite," that would really be like saying, "If there were a sense of abracadabra then it would be all right to talk about abracadabraic sense-perception."[63]

Consequently, he gave up the completed infinite, the idea that there are an infinite number of things. Instead, he held that all we can have and all we need is the notion of infinite possibility, the idea that the finite instances we are acquainted with can be extended indefinitely in a rule-governed manner. Like Kant, he gave the examples of space and time: our experience of space and time is finite, yet it is in their very nature that we can imagine extending them indefinitely.[64]

---

60. MS 108, p. 277. [German in appendix.] Cf. Big Typescript, §1, p. 4; MS 114, II, p. 4, the source for *Philosophical Grammar*, p. 40; MS 116, p. 6; *Philosophical Investigations*, §504.

61. *Tractatus*, 5.535.

62. *Philosophical Remarks*, §124.

63. *Philosophical Remarks*, §144.

64. Wittgenstein's adherence to the Kantian thesis that spatiotemporal experience presupposes a grasp of the concepts of space and time is already partially anticipated in *Tractatus* 2.0121–2.0131:

> Just as we are quite unable to think of spatial objects apart from space or temporal objects apart from time, so too there is *no* object that we can think of apart from the *possibility* of combining with others. . . .
> Each thing is, as it were, in a space of possible states of affairs. I can think of this space as empty, but not of the thing without the space.
> A spatial object must be located in infinite space.

In his "Metaphysical Exposition of the Concept of Space" in the Transcendental Aesthetic, Kant writes: "We can never represent to ourselves the absence of space, though we can quite well think it as empty of objects. . . . Space is represented as an infinite given magnitude" (Kant, *Critique of Pure Reason*, A24/B38–39).

Time appears to us to be essentially an *infinite* possibility.
Indeed, obviously infinite from what we know of its structure.

Surely, it's impossible that mathematics should depend on any hypothesis concerning physical space. And surely in this sense *visual* space isn't infinite.
And if it's a matter, not of the reality, but of the possibility of the hypothesis of infinite space, then this possibility must surely be prefigured somewhere.[65]

As this "infinite possibility" cannot be a contingent empirical fact or hypothesis (for that would undermine the aprioricity of mathematics), and is not to be reduced to a tautology, Wittgenstein is driven to the Kantian answer that it is due to the form of experience:

> In some sense or other, I must have two kinds of experience: one which is of the finite and which cannot transcend the finite (the idea of such a transcendence is nonsense even on its own terms) and one of the infinite. And that's how it is. Experience as experience of the facts gives me the finite; the objects *contain* the infinite. . . . I can see in space the possibility of any finite experience. That is, no experience could be too large for it or exhaust it: not of course because we are acquainted with the dimensions of every experience and know space to be larger, but because we understand this as belonging to the essence of space.[66]

> We are in fact in the same position with time as with space. The actual time we are acquainted with is limited (finite). Infinity is an internal quality of the form of time.[67]

Explanation still comes to an end with the "fact" that the world consists of the objects that it does, but now it is enriched by specifying the contribution made by their finitude and their spatiotemporal constitution. We do not experience an actual infinity, but we can conceive of a law which states that the finite objects we do experience extend to infinity. For instance, we might think of a series of red spheres on an infinite filmstrip which makes possible everything finite that happens on the screen.[68] Of course, we can't actually imagine experiencing an infinite series, so we have to represent it through a proposition which states that for all numbers n, there is an nth thing which is a red sphere.[69] In tracing out his train of thought, we can see how Wittgenstein's conviction that an infinite totality is inconceivable depends on the thesis that experience, the primary realm, must be finite. The connection is brought out

65. *Philosophical Remarks*, §136.
In his "Metaphysical Exposition of the Concept of Time," Kant writes:

> Time is not an empirical concept that has been derived from any experience. . . . Appearances may, one and all, vanish; but time (as the universal condition of their possibility) cannot itself be removed. . . . Different times are but parts of one and the same time; and the representation which can be given only through a single object is intuition. . . . The infinitude of time signifies nothing more than that every determinate magnitude of time is possible only through limitations of one single time that underlies it. The original representation, *time*, must therefore be given as unlimited. (Kant, *Critique of Pure Reason*, A30–32/B46–48; the first set of parentheses was added in the second edition).

66. *Philosophical Remarks*, §138.
67. *Philosophical Remarks*, §143.
68. *Philosophical Remarks*, §139.
69. "It is expressed by a proposition of the form '(n):(∃nx).Φx.'" *Philosophical Remarks*, §139.

in the following passage, which clearly contrasts the nature of the finite space of experience and the potentially infinite space of physical theory:

> You can only answer the objection "But if nevertheless there were infinitely many things?" by saying "But there aren't." And what makes us think that perhaps there are is only our confusing the things of physics with the elements of knowledge.
>
> For this reason we also can't suppose an hypothetical infinite visual space in which an infinite series of red patches is visible.
> What we conceive of in physical space is not that which is primary, which we can only acknowledge [*anerkennen*] to a greater or lesser extent; rather, what we can know [*erkennen*] of physical space shows us how far what is primary reaches and how we have to interpret physical space.[70]

While infinity is grounded in the form of experience, it is not part of its content. Instead, we have to look at the form of our physical theory, at "what we conceive of in physical space." Here we are not limited to what is given in experience; we can also express hypotheses with a potentially infinite series of consequences. That conception of infinity is expressed by the rules for the number system:

> The rules for a number system—say, the decimal system—contain everything that is infinite about the numbers. That, e.g. *these rules* set no limits on the left or right hand to the numerals; *this* is what contains the expression of infinity.[71]

It is striking that Wittgenstein immediately responds by raising an objection that he would pursue much further shortly afterward, only to respond that the rules are unaffected by such merely material considerations:

> Someone might perhaps say: True, but the numerals are still limited by their use and by writing materials and other factors. That is so, but that isn't expressed in the *rules* for their use, and it is only in these that their real essence is expressed.[72]

As a result, Wittgenstein's philosophy of mathematics becomes a matter of understanding the nature of the rules governing our use of numbers and other mathematical expressions, rules that have their own distinctive character. In the *Philosophical Remarks*, Wittgenstein holds that no tautology is equivalent to a mathematical truth. He maintains that while it is a tautology that five things and seven more things make twelve, the tautology is not equivalent to the equation "$7 + 5 = 12$," even though it does show that it is true. His reason is that the equation, unlike the tautology, is supposed to provide a "fundamental insight" into the structures of the numbers in question, the insight that

> the 5 strokes and the 7 combine *precisely to make 12* (and so for example to make the same structure as do 4 and 4 and 4.) —It is always only insight [*Einsicht*] into

70. *Philosophical Remarks*, §147; cf. Big Typescript, §101, p. 492, where the last paragraph is enclosed in quotation marks and is placed immediately after the passage about "that inarticulate sound with which some writers would like to start philosophy" quoted on p. 145.
71. *Philosophical Remarks*, §141.
72. *Philosophical Remarks*, §141.

the internal relations of the structures and not some proposition or other or some logical consideration which tells us this.[73]

While Wittgenstein's notion of insight into the internal relations of numerical structures is not fully spelled out, the position is certainly a radical departure from the *Tractatus*, where he had unequivocally dismissed the role of intuition [*Anschauung*] in mathematics.[74] However, it is clear that his new appeal to to "insight" in mathematics is meant to exclude any account of mathematical truths that makes them dependent on the truth of other propositions: "No investigation of concepts, only direct insight can tell us that $3 + 2 = 5$."[75] A later correction to the text of the *Philosophical Remarks* suggests that the insight in question is only a matter of seeing the place of the equation in a system of equations, for after "direct insight" he added "into the number calculus" and noted his dissatisfaction with the expression "direct insight."[76] The very fact that he made the alteration suggests that he had previously entertained a different conception of "direct insight," however. A remark in the next section suggests a parallel with Kant's treatment of mathematics as arising out the form of temporal intuition:

> What I said earlier about the nature of arithmetical equations and about an equation's not being replaceable by a tautology explains—I believe—what Kant means when he insists that $7 + 5 = 12$ is not an analytic proposition, but synthetic *a priori*.[77]

On the next page, Wittgenstein goes back not just to Kant's terminology, but to his solution to the problem of how mathematics is possible—namely, that it is due to the temporal form of our experience:

> Aren't the numbers a logical peculiarity of space and time?
>
> The calculus itself exists only in space and time.[78]

While his Kantian account explains the aprioricity of mathematics and is supposed to make contingent limitations on its application irrelevant, it does impose limitations of its own. We have already seen that it implies that understanding a mathematical equation consists of an insight into the structures of the expressions it equates:

> We might say, "A mathematical proposition is a pointer to an insight." The assumption that no insight corresponded to it would reduce it to utter nonsense.
>
> We cannot *understand* the equation unless we recognize the connection between its sides.[79]

73. *Philosophical Remarks*, §104; cf. §99 ff., and especially §103.
74. See chapter 2, p. 54.
75. *Philosophical Remarks*, §107.
76. *Philosophical Remarks*, §107, n. 2.
77. *Philosophical Remarks*, §108. According to F. A. von Hayek's unpublished biographical notes, Wittgenstein was well acquainted with the *Critique of Pure Reason*, having studied and read it out loud with a friend while he was interned at the Monte Cassino prisoner-of-war camp after the end of the World War I. See Newton Garver, "Neither Knowing nor Not Knowing," p. 223, n16.
78. *Philosophical Remarks*, §109.
79. *Philosophical Remarks*, §174.

Insight is also needed in applying a rule in a proof, for we have to see that the rule applies to the case in hand. In other words, application of a rule always depends on an act of insight, the insight that the rule can be applied in *this* case:

> Is it like this: I need a new insight at each step in a proof? This is connected with the question of the individuality of each number. Something of the following sort: Supposing there to be a certain general rule (therefore one containing a variable), I must recognise afresh that this rule may be applied *here*. No act of foresight can absolve me from this act of insight. Since the form to which the rule is applied is in fact different at every step.[80]

There is a marginal note in the typescript of the *Philosophical Remarks* that encapsulates the next phase of Wittgenstein's thought: next to "No act of foresight can absolve me from this act of insight" he wrote "Act of *decision*, not *insight*." That is, he gave up the idea that applying the rule depends on seeing that it *must* apply; instead, it is a matter of *my* deciding to apply it here. The note is taken up in the text of the *Philosophical Grammar*, where it provides the basis for the final sentence of a revised version of the paragraph just cited: "But it is not a matter of an act of *insight*, but of an act of *decision*."[81]

In a revision of another remark about mathematical insight in the *Philosophical Remarks*, Wittgenstein wrote that if we are to speak of an act of direct insight at all in such a context, it had best be an insight into the calculus, the system of rules within which we are working.[82]

Taken by itself, the claim that applying a rule is "an act of *decision*" makes it sound as if Wittgenstein had given up the apriority of mathematics for an extreme conventionalism in which one is free to decide how to apply a rule every time one makes use of it. This new position is proposed as a critique of the notion of insight, not of mathematics, however. While it is conceivable that a mathematician experiences an insight at each stage of a series of inferences, the insight is neither necessary nor sufficient for it to be a proof; what matters is whether or not those inferences are according to the rules. All that need happen is that the mathematician writes a sequence of equations—decides to write them down, as Wittgenstein now puts it. Emphasizing decision is intended as a dramatic way of deflating the search for a metaphysical justification and is not meant to affect our confidence in the practice of mathematical inference. The motivation is clearly stated in a parallel passage from *Zettel*:

> One is tempted to justify rules of grammar by sentences like "But there really are four primary colours." And the saying that the rules of grammar are arbitrary is directed against the possibility of this justification, which is constructed on the model of justifying a sentence by pointing to what verifies it.[83]

80. *Philosophical Remarks*, §149. Cf. §164 on "the unbridgeable gulf between rule and application, or law and special case." See also §104, §107, and *Wittgenstein's Lectures, Cambridge, 1932–1935*, pp. 131–134. Cf. the discussion of this passage and subsequent developments in David Pears, *The False Prison*, Vol. 2, pp. 518 ff.

81. *Philosophical Grammar*, p. 301; Big Typescript, §110, p. 545.

82. See the reference to Wittgenstein's emendation of §107 along these lines on p. 113.

83. *Zettel*, §331. Source: MS 114, p. 159, 1933–1934. Cf. *Zettel*, §320, on cookery as nonarbitrary, because there are limits set on what counts as cookery due to its having the aim of producing edible food, while a game or language is arbitrary because it doesn't have any such independently given end.

Similarly, he had once postulated an act of insight lying behind our grasp of an equation: "As the immediate datum is to a proposition which it verifies, so is the arithmetical relation we see in the structure to the equation which it verifies."[84] By "verification" here, Wittgenstein means the procedure we use to establish the truth or falsity of a proposition, whatever it may be, and there is no implication that they must be the empirical methods of verification that are characteristic of the logical positivists' use of the term: "How a proposition is verified is what it says. Compare the generality of genuine propositions with generality in arithmetic. It is differently verified and so is of a different kind."[85]

Shortly after he wrote the *Philosophical Remarks*, Wittgenstein came to see that not only is the difference in kind between arithmetical propositions and those concerning immediate experience, or "genuine propositions," as he called them, much deeper than he had realized, but that *neither* of them can be understood on the model of establishing the truth or falsity of a factual proposition. In the case of arithmetic, there is a procedure for establishing the truth or falsity of a given proposition, but the procedure has more affinities with proof in logic than with empirical investigation. Propositions about immediate experience, on the other hand, do not call for any procedure at all in order to tell whether it is true or false, and so, once again, one's basis for knowing whether it is true or false is quite dissimilar to ordinary empirical investigation:

> "Verifying by inspection" is a wholly misleading expression. For it says that first of all a procedure, the inspection, takes place (it might be compared with looking through a microscope, or with the procedure of turning one's head round *in order to see something*). And that the seeing *has* to succeed. One might speak of "seeing by turning round," or "seeing by looking." But in that case the turning round (or looking) is a process external to the seeing, a process that is thus of only practical concern. What one would like to say is "seeing by seeing."[86]

Wittgenstein thus came to deny that the privileged status of propositions describing immediate experience, or mathematical truths, can be underwritten by appealing to special processes that guarantee the truth of the results; instead, the role of these propositions in our language is to be clarified by setting out the rules that we follow in each case. But he remained a Kantian in the sense that he thought of philosophy as vindicating human knowledge by clarifying the rules to which it conforms. Indeed, in a lecture given in the early 1930s, Wittgenstein described the transcendental method—"Kant's critical method without the peculiar applications Kant made of it"—as "the right sort of approach":

> Descartes and others had tried to start with one proposition such as "Cogito, ergo sum" and work from it to others. Kant disagreed and started with what we know to be so and so, and went on to examine the validity of what we suppose we know.[87]

Wittgenstein now holds that if we get a clear view of our inferential practices, we will see both why one might be misled into believing that mathematical inference

84. *Philosophical Remarks*, §166.
85. *Philosophical Remarks*, §166.
86. *Zettel*, §436. Source: MS 112, p. 230, 1931.
87. *Wittgenstein's Lectures, Cambridge, 1930–32*, pp. 73–74.

needs philosophical support and why that belief is mistaken. We can justify a particular inference by reference to the system of rules it belongs to, but the system has to be self-supporting. There is no higher court of appeal.

While the later Wittgenstein did not give as much emphasis to the conventional aspects of our language as he did when he embraced the calculus conception, the change does not mark a return to his earlier essentialism. Instead, he acts out the tension in dialogues that set out both the attractions and shortcomings of conventionalism and essentialism. The dialectic is summed up in the following exchange:

> If you talk about *essence*—, you are merely noting a convention. But here one would like to retort: there is no greater difference than that between a proposition about the depth of the essence and one about—a mere convention. But what if I reply: to the *depth* that we see in the essence there corresponds the *deep* need for the convention.[88]

The first voice states a conventionalist objection to talk about essences: it simply registers the existence of certain linguistic conventions. The essentialist replies that there is a crucial difference between talking about a convention and talking about an essence—namely, that the essence goes far deeper than mere words. For instance, there is all the difference in the world between the proposition that two and two makes four, and a proposition setting out the conventions that must be in place for "two and two makes four" to mean what it does. To both of these voices, Wittgenstein responds that the depth the essentialist sees is not simply due to the nature of mathematics, but is also due to our nature: we have a deep need to see things that way, and that is itself an important fact that deserves our attention.

Wittgenstein had first thought that inference must be justified by a self-interpreting given lying behind the rule that would fully determine the rule's application, and then realized that such a given was both unnecessary and impossible. It was unnecessary because we do not need an unmoved mover in order to follow a rule; it was impossible because nothing could perform that task. Instead, we have to look at how the rule is actually used. The problem that had motivated the search for something that would unambiguously determine the application of the rule had been that any formulation of a rule is always, in principle, capable of being interpreted in a variety of ways. At first sight, it seems as if a rule determines the result of its application in each of the infinite number of circumstances where it might be applied. But the rule must be expressed in words or actions. The words can always be misunderstood, and any series of actions one performs while following that rule also conforms to any number of other rules. If we begin by worrying that the words I use to express a rule do not guarantee that they will be interpreted correctly, then any interpretation of those words will be open to the same objection. As a result, it can seem as if the regress of interpretations can only come to an end with something which is not open to interpretation, something which cannot be misinterpreted. That is the task of the act of insight.

This act of insight is even more problematic than the regress of interpretations it is meant to end: it is simply a postulate, required in order to bring the regress to an end, and we are never told how it can guarantee that our doubts will be laid to rest.

88. *Remarks on the Foundations of Mathematics*, I §74.

We may never have an insight or an intuition, and, if we do, it is just as open to mis-interpretation as any verbal formulation of a rule:

> "But this initial segment of a series obviously admitted of various interpreta-tions (e.g. by means of algebraic expressions) and so you must first have chosen *one* such interpretation." —Not at all. A doubt was possible in certain circum-stances. But that is not to say that I did doubt, or even could doubt. . . .
>
> So it must have been intuition that removed this doubt? —If intuition is an inner voice—how do I know *how* I am to obey it? And how do I know that it doesn't mislead me? For if it can guide me right, it can also guide me wrong.
>
> ((Intuition an unnecessary shuffle.))[89]

Even in the *Philosophical Remarks*, then, Wittgenstein's work on specific issues in the philosophy of mathematics makes little use of insight or what is given in intu-ition.[90] Instead, most of his work depends on articulating a holistic conception of arithmetic as the "grammar of number" and, more generally, of mathematics as con-sisting of calculi that are determined by systems of rules.[91] For the most part, the chapters on the philosophy of mathematics in the Big Typescript develop the discus-sion of issues already broached in the *Philosophical Remarks*, such as generality, cardinal numbers, mathematical proof, inductive proof, and the infinite. The passages that appeal to insight are either dropped or modified. Wittgenstein writes: "You can't get behind the rules, because there isn't any behind."[92] However, the issue of rule-following had not dropped out of sight. Rather, he had recognized that the ques-tions raised by rule-following in mathematical proof could be applied to any rule at all, and that recognition was connected with important changes in his philoso-phy of mind and language. There is a close parallel between the demand for an an act of insight to close the otherwise "unbridgeable gulf between a rule and its application" and the demand for a mental process to bring about the "leap from the sign to what is signified."[93] Just as no act of insight is necessary to infer or to un-derstand an equation, so no mental process need animate everyday inference or understanding, either.

In the *Philosophical Grammar*, Wittgenstein raises the question whether point-ing at an object should be considered a "primary sign," providing a direct connec-tion between language and reality, as opposed to ordinary words, "secondary signs."

---

89. *Philosophical Investigations*, §213.

90. In fact, the thesis that "arithmetic is the grammar of numbers" comes from §108, the very remark in which Wittgenstein claims he has explained what Kant means by saying that 7 + 5 = 12 is synthetic a priori. On calculi and systems of rules, see *Philosophical Remarks*, §152, and §§148–169.

91. *Philosophical Remarks*, §113, does speak of the natural, rational, and complex numbers as "given in reality":

> The natural numbers are a form given in reality [*Wirklichkeit*] through things, as the ratio-nal numbers are through extensions etc. I mean by real [*wirklich*] forms. In the same way, the complex numbers are given by real manifolds. (The *symbols* are real.)

92. *Philosophical Grammar*, p. 244. For the most part, the chapters on the philosophy of math-ematics in the Big Typescript develop the discussion of issues already broached in the *Philosophical Remarks*, such as generality, cardinal numbers, mathematical proof, inductive proof, and the infinite.

93. *Philosophical Remarks*, §164; §26; see pp. 67–69, 104–110.

Similarly, one could consider a red coloured label a primary sign for the colour red, the word "red" a secondary sign.[94] These considerations lead him to ask:

> Are the signs one wants to call "primary" incapable of being misinterpreted? Can one perhaps say, that they don't really any longer need to be understood?[95]

In reply, he points out that the primary signs and ordinary words are in the same boat: both are usually understood, and both are equally capable of being misunderstood: "—If that means they don't have to be further *interpreted*, that goes for words, too; if it means, they *cannot* be further interpreted, then it's false."[96] As the context here makes clear, "interpreting" is not simply a matter of using a sign in accordance with a rule, but involves explicitly formulating the rule one is following.[97] While we find it hard to imagine that we could misunderstand the primary signs, and so usually feel no need to to state any rule, we are nevertheless acting in accordance with a rule and other rules are possible. Given a sufficiently unusual context, we might have to state the rules we were following in using even the simplest primary signs. Wittgenstein makes his point clear by giving the example of a seemingly straightforward table correlating primary signs—red labels, green labels, etc.—with secondary signs— "red," "green," etc.—and then describing some of the different ways we might use it. The simplest case, of course, is the one in which the words and colour patches are arranged in parallel columns and each word is opposite the corresponding colour patch. But a table in which the red label is opposite "green" and the green label opposite "red" could still be used to connect the appropriate words with the appropriate colours. One could, for instance, simply make different connections within the chart: instead of looking from a patch to the word opposite it, one might look diagonally, so that the old connections were still made. Another possibility would be to look directly across from the word "red" to the green label, but to use the green label as standing for the complementary colour, namely red. In the same way, a red label would represent green; a blue label, yellow; and so forth. The first deviant case illustrates how the table can be further interpreted; the second illustrates how the primary signs can be further interpreted.[98]

The discussion of the colour chart prepares the ground for Wittgenstein's interlocutor to insist that even if we aren't following the obvious rule, there must be some rule that we're following: "'I won't insist that the red pattern in the explanatory chart must be horizontally opposite the word "red," but there must be some sort of law for reading the table or it will lose its sense.'"[99] Wittgenstein responds by asking whether

94. *Philosophical Grammar*, §46–47.

95. *Philosophical Grammar*, §48.

96. *Philosophical Grammar*, §48.

97. Cf. *Philosophical Investigations*, §201: "[T]here is an inclination to say: every action according to the rule is an interpretation. But we ought to restrict the term 'interpretation' to the substitution of one expression of the rule for another." See also *Philosophical Grammar*, §99 = *Zettel*, §234: "What happens is not that this symbol cannot be further interpreted, but: I do no interpreting. I do not interpret because I feel natural in the present picture. When I interpret, I step from one level of my thought to another."

98. *Philosophical Grammar*, §49. In addition to the complementary-colour interpretation of the labels, Wittgenstein also considers the possibility that we use a label as a sample of a colour a shade darker.

99. *Philosophical Grammar*, §52.

there is no law if we read the chart diagonally. In that case, the interlocutor insists, wouldn't we have to give that schema beforehand? Wittgenstein replies with yet another question: Do we have to give a schema specifying horizontal connections in the normal case? His reply provokes a final barrage of interlocutory questions:

> But in that case mustn't there at least be a regularity through time in the use of the table? Would it work if we were to use the table in accordance with different schemata at different times? *How would one know* in that case how the table was to be used?[100]

To which Wittgenstein simply replies: "Well, how does one know *anyway*? Explanations of signs come to end somewhere."[101]

While Wittgenstein's reply is meant to put an end to the search for the ultimate explanation, or the ultimate reason, it is not his last word on the topic. Though misunderstanding is always possible we can, in practice, rely on people to respond to colour charts in a predictable way, reading them horizontally and taking the colour labels as samples of that very colour. Similarly, we expect someone who points their finger to be pointing in the direction from the hand to the fingertip, rather than viceversa: "It is part of human nature to understand pointing with the finger in the way that we do. (As it is also part of human nature to play board games and to use sign languages that consist of written signs on a flat surface.)"[102] While we cannot get outside the rules in order to give them some further justification, facts such as the ones presented above are part of the context of rule-governed activity. In discussing what is involved in teaching someone a language, Wittgenstein emphasizes that we depend on the pupil's reacting in certain ways to our encouragement, and without such responses, teaching would not take place:

> And if the child does not react to our encouragement, like a cat that one wishes to teach to retrieve, then one does not succeed in getting it to understand one's explanation; or rather, understanding begins here with reacting in a determinate way.[103]

In the case of the child learning to speak, understanding begins with such reactions; in this way, more sophisticated reactions become possible.

We try to give our explanations so that they will not be misunderstood, but we never reach a self-evident stopping point: every explanation, even a simple colour chart, can be given a deviant interpretation. No rule can unambiguously determine its application: one can always raise a question as to how it is to be applied in any particular case. The chart cannot compel me to use it in a certain way: "It's there, like a field, with paths leading through it: but I can also cut across. —Each time I apply the chart I make a fresh transition. The transitions aren't made, as it were, once for all the chart."[104] Immediately after making these observations Wittgenstein asks himself, "What kinds of propositions are these?", and replies:

100. *Philosophical Grammar*, §52.
101. *Philosophical Grammar*, §52. Cf. *Philosophical Investigations*, §1: "'But how does he know where and how he is to look up the word 'red' and what he is to do with the word "five"?' —Well, I assume that he *acts* as I have described. Explanations come to an end somewhere."
102. *Philosophical Grammar*, §52.
103. *Eine Philosophische Betrachtung*, p. 131.
104. *Philosophical Grammar*, §52.

—They are like the observation that explanations of signs come to an end some-where. And that is rather like saying "How does it help you to postulate a creator, it only pushes back the problem of the beginning of the world?" This observation brings out an aspect of my explanation that I perhaps hadn't noticed. One might also say: "Look at your explanation in *this* way—now are you still satisfied with it?"[105]

4.4 From Logical Holism to Practical Holism

In the *Tractatus*, Wittgenstein had held that while truth-functional propositional logic limits what can be said, its logical form shows the common structure of language and world: "Logic must take care of itself."[106] Once he gave up the logical atomist doctrine that all relations between propositions are ultimately truth-functional, lan-guage itself takes its place: "Language has to speak for itself."[107] The logical holist conceives of everyday language as consisting of systems of rules, such as the rules of a formal calculus or a scientific theory.[108] On Wittgenstein's post-*Tractatus* con-ception of language, even formal rules must be understood in terms of their practical background, a change of view that emphasizes practice over theory: "rules leave loop-holes open, and the practice has to speak for itself."[109] There is no sharp transition from the calculus model to the language-game model, from logical holism to practi-cal holism: Wittgenstein does not give up the idea that our linguistic practices are rule-governed, but rather comes to see that rule-governed behaviour depends on a practical context. Alternatively, one might say that his conception of language be-comes increasingly broad, until it includes the whole range of human activity. Both the logical holist conception of language as a calculus or a theory and the later prac-tical holist notion of a language-game stress the paramount role of context: an utter-ance is only significant within a larger context. On either view, the meaning of an utterance, an inscription, or a thought is not an entity independent of the rest of our language, but consists in its relation to the rest of language.

Despite these continuities, Wittgenstein's conception of language changed radi-cally during the 1930s. During the early 1930s, he frequently compares language to a calculus, a formal system of rules, stressing the role of explicit rules when discuss-

---

105. *Philosophical Grammar*, §52. Cf. *Philosophical Grammar*, §68; *Philosophical Investiga-tions*, §143, quoted at the end of chapter 1, p. 30.

106. *Tractatus*, 5.473.

107. *Philosophical Grammar*, §2 and §27.

108. There is thus a close affinity between Wittgenstein's logical holism, once he had given up the goal of a phenomenological language, and what Hubert Dreyfus calls "theoretical holism," the view that all understanding is a matter of formulating a theory. I take the term "practical holism" from Dreyfus' interpretation of Heidegger and Wittgenstein in "Holism and Hermeneutics," where he draws a paral-lel distinction between *theoretical* holism, the view that all interpretation is a matter of translating between theories, and *practical* holism, the view that while everyday coping with things and people "involves explicit beliefs and hypotheses, these can only be meaningful in specific contexts and against a background of shared practices," p. 9.

109. *On Certainty*, §139. There is a valuable discussion of the triptych formed by this quotation and the preceding two in K. S. Johannessen, "The Concept of Practice in Wittgenstein's Later Philoso-phy."

ing what is involved in explaining the meaning of a word.[110] Thus, he dismisses the idea that we can think of the meaning of a word as an entity, a "meaning-body" that lies behind the use of our words, in favour of a description of the rules we accept for the use of the word.[111] While he retains the calculus analogy in subsequent writing, it is usually as an object of comparison, as a way of bringing out the *dis*analogies between ordinary language and a calculus. In Wittgenstein's subsequent work, he placed much less emphasis on the act of formulating or expressing a rule. He turned his attention away from the standard models of explaining linguistic meaning in terms of linking words to the world by means of ostensive definition, and words to words by identifying necessary and sufficient conditions for the use of terms, pointing out that such devices only work when most of our language is already in place. In practice, we explain the meaning of words by offering paradigmatic examples. These examples need not be given in such a way that they are protected against all possibilities of misunderstanding; it is enough that they usually work. In place of the single propositional form—"This is how things stand"[112]—that the author of the *Tractatus* had attempted to impose on our language, the author of the *Philosophical Investigations* sketches a variety of widely differing yet interconnected linguistic practices. In response to the objection that "you let yourself off the very part of the investigation that once gave yourself the most headache, the part about the *general form of propositions* and of language," he writes:

> And this is true. —Instead of producing something common to all that we call language, I am saying that these phenomena have no one thing in common which makes us use the same word for all,—but that they are *related* to one another in many different ways. And it is because of this relationship, or these relationships, that we call them all "language."[113]

Immediately after summing up his discussion of the nature of philosophy in the *Philosophical Investigations* with the words "There is not *a* philosophical method, though there are indeed methods, like different therapies,"[114] Wittgenstein returns to the Tractarian claim that "This is how things stand" is the general form of any proposition. In section 135, he replies: "Asked what a proposition is—whether it is another person or ourselves that we have to answer—we shall give examples . . . now in *this* way we have a concept of a proposition." Most of the next 100 sections of the *Philosophical Investigations* are occupied with exploring and undermining the two main avenues of reply which had attracted Wittgenstein: the view that meaning consists in mental processes and the view that meaning consists in implicit rules. One of his principal aims is to discredit the idea of a hidden fact that somehow underlies what our words mean and gives them a fully determinate sense, whether that "fact" is conceived of as a subjective mental process or an objective rule.

110. See *Philosophical Grammar*, §§69–80, and the discussion of the *Blue Book*, p. 25, on p. 104.
111. See *Philosophical Grammar*, §16, where Wittgenstein discusses how one might explain the difference between the "is" of identity and the "is" of predication in these terms. Cf. *Philosophical Investigations*, §§558–560.
112. See *Tractatus*, 4.5, and *Philosophical Investigations*, §134.
113. *Philosophical Investigations*, §65.
114. *Philosophical Investigations*, §133; cf. the discussion of this section in chapter 1, pp. 19ff.

A key argument that continually recurs in one form or another throughout the first 200 sections of the *Philosophical Investigations* is that just as no mental content is intrinsically meaningful, so no strict rule by itself can determine how we go on, as all determination of meaning depends on interpretation. Any given mental process or any formulation of a rule is always, in principle, open to a further, deviant, interpretation. The imaginary case of the wayward child who learns to add small numbers correctly but systematically miscalculates, all the while insisting that he is going on the same way, is just one example of this leitmotif; other examples include the drawing of a man climbing uphill that might also be seen as a man sliding downhill, and Wittgenstein's discussion of different ways of making use of a sample of a leaf, following arrows or signposts, or interpreting a drawing of a cube.[115] No occurrent act of meaning or intending, grasping an essence or deciding to go on in a certain way, can give a rule the power to determine our future actions, because there is always the question of how that act is to be interpreted. As a result, the idea that a rule can determine all its future applications turns out to be misguided. Only if we ignore the context can we think that some isolated act or event can have a determinate meaning regardless of its context. A change in the context of application can yield a change in meaning, and therefore meaning cannot be identified with anything independent of context.

In pursuing these issues in *Philosophical Investigations*, section 138, and in the lengthy discussion of rule-following that is elaborated in the paragraphs that follow, Wittgenstein frequently returns to the question of what it is to understand a word in a flash, to suddenly understand how to use a word. One reason is that the phenomenon of understanding a word can look as though it provides a decisive counterexample to any conception of meaning that stresses context at the expense of "what's in the head." On the one hand, understanding a sentence is a matter of being able to use those words correctly, in applying them "in the course of time"; on the other hand, we may grasp the meaning of a sentence in a flash, when it "comes before our mind in an instant."[116] How do these subjective and objective sides fit together? Another reason is that the problem of "understanding the sense in the moment of application"[117] had occupied him since his return to philosophy in 1929. The questions in the *Philosophical Investigations* about what goes on when one suddenly understands how to use a word are a reformulation of his earlier questions about the relationship between the words I use in describing my experiences and the experiences themselves. In the same spirit, he had once asked why the words he used to describe his experiences seemed unable to describe "that which goes on in the reading of the description,"[118] the mental processes animating our words. At that stage in his development he had thought of the process of sudden understanding as illuminating the processses of

---

115. For the wayward child, see *Philosophical Investigations*, §§143 ff. and §§185 ff., quoted in part at the end of chapter 1. For the other examples, see *Philosophical Investigations*, p. 54; §73–74; §§85–86; §§139 ff.

116. *Philosophical Investigations*, §141, §139.

117. MS 107, p. 233. [For the German, see the passage in the appendix attached to chapter 5, n. 38, where this passage is quoted at greater length.]

118. Big Typescript, §102, p. 496. [For the German, see the passage in the appendix attached to chapter 5, n. 74, where this passage is quoted at greater length.]

understanding that animate our ordinary use of words, processes that cannot themselves be put into words.

The Wittgenstein of the *Philosophical Investigations* was well aware that people do sometimes understand words in a flash, but he saw that the phenomenon of sudden understanding is a dangerously limited basis for any insight into the essence of understanding. The same image can mean different things in different contexts: "What is essential is to see that the same thing can come before our minds when we hear the words and the application still be different. Has it the *same* meaning both times? I think we shall say not."[119] Wittgenstein holds that what justifies someone in saying that he or she has understood is not the accompanying experience considered in isolation from its surroundings, but the circumstances in which the experiences occur. The therapy he proposes is that we consider relatively simple cases of mental activity, such as what goes on when we read out loud, in order to see how the temptation of thinking that ineffable mental processes are involved arises.[120] In other words, he asks us to consider "the activity of rendering out loud what is written or printed; and also of writing from dictation, writing out something printed, playing from a score, and so on."[121]

The first point Wittgenstein makes in his discussion of "reading" in the *Philosophical Investigations* is that, although we are all very familiar with such activities, we would find it difficult to describe the part they play in our life, "even in rough outline." The observations that follow suggest that the difficulty is due to the differences between what happens when a skilled reader reads, when all kinds of things may go on, and often nothing at all over and above the successful completion of the task, with what goes on with a beginner who makes a conscious effort to read, or a skilled reader who makes a special effort to direct his or her attention to the process of reading. If we concentrate on the case of the beginner or the self-conscious reader, we shall indeed be inclined to say that it is "a special conscious activity of the mind."[122] The idea is that there must be some special conscious act of reading, "the act of reading the sounds off from the letters."[123] Here Wittgenstein replies by thinking of cases in which the experience goes on, but the "reader" does not really understand (perhaps he or she has been drugged), and cases in which the reader does understand, but nothing or something else goes on. Whether something is reading or not is a matter of whether the activity is successful, not a matter of whether I consciously apply a rule or feel guided or whatever. One wants to say that in reading "the words *come* in a special way"[124] or that "I experience the because"[125] but in practice, the words do not have to come in a special way and we need not experience anything in particular.

In most cases of proficient reading, we just get on with it and do it. Here we have an example of what Heidegger calls "readiness-to-hand" [*Zuhandenheit*]: our ordi-

119. *Philosophical Investigations*, §140.

120. Cf. *Philosophical Investigations*, §§431–432, on the idea that understanding animates signs and §§435–436, on the idea that understanding is a hidden rapid process.

121. *Philosophical Investigations*, §156.

122. *Philosophical Investigations*, §156.

123. *Philosophical Investigations*, §159.

124. *Philosophical Investigations*, §165.

125. *Philosophical Investigations*, §177.

nary use of everyday things does not call for reflective awareness of what we are doing. We only become aware of these things when something goes wrong or some other unusual circumstance draws our attention to them, making them "present-at-hand" [*vorhanden*].[126] Thus, under normal circumstances, reading a familiar language, "can we say anything but that . . . this sound comes automatically when we look at the mark?"[127] But if we try to understand the cases in which we are proficient on the model of what goes on in abnormal or problematic cases, we shall inevitably look at what goes on when we make an effort to read as revealing the essence of being influenced, an essence that is concealed in normal usage.[128] We think of particular cases of being guided or being influenced, and think that the experience we have in this or that case is paradigmatic, what goes on in every case.

The possibility of unanticipated deviant ways of following a rule arises again in the *Brown Book* in an early version of the rule-following discussion in *Philosophical Investigations*, beginning in section 185. Wittgenstein discusses the possibility that someone might learn how to add 1, as we do with small numbers, but does what we would call adding 2 when asked to add 1 to numbers between 100 and 300, adds 3 when asked to add 1 to larger numbers, and persists in regarding the procedure as a correct application of the rule he or she was taught. In response, Wittgenstein's interlocutor suggests that an act of intuition will always be needed to protect us against the possibility of a deviant interpretation of the rule: "'I suppose what you say comes to this, that in order to follow the rule "Add 1" correctly a new insight, intuition is needed at every step.'"[129] Instead of giving a direct answer to the question, Wittgenstein replies by asking the interlocutor to explain the notion of following the rule correctly, a notion he has simply taken for granted in his question: "—But what does it mean to follow the rule *correctly*? How and when is it to be decided which at a particular point is the correct step to take?"[130] The interlocutor responds by appealing to the rule-giver's intentions: "'The correct step at every point is that which is in accordance with the rule as it was *meant*, intended.'"[131] In the ensuing dialogue, the interlocutor tries to specify what the rule-giver's intentions consist in, and Wittgenstein repeatedly undermines him by asking how the application of the intention, meaning, mental act, or whatever other candidate is offered can be guaranteed in advance: the same deviant possibilities can always be raised. A page later, Wittgenstein sums up:

> If the mere words of the rule could not anticipate a future transition, no more could any mental act accompanying these words.
>
> We meet again and again with this curious superstition, as one might be inclined to call it, that the mental act is capable of crossing a bridge before we've got to it. This trouble crops up whenever we try to think about the ideas of think-

126. See Martin Heidegger, *Being and Time*, §§15–16.
127. *Philosophical Investigations*, §166.
128. This is very clearly stated in *Philosophical Investigations*, §170, and in the last paragraph of §175.
129. *Brown Book*, p. 141. Cf. *Eine Philosophische Betrachtung*, pp. 214–216; *Philosophical Investigations*, §185 ff.
130. *Brown Book*, p. 142.
131. *Brown Book*, p. 142.

ing, wishing, expecting, believing, knowing, trying to solve a mathematical problem, mathematical induction, and so forth.

It is no act of insight, intuition, which makes us use the rule as we do at the particular point of the series. It would be less confusing to call it an act of decision, though this too is misleading, for nothing like an act of decision must take place, but possibly just an act of writing or speaking. And the mistake which we here and in a thousand similar cases are inclined to make is labelled by the word 'to make' as we have used it in the sentence 'It is no act of insight which makes us use the rule as we do,' because there is an idea that 'something must make us' do what we do. And this again joins on to the confusion between cause and reason. *We need have no reason to follow the rule as we do.* The chain of reasons has an end.[132]

Here there is no suggestion that there must be an act of decision; only that if any mental process at all is involved, it is a decision, not an insight or an intuition. The search for a self-interpreting interpretation only arises if one treats the words and actions that express the rule as an interpretation, a construal of the rule that still needs to be made completely determinate. In some cases, of course, our words or actions will be ambiguous; in others, we can just get on with it and write or say the next term in the series. Wittgenstein is proposing that we look at these latter cases, when we do not do any interpreting, but simply grasp the rule in practice, such as everyday conversation and arithmetic, as prototypical instances of rule-following.

In the *Philosophical Investigations*, Wittgenstein illustrates his conception of a rule by elaborating the similarities between a rule and a signpost:

A rule stands there like a sign-post. —Does the sign-post leave no doubt about the way I have to go? Does it show which direction I am to take when I have passed it; whether along the road or footpath or cross-country? But where is it said which way I am to follow it; whether in the direction of its finger or (e.g.) in the opposite one? And if there were, not a single sign-post, but a chain of adjacent ones or of chalk marks on the ground—is there only one way of interpreting them? —So I can say, the sign-post does after all leave no room for doubt. Or rather: it sometimes leaves room for doubt and sometimes not. And now this is no longer a philosophical proposition, but an empirical one.[133]

Whether or not a given rule or sign-post gives rise to doubts about what it means will depend both on its context and on our interpretation of that context. If a doubt does arise, then it will be appropriate to ask a question. What Wittgenstein denies is that every possible question must be answered for the sign to be any use. We do not need to explain how a potential ambiguity is to be resolved unless it actually arises. In turn, that explanation may call for further explanations, but once again, only if it is necessary to prevent a misunderstanding:

An explanation may indeed rest on another one that has been given, but none stands in need of another—unless *we* need it to prevent a misunderstanding. One might say: an explanation serves to remove or to avert a misunderstanding—one, that is, that would occur but for the explanation; not every one that I can imagine.

---

132. *Brown Book*, p. 143. Cf. *Eine Philosophische Betrachtung*, p. 216; *Philosophical Investigations*, §§185 ff.
133. *Philosophical Investigations*, §85.

It may easily look as if every doubt merely *revealed* an existing gap in the foundations; so that secure understanding is only possible if we first doubt everything that *can* be doubted, and then remove all these doubts.

The sign-post is in order—if, under normal circumstances, it fulfils its purpose.[134]

This flat rejection of the philosophical demand that every possible doubt must be answered is itself the result of an intricate and complex dialogue with that demand. Sections 198—199 of the *Philosophical Investigations* amount to a compressed summary of the dialectic between the authorial voice that insists that the sign-post is in order if it usually does the job, and the sceptical interlocutor who attempts to raise every imaginable doubt. The first section recapitulates the dialogue with a voice that asks the sceptical question: How can I ever know how to follow a rule, if any action can follow from any rule, given a sufficiently ingenious interpretation? The second remark presents certain facts about the role of language and practice in our lives as a response to the sceptical challenge:

> "But how can a rule show me what I have to do at *this* point? Whatever I do is, on some interpretation, in accord with this rule." —That is not what we ought to say, but rather: any interpretation still hangs in the air along with what it interprets, and cannot give it any support. Interpretations by themselves do not determine meaning.
>
> "Then can whatever I do be brought into accord with the rule?" —Let me ask this: what has the expression of a rule—say a sign-post—got to do with my actions? What sort of connexion is there here? —Well, perhaps this one: I have been trained to react to this sign in a particular way, and now I do so react.
>
> But this is only to give a causal connexion, only to explain how it has come about that we now go by the signpost; not what this going-by-the-sign really consists in. On the contrary; I have further indicated that a person goes by a sign-post only in so far as there exists a regular use of sign-posts, a custom.
>
> Is what we call "obeying a rule" something that it would be possible for only *one* man to do, and to do only *once* in his life? —This is of course a note on the grammar of the expression "to obey a rule."
>
> It is not possible that there should have been only one occasion on which someone obeyed a rule. It is not possible that there should have been only one occasion on which a report was made, an order given or understood; and so on. —To obey a rule, to make a report, to give an order, to play a game of chess, are *customs* (uses, institutions.)
>
> To understand a sentence means to understand a language. To understand a language means to be master of a technique.[135]

Wittgenstein's first response to his interlocutor's sceptical question is that interpretation is not enough: imagining deviant interpretations on which my words do not mean what I ordinarily take them to mean shows only that there is more to following a rule than simply formulating an interpretation of the rule. His second reply takes the form of another question: "What is the relationship between the expression of a rule and my actions?"[136] Instead of just imagining possible deviant interpreta-

---

134. *Philosophical Investigations*, §87.

135. *Philosophical Investigations*, §198, §199.

136. See p. 108 on passages where Wittgenstein advocates this approach as a way of dealing with "What is x" questions that avoids the danger of thinking that there must be some thing, the nature of x, that we are attempting to specify.

tions, we are to think about how a particular expression of a rule and my actions are connected. Wittgenstein then turns to the case of seeing a signpost and going one way rather than another. His initial answer is to point to a causal connection: he asks his interlocutor to consider that he was once *trained* how to make use of signposts, and that is what the connection depends on. The interlocutor objects that it is not enough to point to a causal connection, for it commits the genetic fallacy of confusing causes and reasons: it only states the causal conditions for my using the signpost as I do, not what justifies my using it as I do. Wittgenstein's response is that he is not simply stating the causes that led one to act as one does, he is also insisting on the importance of the social and practical dimensions of our use of language: the training only has the significance that it does within the context of other customary uses and institutions. Considered in abstraction from that context, a rule, like an ostensive definition, can be made to conform with every course of action. In such a case, "we give one interpretation after another; as if each one contented us at least for a moment, until we thought of yet another lying behind it."[137] It is only when we return to the "rough ground" and consider the background of practices to which a rule belongs that the rule takes on a determinate form.

Our explicit beliefs and interpretations are only meaningful against a background of shared practices, which include the skills and customs we have learned—ways of acting that were not acquired as beliefs, even though we may express them in beliefs. It is this "way of grasping a rule which is *not* an *interpretation*, but which is exhibited in what we call 'obeying the rule' and 'going against it'" that ultimately ends the regress of interpretations.[138] In other words, "it is our *acting*, which lies at the bottom of the language-game."[139] Some readers have taken the practical turn in Wittgenstein's later work to amount to a form of linguistic relativism or idealism that makes the beliefs of a particular group or linguistic community immune to criticism, because they are part of the language-games that the community uses. But the agreement in what we call obeying a rule and going against it Wittgenstein appeals to here is not comparable to agreement over specific doctrines or views. The point of drawing our attention to the role of training and custom and other facts of our natural and social history is not to establish a positive theory of concept formation, but to emphasize what such theories overlook: that language depends on these facts being in place.

Wittgenstein's first steps away from the *Tractatus* in 1929 led him to a conception of language as a number of rule-governed systems or "calculi," capable of being systematically elucidated. He began work on the philosophy of mathematics and mind, attempting to analyse the structure of the rules governing mathematical and psychological language. In the philosophy of mathematics, he focussed on such topics as the rules governing the use of equations, or talk of the infinite. In the philosophy of mind, he began by looking for a language that would provide an analysis of the phenomena of immediate experience.

137. *Philosophical Investigations*, §201.
138. *Philosophical Investigations*, §201.
139. *On Certainty*, §204.

5

The Description
of Immediate Experience

5.1 Philosophical Analysis and Primary Language

To see how the changes I have just outlined came about, we must start with "Some Remarks on Logical Form," the only paper Wittgenstein ever published, and the last piece of his philosophical writing he saw to press. Written for the Aristotelian Society's annual meeting in summer 1929, it gives us a very clear idea of some of the main issues that occupied him at the time.[1] In a few pages, the paper sets out a programmatic conception of philosophical analysis and the relationship between language and experience. It also gives Wittgenstein's initial response to the problem of the logic of colour: he tried to rescue the *Tractatus* ontology by giving an account of elementary propositions on which they do stand in logical relations with one another. These interconnected changes in Wittgenstein's outlook show him beginning to modify the doctrines of the *Tractatus*. These changes are part of a change in his conception of analysis, at a time when he still he thought of it as a matter of formulating a surveyable language for the description of immediate experience. The paper, which is quite short, must have been written soon after Wittgenstein's return to Cambridge, as the *Proceedings* are published before the summer meeting. According to G. E. M. Anscombe in an editorial footnote that appeared in the reprinted version in *Essays on Wittgenstein's Tractatus*, Wittgenstein later described it as "quite worthless" and "weak and uncharacteristic."[2] As the letter has since been lost, we will probably never know Wittgenstein's reasons for this dismissive judgment. Despite her insistence that "little value can be set upon it as information about Wittgenstein's ideas,"[3] the paper does contain ideas about the relationship between language and experience that are certainly not found in the *Tractatus*, ideas that are important precisely because Wittgenstein soon repudiated them, giving up this conception of philosophy for a study of the structure of everyday language.

Wittgenstein begins by distinguishing between the form and the content of a proposition. He says that the philosopher is interested in the form, the logical structure of the proposition, which can be found by substituting variables for every refer-

---

1. Wittgenstein did not present the paper at the meeting, where he spoke about mathematical infinity instead.
2. Copi and Beard, *Essays on Wittgenstein's* Tractatus, p. 31.
3. Copi and Beard, *Essays on Wittgenstein's* Tractatus, p. 31.

ring term in the proposition. That procedure clarifies the syntax of our language, the rules that govern the combination of the symbols, and so tells us which arrangements of words make sense and which do not. Some propositions are composed of simpler propositions linked together by logical connectives. But eventually analysis must lead to propositional forms that cannot be analysed into simpler propositions—atomic propositions. Wittgenstein's recapitulation of the conception of logic and language he had set out in the *Tractatus* now leads him to stress the central role of atomic propositions in the whole edifice:

> [Atomic propositions] are the kernels of every proposition, *they* contain the material, and all the rest is only a development of this material.
>
> It is to them we have to look for the subject matter of propositions. It is the task of the theory of knowledge to find them and to understand their construction out of the words or symbols. This task is very difficult, and Philosophy has hardly yet begun to tackle it at some points. What method have we for tackling it? The idea is to express in an appropriate symbolism what in ordinary language leads to endless misunderstandings.[4]

The method he describes for investigating the nature of atomic propositions is the one advocated, if not always practised, in the *Tractatus*: we are to look for a symbolism that clearly displays its linguistic rules and so eliminates the misunderstandings generated by ordinary language. The task he sets himself in this passage—providing an analysis of the particular logical forms of elementary propositions—raises the very epistemological questions about our knowledge of the ultimate level of analysis that he had left unanswered in the *Tractatus*.[5] Wittgenstein speaks of this investigation of the logical form of atomic propositions, concealed by the subject-predicate and relational forms of our ordinary language, as "the logical investigation of the phenomena themselves."[6] As a result, he complains, our language itself is misleading. He offers a simile as an explanation of his predicament, a simile that captures both his current conception of his philosophical research and his difficulties in putting it into words:

> Let us imagine two parallel planes, I and II. On plane I figures are drawn, say, ellipses and rectangles of different sizes and shapes, and it is our task to produce images of these figures on plane II. Then we can imagine two ways, amongst others, of doing this. We can, first, lay down a law of projection—say that of orthogonal projection or any other—and then proceed to project all figures from I into II, according to this law. Or, secondly, we could proceed thus: We lay down the rule that every ellipse on plane I is to appear as a circle in plane II, and every rectangle as a square in II. Such a way of representation may be convenient for us if for some reason we prefer to draw only circles and squares on plane II. Of course, from these images the exact shapes of the original figures on plane I cannot be immediately inferred. We can only gather from them that the original was an ellipse or a rectangle. In order to get in a single instance at the determinate shape of the original we would have to know the individual method by which, e.g., a particular ellipse is projected into the circle before me. The case of ordinary language is quite

4. "Some Remarks on Logical Form," p. 163.
5. Cf. *Tractatus*, 4.1121, 5.55 ff.
6. "Some Remarks on Logical Form," pp. 163–164.

analogous. If the facts of reality are the ellipses and rectangles on plane I the sub-ject-predicate and relational forms correspond to the circles and squares in plane II. These forms are the norms of our particular language into which we project in *ever so many different* ways *ever so many different* logical forms. And for this very reason we can draw no conclusions—except very vague ones—from the use of these norms as to the actual logical form of the phenomena described.[7]

The projective geometry that provides the basis for Wittgenstein's analogy can be drawn as shown in Figure 5.1.

The point of the analogy is that a fully analysed language would allow us to re-produce the full variety of logical forms to be found in the world so that they can be taken in at a glance, just as the first law lets us reproduce the full variety of ellipses and rectangles on plane I. Ordinary language, on the other hand, like the second version of plane II, is restricted to far fewer forms. In this version of plane II, two squares can be different symbols, representing differently proportioned rectangles on plane I, because the two squares have different methods of projection associated with them. Both ordinary language and a fully analysed language represent the same facts, and so both must have the same representational resources. While those re-sources are clearly surveyable in the syntax of a fully analysed language, ordinary language hides its rules behind a misleadingly simple surface structure and a corre-spondingly complex set of tacit conventions concerning how its words are to be applied.

What is the multifarious variety of ellipses and rectangles on plane I supposed to represent? In other words, what are the "phenomena" Wittgenstein refers to, the phenomena that are supposed to be clearly represented by a fully analysed language? How are we to get at the varied methods of projection that link the superficially similar grammatical forms we find ourselves using with the full variety of phenomena? Wittgenstein's answer, baldly stated, is that the forms in question are very different from those we find in our ordinary language; they are the forms we encounter in describing the phenomena of immediate experience:

> If, now, we try to get at an actual analysis, we find logical forms which have very little similarity with the norms of ordinary language. We meet with the forms of space and time with the whole manifold of spacial and temporal objects, as colours, sounds, etc., etc., with their gradations, continuous transitions, and com-binations in various proportions, all of which we cannot seize by our ordinary means of expression.[8]

Ordinary language is not appropriate for a full description of these phenomena be-cause, for instance, it does not let us distinguish the many different degrees of bright-ness we can see, or the variety of subtle gradations of shades between red and yel-low, let alone fully specify the contents of an entire visual field at any one time. Nor does our colour vocabulary bring out the structure of the relationship between the four colours that Wittgenstein, following one of the leading theories of colour of his time, considered primary—red, blue, green, and yellow—and the other colours we see.

---

7. "Some Remarks on Logical Form," pp. 164–165. Cf. *Philosophical Remarks*, §93; *Philosophical Grammar*, pp. 204–205.
8. "Some Remarks on Logical Form," p. 165.

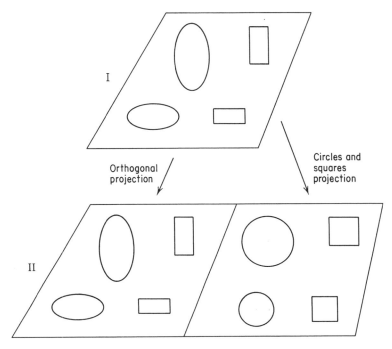

Figure 5.1

In "Some Remarks on Logical Form," Wittgenstein goes on to propose analytic techniques that might overcome some of these limitations. For instance, he suggested that one could imagine using Cartesian coordinates to specify any location within the visual field and thus describe the distribution of coloured patches by specifying the boundaries of each patch together with its colour. Consider the example of a rectangular red patch located on a flat plane. We could begin analysis with a proposition that consists of the appropriate coordinates. Wittgenstein suggests we might use a symbolism such as "[6–9, 3–8] R", where the two numerical terms would specify a rectangular patch that extended from 6 to 9 in the x-dimension and from 3 to 8 in the y-dimension, while R would stand for the as yet unanalysed colour predicate.

Wittgenstein introduces the new rules for the relationship between elementary colour propositions as an extension of the rules for truth functions. For instance, he says that the principle that one shade of colour cannot have two different degrees of brightness or redness does not express an experience but is "in some sense" tautologous.[9] Rules such as these, concerning the structure of a phenomenal field, the structure of our language, and the projective relationship between the two, are used to introduce a new conception of analysis as the activity of uncovering the structure of experiential phenomena. In effect, the explanation of a new notion of logical exclusion using a modified truth-table and the description of the contents of a simplified visual field using Cartesian coordinates are presented as the first two steps toward a fully analysed language for immediate experience.

9. "Some Remarks on Logical Form," p. 167.

Wittgenstein recognized that he had not given a complete analysis, acknowledging that he had not taken account of time and that a two-dimensional space is an oversimplification, even in the case of what is seen with a single eye. Despite this, he maintained that he had shown that a system of coordinates is a "part of the method of projection by which the reality is projected into our symbolism"—that is, that the use of a system of coordinates is implicit in the relationship between what we say about visual experience ("our symbolism") and the experience itself ("the reality.")[10] That initial analysis was supposed to indicate "the direction in which, I believe, the analysis of visual phenomena is to be looked for, and that in this analysis we meet with logical forms quite different from those which ordinary language leads us to expect."[11] In a similar vein, he ended by saying that the syntactic rules for atomic propositions "cannot be laid down until we have actually reached the ultimate analysis of the phenomena in question. This, as we all know, has not yet been achieved."[12] Thus, while he conceded that much work remained undone, he appeared quite confident as to which questions needed to be answered.

In "Some Remarks on Logical Form," Wittgenstein repeatedly emphasizes the complexity and problematic character of the phenomena he is analysing. But his assumption that an analysis of the phenomena must deal with the contents of the visual field and other sensory experience makes it clear that he takes it for granted that the phenomena in question are experiential. In fact, the question of the proper objects of analysis, the "phenomena" that he refers to, is not raised explicitly at all. Later, in the *Philosophical Remarks*, Wittgenstein does speak of these phenomena as "givens": "The things themselves are perhaps the four basic colours, space, time and other such givens."[13] In such passages, we can see an embryonic ontology, a move comparable to Kant's production of the table of categories at the beginning of the Transcendental Analytic.[14] Like Kant, Wittgenstein presents his readers with a set of basic concepts that are supposedly constituents of every experiential judgment and in lieu of any elaboration of his rationale for choosing this set of concepts, presents them as though their choice were a matter of elementary logic. Elsewhere in Wittgenstein's writing from the early 1930s he provides a much more detailed description of what he takes the structure of colour, space, time, and other such givens to consist. In each case, he tries to specify the relevant rules and give the reader an overview of their structure, often by using striking models or metaphors. For instance, in discussing the case of the relations between colours, he made use of a diagram of a "colour octahedron," an octahedron with a white apex and a black base, with the four primary colours—red, blue, green, and yellow—arranged in that order on the other four corners. The surfaces are supposed to be shaded so that there is an even transition between each colour. In the *Philosophical Remarks* and Big Typescript, Wittgenstein maintains that the colour octahedron "*approximately* represents" colour space, and that this representation is a priori and grammatical and therefore not a matter for psychological experiment:

10. "Some Remarks on Logical Form," p. 166.
11. "Some Remarks on Logical Form," p. 166.
12. "Some Remarks on Logical Form," p. 171.
13. *Philosophical Remarks*, §147.
14. Kant, *Critique of Pure Reason*, A70/B95.

The colour octahedron is grammar, since it says that you can speak of a reddish blue but not of a reddish green, etc.

The octahedral representation is a *perspicuous* representation of the grammatical rules.[15]

The discussion of the logic of colour propositions that follows the remarks about the relationship between language and reality in "Some Remarks on Logical Form" quoted here, is one of the few passages from this period to have attracted attention in the secondary literature. What were Wittgenstein's reasons for treating the analysis of colour propositions as a central problem, when ten years earlier he had been prepared to dismiss the problem of colour incompatibility as a minor anomaly?[16] The change in Wittgenstein's conception of analysis is a change in his conception of what *counts* as a philosophical problem, a change that turned a minor anomaly into a refutation of his conception of logic and lanugage. Why did he now think it necessitated revising his conception of the nature of the proposition? What had led him to think of colour propositions as a paradigm case for analysis?

In the *Tractatus*, Wittgenstein had maintained that language and the world must have a common structure. But the very abstractness of the Tractarian view lends itself to a certain scepticism about our ability to specify this common structure: for all we know, it might be far too complex. If one literally examines a proposition and the state of affairs to which it refers, looking for the common structure, one is likely to feel at a loss: How is one to get at what they have in common? Certainly, my saying my watch is on the table when my watch is on the table is true, and this is so because certain objects stand in certain relations. In other words, what I say is true because my watch is on the table. But how are we to say in what that relationship between my words and the objects they refer to consists? Perhaps even the simplest everyday sentences have an infinite analysis, dividing into statements about the parts of the objects in question and their parts in turn without end, or one so convoluted that we could not live long enough to set it out.

Wittgenstein's abstract intuition that there must be a pictorial relationship between language and world, together with the apparent intractability of the task of specifying that relationship, had led him to the conclusion that such an analysis was unnecessary. Now he had seen that he could not insist that an analysis must be possible in principle while being unable to actually give any examples, he was forced to return to the problem he had previously put to one side.[17] As the surface structure of our ordinary language—the subject-predicate grammar of everyday English or German—conceals its underlying structure, Wittgenstein turns to the structure of the world. What does it mean to turn to the structure of the world? Instead of directly addressing the question, Wittgenstein relies on analogies and metaphors that allow him to

15. Big Typescript, §94, p. 441. The first sentence occurs in *Philosophical Remarks*, §39; the other is in §1. The words quoted immediately before this passage are from *Philosophical Remarks*, §1, and are repeated in the Big Typescript, p. 440. The title of §94 is: "Phenomenology Is Grammar" [*Phänomenologie ist Grammatik*]. For further discussion of colour along these lines, see *Philosophical Remarks*, §§37–46 and §§218–224.

16. See the discussion of *Tractatus* 6.3751 on p. 65.

17. Cf. chapter 3, §§1–2, on the treatment of objects in the *Tractatus*, and chapter 4, §2, pp. 101–104 on Wittgenstein's criticism of the *Tractatus'* "dogmatism."

suggest the answer is obvious, so obvious that no alternative is possible. That is the real force of the analogy he offers of the two planes, one of them covered with ellipses and rectangles, the other with circles and squares. By comparing the relationship between language and world with the projective geometrical relationship between two sets of plane geometrical figures whose form is clearly visible, Wittgenstein suggests that we just have to look in the right way at what is given in experience to grasp its form. But it is the geometrical model that had been projected onto our language that motivated this account of the nature of representation. The problem is that Wittgenstein had not seen the limitations of this analogy. Specifically, it had led him to expect that we should be able to identify the language that is analogous to the orthogonal projection in his analogy, the language that directly reflects the nature of the phenomena.

The idea that immediate experience is a direct, nonlinguistic presentation of the true nature of the world must have struck Wittgenstein as a compelling solution to his methodological problems. While the surface grammar of ordinary language is philosophically misleading, one can just look at the structure of the phenomena, bypassing the process of linguistic analysis. The form of the final level of analysis would be right in front of our eyes.

Consider Wittgenstein's example of a blue patch's place in colour space. The experience of something blue is also an experience of something that is not red, green, or yellow: these relations must be mirrored in the grammar of colour language. A fact containing coloured givens is located at a certain point in colour space; the proposition expressing that fact is located at the corresponding point in an isomorphic logical framework. Linguistically considered, that structure shows itself in the grammar of our language. The strategy of reading off the logical form of the phenomena from the "shape" of the phenomena holds out the hope of a quick and simple way of getting to the heart of the matter. In this way, perceiving a coloured plane provides Wittgenstein with a new model for understanding the structure of our language.

In effect, Wittgenstein had transformed the picture theory from a schematic account of the structure of our language into a conception of mind and world that treats both thought and experience as analogous to a picture. Just as we know that propositions must have whatever features enable them to depict, so experience must have whatever features enable it to be depicted. But the analogy can be pushed further in the case of visual experience. Unlike language, it actually looks like a picture, for it is a field composed of an arrangement of coloured shapes. As a result, we can just *see* its structure. Here Wittgenstein was so sure of his ground that he thought a justification either unnecessary or impossible: the experiential character of the "phenomena" is simply treated as a given. And so an interpretation of this passage calls for a certain kind of double vision: it must convey the philosophical picture that made it possible for the author to regard this move as "seeing something closer up and in a more definite manner,"[18] but it must also explain how the picture came to be taken for granted.

In retrospect, we can separate two distinct problems that Wittgenstein faced at

18. *Ludwig Wittgenstein and the Vienna Circle*, p. 184, 9 December 1931.

this point. On the one hand, there was the problem of how to describe primary experience: how to provide a pure, nonhypothetical description of that which is given in experience and provides a basis for our ordinary talk of physical objects. On the other hand, there was the problem of how to describe the mental: how to understand the relationship between language and the content of immediate experience. The interpretation that I offer in this chapter makes it clear that Wittgenstein ran the two problems together during this period because he took it for granted that primary experience is mental. Even in the case of an experience that we would ordinary describe as an experience of a physical object, he treats the physical object as a construct and assumes that the immediate object of the experience—the object that the primary language is supposed to describe—must be a mental event. As a result, his discussion of the relation between the primary and the secondary in 1929 and the early 1930s is not only a discussion of whether it is possible to provide a nonhypothetical description of the content of experience, but also amounts to a discussion of the question whether an autonomous self-contained description of experience is possible at all. By the time he came to write the *Philosophical Investigations*, the whole project of describing primary experience no longer had the same importance, and his attention was directed at the second problem, the problem of understanding the relationship between language and experience. As a result, his chosen example changed accordingly; the examples of describing simple geometrical arrangements of coloured objects are replaced by references to pain experience or other sensations that are quite straightforwardly mental. His attention had shifted from the question of the possibility of a pure description of the experientially given to the question of a discussion of the possibility of a private language. To see how he arrived at his later approach to the problem of the relationship between language and the mind, we need to look more closely at the solutions he had earlier proposed.

On the conception Wittgenstein set out in "Some Remarks on Logical Form," all that would be left for the philosopher to do would be to find the "appropriate symbolism,"[19] the language that describes the phenomena directly, without any hypothetical additions. This is what Wittgenstein meant by "phenomenology."[20] Phenomenological language would be the linguistic equivalent of the orthogonally projected representation of the "facts of reality."[21] In "Some Remarks on Logical Form" he wrote:

> [W]e can only substitute a clear symbolism for the unprecise one by inspecting the phenomena which we want to describe, thus trying to understand their logical multiplicity. That is to say, we can only arrive at a correct analysis by, what might be called, the logical investigation of the phenomena themselves, i.e., in a certain sense *a posteriori*, and not by conjecturing about *a priori* possibilities.[22]

Wittgenstein soon gave up this conception, however, so that his most detailed exposition of it is to be found in his later criticism of these views.

19. "Some Remarks on Logical Form," p. 163.
20. For further discussion of phenomenological language, see section 2, this chapter.
21. "Some Remarks on Logical Form," p. 164.
22. "Some Remarks on Logical Form," p. 163.

5.2 Wittgenstein's Rejection of Primary Language

Like "Some Remarks on Logical Form," the *Philosophical Remarks* begin with a terse summary of Wittgenstein's conception of analysis. The first paragraph reads as follows: "A proposition is completely logically analysed if its grammar is made completely clear: no matter what way it may be written or expressed."[23] This amounts to a fundamental break with both the *Tractatus* and the revisions he had proposed in "Some Remarks on Logical Form." To hold that whatever proves effective in clarifying propositions is to count as an analysis is to reject the Tractarian thesis that "a proposition has one and only one complete analysis."[24] While he had already modified his conception of analysis in "Some Remarks on Logical Form" he had not questioned the thesis that every proposition has an unique analysis, and he had still aimed at "the ultimate analysis of phenomena,"[25] thus retaining the Tractarian conviction that analysis would lead to a formal symbolism of the kind used by a mathematical logician. Now he realized that this whole conception of analysis was fundamentally mistaken and had to be eliminated, not modified, for it implies that our present language is inadequate, and that we won't really understand what we are saying until it has been analysed. Instead, what we need is a clear view of our current use of language. As a result, Wittgenstein came to see that there might be any number of ways of conveying the structure of a language. On this conception, the value of any new notation can only consist in the light it casts on everyday language use:

> How strange if logic were concerned with an "ideal" language and not with *ours*. For what would this ideal language express? Presumably, what we now express in our ordinary language; in that case, this is the language logic must investigate.[26]

The second paragraph of the *Philosophical Remarks* amplifies the rejection of his earlier views, specifically repudiating the conception of analysis he had accepted earlier that year and sharply contrasting "phenomenological language" with the language we ordinarily speak. In this passage, drafted in October 1929, he wrote that he no longer had "phenomenological language, or 'primary language' as I used to call it, in mind as my goal. I no longer hold it to be necessary. All that is possible and necessary is to separate what is essential from what is inessential in *our* language."[27] The original manuscript volume entry reads instead "I no longer hold it to be possible."[28] Some commentators regard the replacement of this impossibility claim by the seemingly weaker claim that a phenomenological language is not necessary as a qualification that implies that Wittgenstein had recognized that he could not yet prove that phenomenological language is impossible. Hintikka and Hintikka, for instance, argue that this lacuna would only be filled much later by the private language argument.[29] However, the surrounding material suggests a much simpler explanation for

23. *Philosophical Remarks*, §1.
24. *Tractatus*, 3.25.
25. "Some Remarks on Logical Form," p. 171.
26. *Philosophical Remarks*, §3.
27. *Philosophical Remarks*, §1.
28. MS 107, p. 205, 29 November 1929. [German in appendix.]
29. Hintikka and Hintikka, *Investigating Wittgenstein*, pp. 137 ff. 172, 241 ff.

the rewording: Wittgenstein sometimes uses the term "phenomenological language" in a restricted sense, to mean a canonical analysis of the experience of the present moment. In this sense, he consistently maintained after 1929 that such a primary language was indeed impossible. A few pages earlier, he had described the very idea that a phenomenological language is possible as absurd:

> The assumption that a phenomenological language were possible and that only it would actually say what we must /want to/ express in philosophy is—I believe—absurd. We must make do with our ordinary language and just correctly understand it. That is to say, we shouldn't allow ourselves to be seduced by it into talking nonsense.
>
> I mean: what I call a sign must be what one calls a sign in grammar, something on the film, not on the screen.[30]

But he also spoke of "phenomenological language" in a looser sense, meaning by it any way of talking about the content of experience, and, in this sense of the term, he holds that a phenomenological language is possible but not necessary. Giving up the goal of a phenomenological language in the narrow sense meant giving up the goal of constructing an artificial philosophical language that would be capable of fully clarifying the structure of present experience, in favour of a study of the structure of the language we ordinarily speak. But this new project still included a study of phenomenological language in the looser sense of the term: a study of how we actually talk about experience, and how we might be misled into misunderstanding that talk. So, in this sense, Wittgenstein still thought of himself as making use of "perspicuous language" to describe experience. Thus, even after he rejected the goal of a single phenomenological language, he was still prepared to speak of himself, in a sense, as constructing phenomenological language.

In his work in the early 1930s, Wittgenstein approached the language we use to talk about experience as though it were made up of a number of autonomous forms of speech, each of which could be elucidated by comparison with an unambiguous, well-organized artificial language. The program he had in mind is elaborated in the rest of the first section of the *Philosophical Remarks*:

> That is, if we so to speak describe the class of languages which serve their purpose, then in so doing we have shown what is essential to them and given an immediate representation of immediate experience.
>
> Each time I say that, instead of such and such a representation, you could also use this other one, we take a further step towards the goal of grasping the essence of what is represented.
>
> A recognition of what is essential and what inessential in our language if it is to represent, a recognition of which parts of our language are wheels turning idly, does the same job as the construction of a phenomenological language.[31]

Wittgenstein set out much the same the same train of thought in his conversations with Schlick and Waismann in December 1929, but the passage is worth quoting for its specification of his reasons for giving up his old conception of language, which

30. MS 107, p. 176, 22 October 1929. [German in appendix.]
31. *Philosophical Remarks*, §1.

had contrasted everyday language with a primary language for experiential phenomena:

> I used to believe that there was the everyday language that we all usually spoke
> and a primary language that expressed what we really knew, namely phenomena.
> I also spoke of a first system and a second system. Now I wish to explain why I do
> not adhere to that conception any more.
>
> I think that essentially we have only one language, and that it is our everyday
> language. We need not invent a new language or construct a new symbolism, but
> our everyday language already is *the* language, provided we rid it of the obscuri-
> ties that lie hidden in it.
>
> Our language is completely in order, as long as we are clear about what it
> symbolises. Languages other than the ordinary ones are also valuable in so far as
> they show us what they have in common.[32]

With hindsight, one can see his new approach as a natural development of the
Tractarian conviction that all languages share the same underlying structure, so that
any language we construct will have that structure in common with our ordinary language.[33] In this sense, even when he wrote the *Tractatus*, Wittgenstein accepted the
Investigations' dictum that "every sentence of our language 'is in order as it is.'"[34] It
had seemed clear to the author of the *Tractatus* that "where there is sense there must
be perfect order,"[35] a single, unitary order that was concealed by our ordinary language. It is that notion of underlying order, of the general form of the proposition,
shown by the structure of our language as a whole, that Wittgenstein now gave up.
He saw that the single clear view he had hoped for was an illusory goal: instead, one
must dispel individual problems one at a time. Thus, Wittgenstein's claim near the
beginning of the *Philosophical Remarks* that "all that is possible and necessary is to
separate what is essential from what is inessential in *our* language"[36] sums up his
turn from an analysis of the language of phenomena, "primary language," to an
investigation of ordinary language. This was a crucial development, for it soon led
him not only to reject his earlier conception of the primacy of immediate experience
but also to give up the idea that our use of language is animated by intrinsically representational mental processes, in favour of a conceiving of the meaning of a sentence as determined by its grammar, the rules for its use. During the early 1930s,
Wittgenstein conceived of ordinary language as consisting of a number of autonomous systems of representational conventions, each with its own logical structure.

It would be misleading, however, to suggest that any of the changes just summarized, even the rejection of phenomenological language announced in the opening
paragraph of the *Philosophical Remarks*, occurred at a single point in time, or
amounted to an immediate and radical break with his earlier views. As we shall see,
Wittgenstein composed a lengthy discussion of the difficulties with his earlier conception of phenomenological language before drafting his rejection of it in October
1929, and this discussion provides the basis for his criticisms of phenomenological

---

32. *Ludwig Wittgenstein and the Vienna Circle*, pp. 45–46, 22 December 1929.
33. *Philosophical Remarks*, §1; see n. 23 this chapter.
34. *Philosophical Investigations*, §98.
35. Wittgenstein's retrospective description in *Philosophical Investigations*, §98.
36. *Philosophical Remarks*, §1; see n. 27 this chapter.

language in the early 1930s. On the other hand, even after rejecting phenomenological language in the strict sense, he still pursued the project of formulating phenomenological languages, descriptions of immediate experience. At first he did this in terms that still owed much to his earlier conception of the primacy of immediate experience, maintaining that the significance of a sentence rests on its verification, where that is understood as its application to present experience.

For some time after his emphatic rejection of the goal of a phenomenological language, Wittgenstein still treated phenomenology, the logical study of the phenomena of experience, as primary. Although he had given up the goal of formulating a primary language, he still thought of the looser notion of a phenomenological language as extremely important. For instance, a few weeks after drafting his rejection of the possibility of a primary language, Wittgenstein reaffirmed his conception of the fundamental role of the phenomena, characterizing them as what there really is, what makes sentences true or false:

> The phenomenon is not a symptom of something else; rather, it is reality.
>
> The phenomenon is not a symptom of something else which then makes the sentence true or false; rather, it is itself that which verifies it [the sentence].[37]

While the representation of the events we ordinarily talk about may seem unproblematic when considered by themselves, our ability to think about those events, to grasp that certain signs mean those events, became highly puzzling. Thus, Wittgenstein wrote in late 1929:

> The application of words considered as extended in time is easy to understand; in contrast, I find it infinitely difficult to understand the sense in the moment of application.
>
> What does it mean e.g. to understand a sentence as a member of a system of sentences?[38]

The conception of language as a set of rules for the use of words, words that are only significant in virtue of their connection with immediate experience, was gradually modified during the early 1930s as Wittgenstein came to see that language is more like a family of interrelated games than the systems of rules found in mathematics. At the same time, he acquired a greater respect for the depth and the difficulty of the misconceptions that had misled him in his earlier work, and he came to regard the formulation of phenomenological languages as a therapeutic device for understanding the motivations that had led him to an obsession with fully describing the nature of immediate experience, rather than as a tool for grasping the essence of our language. While the earliest remarks in the *Investigations* were drafted during

---

37. MS 107, pp. 223–224, 1 December 1929. [German in appendix.] Cf. *Philosophical Remarks*, §1:

> Physics differs from phenomenology in that it is concerned to establish laws. Phenomenology only establishes the possibilities. Thus, phenomenology would be the grammar of the description of those facts on which physics builds its theories.

38. MS 107, p. 233, 13 January 1930. [German in appendix.] See also the discussion of this passage in chapter 4, p. 122 [partially quoted in n. 117.]

this period, and most of them stress the importance of ordinary language, it would be a mistake to conclude that Wittgenstein arrived at his later conception of philosophy during this period. Although he had committed himself to a study of particular cases and a repudiation of aprioristic theorizing, he initially thought of this work in much more systematic terms than he would do later on and, as we shall see, the analyses of the everyday he developed in the early 1930s owed much more to the solipsistic side of the *Tractatus* than his programmatic statements might lead one to expect.

5.3 The Magic Lantern Simile:
Inside and Outside the Picture Theory

Wittgenstein often used the relation between what one sees at the movies and the pictures on the reel of film in the movie projector as a starting point when the question of the relation between experience and the world came up in conversation. In one of his discussions with the Vienna Circle in December 1929, he introduced it with the words, "I would like to use an old simile: the 'magic lantern.'"[39] Although the analogy is never fully elaborated in any of the published works, there are a number of references to it in Wittgenstein's manuscripts, in the *Philosophical Remarks* and Big Typescript, and in the notes of his lectures and conversations in the years following 1929. Talking to O. K. Bouwsma in 1949, Wittgenstein mentioned that the "figure of the cinema lamp," as he called it, had first struck him when he was talking to Frege in 1911.[40] Bouwsma recalls a meeting of Malcolm's discussion group in Cornell where Bouwsma began the conversation by briefly talking about Descartes's *Cogito, ergo sum*. Wittgenstein responded by saying that the real question was "How did Descartes come to do this?" Bouwsma asked whether he meant to ask what led up to the *cogito* in Descartes's own thought, to which Wittgenstein replied:

> No. One must do this for oneself. . . . I always think of it as like the cinema. You see before you the picture on the screen, but behind you is the operator, and he has a roll here on this side from which he is winding and another on that side into which he is winding. The present is the picture which is before the light, but the future is still on the roll to pass, and the past is on that roll. It's gone through already. Now imagine that there is only the present. There is no future roll, and no past roll. And now further imagine what language there could be in such a situation. One could just gape. This![41]

Wittgenstein contrasts the picture on the film reel in front of the projector, part of a sequence of neighbouring pictures that have been or will be projected, and the picture on the screen, which has no such neighbours. If we are to represent the pic-

39. *Ludwig Wittgenstein and the Vienna Circle*, p. 50, 22 December 1929. Unfortunately, Waismann never wrote up most of his notes on that topic, the last of the day, so that we only have a few cryptic notes concerning the relationship between the soundtrack, which is on the roll of film; the music, which accompanies the film; and language, which accompanies the world.

40. O. K. Bouwsma, *Wittgenstein: Conversations, 1949–1951*, p. 10, 5 August, 1949.

41. Bouwsma, *Wittgenstein: Conversations, 1949–1951*, p. 13, 7 August 1949. See also Big Typescript, §102.

ture on the screen without any hypothetical additions, we must take it by itself, excluding the sequence of past, present, and future pictures on the film reel; in fact, we must exclude everything but the picture itself. But any description of the picture would be a sequence of signs, external physical objects. Because language as a system of signs is part of the physical world, Wittgenstein thinks of it as on an altogether different level from the phenomena of experience. In the *Philosophical Remarks*, he explains the problem of the relationship between language and experience in terms of the movie metaphor: "We find ourselves, with our language so to speak, not in the domain of the projected picture but in the domain of the film."[42]

The passage from Bouwsma's notes also hints at a related difficulty, one that Wittgenstein develops elsewhere: the use of language occurs in time; how is it to be applied to an atemporal, self-contained world? In the end, Wittgenstein's objection to the idea of a self-contained description that contains nothing hypothetical is that it is unavoidably self-contradictory, for a description would have to be linguistic, and language brings in the very system of relations that is supposed to be excluded from a pure description of immediate experience. The closest one could come to such a nonlinguistic relationship to one's present experience would be to just stare at it intently.

Wittgenstein sometimes expressed his conception of a categorical distinction between experience and the world by saying that the picture on the screen, unlike the picture on the film reel, "has no neighbours." To say that is not to say that my experiential field has a certain location, and that that there is nothing next to it. Rather, it is to say that it makes no sense to think of my immediate experience as adjoining anything else—that it is essentially neighbourless: self-contained and complete. In lectures given in the early 1930s, Wittgenstein said:

> [T]he pictures in the lantern are all "on the same level" but that the picture which is at any given time on the screen is not "on the same level" with any of them, and that if we were to use "conscious" to say of one of the pictures in the lantern that it was at that time being thrown on the screen, it would be meaningless to say of the picture on the screen that it was "conscious." The pictures on the film, he said, "have neighbours," whereas that on the screen has none.[43]

This is closely connected with the idea that it makes no sense to speak of experience as "present": just as Wittgenstein denies that experience has a spatial location, he also denies it has a temporal location. In both cases, he wants to resist the temptation to project our everyday grammar onto the phenomena, for he holds that there is a "grammatical" difference between the two: the picture on the film and the picture on the screen are not "'on the same level.'" The pictures are not two related objects in a

---

42. *Philosophical Remarks*, §70. Source: MS 107, p. 2. Cf. Big Typescript, §102, p. 496:

> (We find ourselves with our language (as physical appearance), so to speak, not in the domain of the picture projected on the screen but in the domain of the film that goes through the lantern.) [German in appendix.]

43. Moore, "Wittgenstein's Lectures in 1930–33," p. 310. Cf. Wittgenstein's use of the term "neighbour" in the "Notes for Lectures on 'Sense Data' and 'Private Experience,'" p. 297; *Philosophical Occasions*, p. 255; and the *Blue Book*, p. 71.

common space; instead, they represent two different spatialities.[44] If we try to bring the two together, we shall run up against the limits of language.

Section 102 of the Big Typescript, entitled "The experience of the present moment, the actual reality," is devoted to a discussion of the relationship between primary and secondary time and their role in resolving problems about the description of immediate experience. There, Wittgenstein describes his predicament in the following terms:

> We imagine experience like a filmstrip, so that one can say: this picture, and no other, is before the lens at this instant.
>
> But only in film can one talk about the picture that is present at this moment; not if one moves over from physical space and its time to visual space and its time.[45]

Similarly, he maintains that the visual field is not part of a larger whole, but a "complete space":

> Visual space and retina. It's as if you were to project a sphere orthogonally onto a plane, for instance in the way in which you represent the two hemispheres of the globe in an atlas, and now someone might believe that what's on the page surrounding the two projections of the sphere somehow still corresponds to a possible extension of what is to be found on the sphere. The point is that here a *complete space* is projected onto a *part* of another space; and it is like this with the limits of language in a dictionary.[46]

"Inside" the experiential realm, it is inconceivable that it is related to anything else, for it is the world. To speak of one's experience as connected with other experiences, or as belonging to an owner would be to attempt to step "outside" the charmed circle, to stand in a place from which one can say that one's experience stands in a certain relationship to something else. Because experience is *logically* complete, it makes no sense to talk of it as part of a larger space. If that is the case, one might well ask, how did we ever form the notion of an outside? Essentially, Wittgenstein's answer is that we are misled by thinking of *another* space—physical space—a space that is arranged so that part of the new space is analogous to the whole of experiential space. He maintains that physical space is an entirely *new* space: one is no longer talking about the first space at all. Similarly, while one might expand one's frame of reference in the map example and offer a place on the moon as an example of a location that is not on a map of the world, it could not be a neighbouring location. Experience is not just contingently isolated, its isolation is supposed to be a matter of logic: "Experience isn't something that one can demarcate by determinations of something else which isn't experience; rather a logical form."[47] But while the notion of "something else which isn't experience," the domain of secondary, physical phenomena,

---

44. Cf. *Zettel*, §648: "One language-game analogous to a fragment of another. One space projected into a limited extent of another. A 'gappy' space. (For 'inner and outer.')" The first two sentences are also in *Remarks on the Philosophy of Psychology*, I §936. Cf. *Remarks on the Philosophy of Psychology*, I §943: "The concept of a 'fragment.' It is not easy to describe the use of this word *even only roughly*."

45. Big Typescript, §102, p. 495. [German in appendix.]

46. *Philosophical Remarks*, §66.

47. Big Typescript, §107, p. 528. [German in appendix.]

is said to be irrelevant to the conception of experience as autonomous, it is nevertheless invoked in the very contrast between experience as a logical form and experience as part of a larger world. Wittgenstein cryptically summed up this fatal flaw— the contrast with the nonexperiential is essential to setting up the conception, but the whole point of the conception is to exclude the nonexperiental as a matter of logic— in a note included in an appendix to the Big Typescript: "Experience as logical form. Experience in contrast to what?"[48]

The best exposition of this paradoxical conception of experience and the difficulties it leads to can be found in a lengthy passage that Wittgenstein recorded in his notebooks during spring or summer 1929. Most, but not all, of this material was included in the *Philosophical Remarks* in spring 1930, indicating that there was considerable continuity in his views on the topic of experience and its description during this period, despite his repudiation of "primary language" in October 1929. The passage begins with a statement of his conception of the relationship between physical and phenomenological language: they both describe the same primary world, but the propositions of a physical language include hypotheses about unobserved objects, while phenomenological language restricts itself to asserting what can be verified. He immediately goes on to question that compromise, however:

> The phenomenological language describes just the same as the usual physical one. Only it must restrict itself to what is verifiable.
>
> Is that really possible?[49]

Wittgenstein's reason for questioning this conception of a phenomenological language is set out in the paragraphs that follow: perhaps all languages must include a hypothetical component, just as our ordinary ways of speaking do. In that case, one could never simply describe the content of what is seen, but would always have to use a vocabulary that commits one to further hypotheses about what has happened or will happen:

> Again, let's not forget that the physical language, too, only describes the primary world and not a hypothetical world. The hypothesis is only an assumption about the most practical /most suitable ?/ kind of representation.
>
> Now, is this hypothetical aspect essential to any representation of the world?[50]

The implicit alternative to such a language is the one he mentioned a few paragraphs before, a phenomenological language, a language restricted to describing the nonhypothetical primary givens. In the Big Typescript, he sums up this conception with the following formula: "Phenomenological language: the description of immediate sense perception, without hypothetical addition."[51] Unlike our ordinary ways of describing sense perception, in terms of objects which are there even when we

---

48. TS 219, p. 20. [German in appendix.]

49. MS 105, p. 108, spring or summer 1929. [German in appendix.] While this passage and the next passage I quote were not included in the *Philosophical Remarks*, Wittgenstein did include the whole of the next three pages of the manuscript almost verbatim in *Philosophical Remarks*, §§67–69, a passage that explores Wittgenstein's question and offers some programmatic answers.

50. MS 105, p. 108. [German in appendix.]

51. Big Typescript, §101, p. 491. [German in appendix.]

turn away, a phenomenological language would be restricted to representing whatever is immediately experienced without such hypothetical commitments. The goal of finding a language that avoids hypotheses had been the motive for the project of describing experience that Wittgenstein had pursued: "The point of talking of sense data and immediate experience is that we're after a description that has nothing hypothetical in it."[52] But one of Wittgenstein's later objections to any such conception is already implicit in the broken underlining under "<u>language</u>," his way of indicating that he was not satisfied with his choice of words. For he had come to see that the very motives that had led him to seek a phenomenological language ensured that no language could be adequate. What one really wants to do, he suggests, is to directly present what is experienced: "If anything, then something like it must surely be depiction by means of a painted picture or such a description of immediate experience. As when we, e.g., look in a telescope and record or paint the constellations seen."[53] Even the most direct language cannot be more than a representation, so the very idea of a primary language, a language that directly presents the contents of immediate experience, turns out to be incoherent. The desire for a transparent intermediary, present to consciousness, that guarantees that my thoughts are about their objects, and so provides the ultimate basis for language, is the product of philosophical confusion. In a sense, Wittgenstein had already recognized the impossibility of specifying such an intermediary when he wrote his earlier discussions of the topic in 1929 and 1930, but, at that time, he was still tempted by the response that it only indicates the limits of language, limits that can be left behind within the realm of immediate experience.

   In the discussion that follows his initial exposition of his questions about phenomenological language in his 1929 notebook, Wittgenstein first attempts to imagine a phenomenological language by asking us to suppose that he has such a good memory that he could remember all of his sense impressions and describe them without using any hypotheses. In effect, this would be a complete description of what he had previously called "the world as I found it."[54] He elaborates on this fantasy by imagining himself constructing three-dimensional plaster models of the objects that make up this world. Only those parts of the objects that he had actually seen would be finished off, while the rest of the model would be shaded to show that it was not part of the "visual world." Although at first he has no trouble in taking the production of an empirical simulacrum of the phenomena of visual experience for granted—"So far everything would be fine"[55]—he sees that the time it would take to construct his models would turn the models into hypothetical descriptions of a past event. At the point where we might think of a video camera, Wittgenstein proposes an equally elegant solution, imagining a mechanism in which the bodies I seem to see are moved so that

> they would give the visual images to be represented to two eyes fixed at a particular place in the model. The visual image described is then determined from the position of the eyes in the model and from the position and motion of the bodies.

52. *Philosophical Remarks*, §226.
53. Big Typescript, §101, pp. 491–492. [German in appendix.]
54. *Tractatus*, 5.631.
55. *Philosophical Remarks*, §67.

We could then imagine that the mechanism could be driven by turning a crank and in that way the description "read off."[56]

The moral Wittgenstein draws from this story is that nothing descriptive could be as immediate as he wants—that any description of experience will always leave out something crucial, something that cannot be put into words:

Isn't it clear that this would be the most immediate description we can possibly conceive? That is to say, that anything which tried to be more immediate still, would have to give up being a description.

Instead of a description, what would then come out would be that inarticulate sound with which some writers would like to begin philosophy. ("I am, knowing of my knowledge, conscious of something.")
You simply can't begin before the beginning.[57]

In the Big Typescript, Wittgenstein made use of a slightly revised version of this passage in a section entitled "The representation of immediate experience." There, it forms part of a section in which he rejects the very idea that it makes sense to talk of recognizing a visual picture in every detail and describes the comparison of the visual field with a painted surface or a spatial model as "most dangerous." Wittgenstein sets out his objections to his earlier conception of phenomenological language by asking us to consider how we might go about actually reproducing sense perception. He suggests that we imagine attempting to do this by constructing a detailed mechanical model of what is seen. Seen from the correct point, the model could give the observer the appropriate sequence of experiences:

[T]he model could be set in the right motions by a crank-drive and we could read off the description by turning the crank. (An approximation to this would be a representation in film.)
If *that* is not a representation of the immediate—what would be one? —Anything that tried to be more immediate still would have to give up being a description. Instead of a description what would then come out would be that inarticulate sound with which some writers would like to begin philosophy. ("I am, knowing of my knowledge, conscious of something" Driesch.)[58]

The cinematic model, which Wittgenstein had once used to set out a solipsistic conception of present experience as uniquely privileged, thus became a device for explaining the dangers of turning talk about what we see into a philosophical myth about the nature of experience. In fact, Wittgenstein's most detailed exposition of the solipsist's "enormously important"[59] ideas can be found in his criticism of his earlier conception of those ideas in his writing and lectures from the 1930s. The analogy between the self, the subject of experience, and the centre of the visual field

56. *Philosophical Remarks*, §67.
57. *Philosophical Remarks*, §68. Source: MS 105, p. 115.
58. Big Typescript, §101, p. 492. [German in appendix.] The quotation from Hans Driesch is taken from page 19 of his *Ordnungslehre*, where he calls it "our first philosophical proposition, the primal philosophical proposition. It still points to the birthplace of all philosophy, 'experience,' [*Erleben*] but it nevertheless lifts itself out of the everyday toward language." Cf. Hans Driesch, *Wirklichkeitslehre*, p. 8.
59. Moore, "Wittgenstein's Lectures in 1930–33," p. 311.

in *Tractatus* 5.633–5.634 was applied to the objects of experience, which were construed by analogy with the contents of the visual field. That interest in specifying the character of the contents of experience was connected with his new focus on the relationship between the primary world and secondary world of physical objects, and the closely related problem of the relationship between ordinary language and its analysis. He soon came to see that the distinctions between phenomenal and physical, and primary and secondary, were only an overblown misinterpretation of two different ways of talking. His most detailed criticism and rejection of these earlier views can be found in his discussions of solipsism and private experience in a series of notes he wrote preparing for lectures in 1935–1936[60] and in more polished drafts from 1937 to 1938.[61] His exposition of these themes in the *Philosophical Investigations* is very compressed, and for the most part he simply avoids explicit reference to his earlier work on the description of visual experience. At one point in his discussion of private language in the *Philosophical Investigations*, he simply repeats the words he had used in the *Philosophical Remarks* and Big Typescript to characterize the inadequacy of language in describing the nature of experience: "—So in the end when one is doing philosophy one gets to the point where one would like just to emit an inarticulate sound."[62] While he had used these words in the *Philosophical Remarks* to gesture at the inexpressible nature of what one is directly acquainted with in immediate experience, in the *Investigations*, Wittgenstein responds that such sounds are intelligible if we consider their context: "—But such a sound is an expression only as it occurs in a particular language-game, which should now be described."[63] In other words, the later Wittgenstein proposes that we describe the circumstances in which people are misled in this, and similar, ways; in the *Investigations*, however, his treatment is much more general and he does not describe the particular language-game in which he had used those words. Let us therefore return to the context where he had originally been driven to express the desire to "emit an inarticulate sound."

Immediately after his discussion of a mechanism for the depiction of experience in the *Philosophical Remarks*, Wittgenstein asks himself how the relation between physical language and phenomenological language is possible at all: "Language itself belongs to the second system. If I describe a language, I am essentially describing something that belongs to physics. But how can a physical language describe the phenomenal?"[64] In effect, the first part of his answer elaborates a distinction between two fundamentally different kinds of time: the time of physical space and the time of visual space. In the *Tractatus*, Wittgenstein had insisted that time is not an object of experience, that we cannot compare a physical process with "the passage of time," but only with another process, such as the working of a chronometer.[65] The present, on the other hand, is said to be timeless.[66] Wittgenstein treats our ordinary temporal concepts as based on the duration of physical processes, and so holds that they are

60. "Notes for Lectures on 'Sense Data' and 'Private Experience.'"
61. MSS 119–121.
62. *Philosophical Investigations*, §261.
63. *Philosophical Investigations*, §261.
64. *Philosophical Remarks*, §68. Source: MS 106, p. 114.
65. *Tractatus*, 6.3611.
66. *Tractatus*, 6.4311.

not applicable to immediate experience. Nevertheless, even though he was convinced that the phenomena of immediate experience are not part of the order of physical events, he felt the need to give some account of how we can come to think and talk about temporal processes on the basis of a supposedly atemporal experience. In response, he turned to the Kantian thesis that time is part of the *form* of experience:

> Isn't it like this: a phenomenon (specious present) contains time, but isn't in time?
> Its form is time, but it has no place in time.
> Whereas language unwinds in time.[67]

What Wittgenstein is proposing is that while experiential phenomena are not, strictly speaking, "in time," they nevertheless "contain" time as their form. That temporal form is what makes possible the constitution of physical processes, which really do "unwind in time." We can find the same paradoxical distinction in a parallel discussion of whether we can speak of experiential phenomena as "present":

> Of course, the word "present" is also out of place here. For to what extent can
> we say of reality that it is present? Surely only if we embed it once more in a time
> that is foreign to it. In and of itself it isn't present. Rather, on the contrary, it con-
> tains a time.[68]

So far, of course, this is no more than a first step toward an account of the nature of the time of visual space, and it is striking that this idea, like so many others Wittgenstein throws out in his discussions of immediate experience from this period, never receives any systematic elaboration. But he does hint at two ways that his suggestion could be developed into a full-blown conception of the nature of time. One is that our concept of physical time is derived from the temporality of experiential memory of past events. The other is the thought that while the present is not in time—and so saying that primary time is in flux would be a mistake—primary time does contain the "the possibility of change"[69]: "What we are looking at here is really the possibility of motion: and so the logical form of motion."[70] This suggests that for the phenomena to contain time, to have a temporal form, is for them to contain the possibility of temporal processes such as change and motion. But it is no more than a suggestion, and it is never worked out in any detail. Wittgenstein's problem here is akin to Kant's difficulties with the "unsynthesized manifold," Kant's term for the initial data that are the basis for the mental activity that constitutes our ordinary experience on the basis of that input. While the unsynthesized manifold does not itself have a categorial structure, for that structure is precisely what is given to it by the mind's activity, it seems that it must have some prior structure, if it is to serve as the basis for the appropriate kind of experience, to give rise to an experience of a table now, say, rather than a chair then. But if those data do not yet possess the structure that makes it possible for us to grasp them, how are we to conceive of that structure? In Kant's case, it is possible to simply reply that this only shows that we cannot ex-

---

67. *Philosophical Remarks*, §69. Source: MS 106, p. 114.
68. *Philosophical Remarks*, §75.
69. *Philosophical Remarks*, §52; Big Typescript, §91, p. 428.
70. *Philosophical Remarks*, §52. (Although this is printed as the last line of the remark in question in the English translation, it is a separate paragraph in the German.)

pect to fully grasp the character of the preexperiential with our concepts, which are derived from experience. But that reponse is not available to Wittgenstein, for he is discussing the structure of immediate experience, not the conditions for the synthesis of experience. As a result, he has to deny that our usual spatial and temporal concepts can be applied to immediate experience. Yet, rather than deny that experience is altogether spatiotemporal, he distinguishes between phenomenological and physical concepts of space and time and identifies the phenomenological concepts that supposedly provide the basis for our everyday spatiotemporal concepts.

The second part of his answer to the question of the nature of the relationship between physical and phenomenological language is to transpose his way of dealing with physical and phenomenal temporality to the case of language itself:

> What we understand by the word "language" unwinds in physical time. (As is made perfectly clear by the comparison with a mechanism.)
> Only what corresponds to this mechanism in the primary world could be the primary language.[71]

Our ordinary language is just one more physical process; like a clock, it "unwinds in physical time." It belongs on the filmstrip, not on the screen. Considered as a physical process, it is just one more lifeless mechanism that only has significance insofar as it is animated by the phenomena of immediate experience. No physical representation could ever be equivalent to a phenomenological language, for the signs would have to be applied and brought into a projective relationship with the world. That relationship is a precondition for understanding any language whatsoever; it is not something that can be stated *in* language. Language, considered as a system of signs, always needs to be interpreted, supplemented by "primary language," intrinsically meaningful processes. The image of the magic lantern, or the mechanism for the reproduction of immediate experience, each in turn an elaboration of the image of the two planes he had put forward in "Some Remarks on Logical Form," is supposed to provide the key to understanding the relationship between language and experience. The relationship is supposedly inexpressible, but can be conveyed by the use of the appropriate examples, which show us its true nature.

In the paragraphs that follow this exposition of his conception of the relationship between language and experience in the original manuscript notes, material that was not included in the *Philosophical Remarks*, Wittgenstein recorded his growing uneasiness with this conception of a language for the immediate description of experience:

> It's as if the phenomenological language led me into a bewitched morass where everything graspable disappears.
>
> Assuming that the world consisted of an unchanging visual field, wouldn't it then be possible to describe it?
> For instance: There is a blue circular patch in the middle of a red visual field.

---

71. *Philosophical Remarks*, §69. Source: MS 105, p. 117. Cf. Big Typescript, §102, p. 495:

> What we could call phenomenal time (specious present), is not in the time (past, present, and future) of history, is not a stretch of time. Whereas what we understand by language // Whereas the process of "language" // unwinds in homogenous, historical time. (Think about the mechanism for the description of immediate perception.) [German in appendix.]

Even though here also that which goes on in the reading of the proposition cannot be described in the proposition.

But what can be the importance of this description of the present phenomenon? It seems as though the preoccupation with this question is downright childish and will lead us /me/ to a dead end. And yet it is a significant dead end, for it tempts everyone to go down it as though the final solution to the problems of philosophy were to be found there.[72]

Here, Wittgenstein recounts how the description of immediate experience had seemed to contain the key to the "final solution to the problems of philosophy," echoing the words he had once used to sum up the claim that he had brought philosophy to an end in the *Tractatus*.[73] On the other hand, he simultaneously characterizes his preoccupation with phenomenological description as a "dead end," and a temptation. Even if one considers an artificially simplified case, so that most of the difficulties involved in representing everyday experience can be put to one side, no description of the phenomena will describe "that which goes on in the reading of the proposition," the mental act that transforms the dead signs into meaningful symbols.[74] That relationship is a precondition for understanding any language whatsoever; it is not something that can be stated *in* language.

The objection that I have just indicated needs to be handled extremely carefully if we are to do justice to Wittgenstein's changing treatment of "the description of the present phenomenon." It was not as if he had once tried to describe what goes on in reading a description and other such processes and had now recognized that this was impossible; rather, he had conceived of these processes as one aspect of the ungraspable flux of present experience, lying beyond the limits of language. The closest one could get to describing them would be a phenomenological language, but even it would leave the essence of the phenomena unexpressed. On this conception of mind and language, pure reality lies beyond language, and if the philosopher steps into this realm, he or she must leave language behind. Language is like a roll of film in a projector; the phenomena are like the pictures on the screen. There is a projective relation between the two, yet they belong to different worlds. At the same time, it is part of this conception that a certain kind of more limited description of the phenomena of immediate experience is both desirable and possible. Thus, the passage just quoted from Wittgenstein's manuscripts, where he expresses his con-

72. MS 105, pp. 116–118. [German in appendix.] No parallel passage in the *Philosophical Remarks*; cf. Big Typescript, p. 496, in note 74.

73. In the preface to the *Tractatus*, Wittgenstein said he was of the opinion that he had finally solved [*"endgültig gelöst"*] the problems.

74. Wittgenstein rewrote this passage in the Big Typescript, §102, p. 496, so that it points quite explicitly in the direction he had only hinted at in the earlier drafts:

(What, then, is the importance of this description of the *present* phenomenon, which can become an idée fixe for us, as it were. That we suffer from this: that the description cannot describe that which goes on in the reading of the description. It seems as though the preoccupation with this question is downright childish and will lead us down a dead end. And yet it is a significant dead end, for it tempts everyone to go down it; as though the final solution to the problems of philosophy were to be found there. It is as though one came, with the representation of the present phenomenon, in an enchanted swamp, where everything graspable disappeared.) [German in appendix.]

viction that "that which goes on in the reading of the proposition cannot be described in the proposition," a passage that was not included in the *Philosophical Remarks*, is immediately followed by a passage that reiterates the need for a language for the description of experience, a passage that is repeated verbatim in the *Philosophical Remarks*. It begins: "On the other hand, it's clear we need a way of speaking with which we can represent the phenomena of visual space, isolated as such."[75] This leads, in turn, to a discussion of how ordinary talk such as "I can see a lamp standing on a table" says more than a description of what is seen, for it carries further hypothetical commitments concerning what will be seen on other occasions.

A few pages further on in the manuscript source, Wittgenstein attempts to characterize his starting point—his conception of visual space as an autonomous, subjectless, primary realm, a realm that is extremely difficult to describe using our everyday language:

> It is not necessary to make eliminative experiments (e.g., thought experiments). Visual space, just as it is, has its own independent reality.
> Taken by itself, it contains no subject. It is autonomous.
>
> It can be immediately described (but we are far from knowing a means of expression which describes it). Everyday physical language is related to it in an *extremely* complicated way which we grasp instinctively.[76]

Next, Wittgenstein states the focus of his attempts to understand the relation between language and experience: the "application" of language, the relationship that connects words with their objects: "The decisive aspect of a language is its application. Thinking with its help."[77] He then states the philosophical problem that prevents him understanding the applications of language: conceiving of the present as "the only reality." On this conception, the present is like a stream continually flowing away from one so that it cannot be grasped:

> The approach that leads us into an enchanted valley, as it were, from which there is no escape into the open countryside is taking the present as the only reality. This present, constantly flowing or, rather, constantly changing, cannot be arrested or caught hold of. It disappears before we can think of grasping it. We stick in this valley, as though bewitched, in a whirl of thoughts.[78]

He then proposes that the confusion he has just described is due to attempting to grasp the present using an inappropriate method, for our physicalistic, scientifically oriented language is incapable of capturing the nature of the present:

> The mistake must be that we try to grasp the fleeting moment by scientific methods. It must be as though we wanted to determine the solidity of a beam in abstraction from it. To distill the one from the other, as it were.[79]

75. *Philosophical Remarks*, §70. Source: MS 105, p. 118.
76. MS 107, p. 1. [German in appendix.]
77. MS 107, p. 1. [German in appendix.]
78. MS 107, p. 1. [German in appendix.] Cf. Descartes, who after having raised the problem of how we can know we are not deceived in all our beliefs, wrote that it felt "as though I have fallen unexpectedly into a deep whirlpool which tumbles me around so that I can neither stand on the bottom nor swim up to the top" (René Descartes, *Meditations on First Philosophy*, p. 16).
79. MS 107, pp. 1–2. [German in appendix.]

Next, he offers his solution. We are to recognize that this is an inappropriate use of language: "We must be saved from trying to do this impossible thing by the knowledge that we talk nonsense if we try to use our language in this undertaking."[80] The solution is set out in more detail by appeal to the cinematic analogy. Language is analogous to the mechanism used to project the picture on the screen, not the picture itself, and so it belongs to the physical, not the phenomenal, realm:

> With our language we find ourselves, so to speak, in the domain of the film, not of the projected picture. And if I want to make music to accompany what is happening on the screen, whatever produces the music must again happen in the sphere of the film.[81]

Once we recognize the role of language, we will no longer attempt to use it to perform a task it cannot carry out. The moral is drawn in Tractatarian terms: the problematic approach to understanding the application of our language, the approach which seems to lead to an inexpressible and inescapable solipsism, cannot be put into words, and so cannot be a problem:

> That which I can't think, language can't express. That is our comfort.

> But if one says: the philosopher must step down into this encircled area, grasp the pure reality itself and bring it to the light of day, then the answer runs that he must in so doing leave language behind and so come back without achieving anything.[82]

Yet Wittgenstein was clearly unable to rest content with this resolution, for he immediately continued his discussion by returning to the problem of how to formulate a phenomenological language in the face of these limitations: "And yet there can be a phenomenological language. (Where must it stop?)"[83]

This train of thought leads to the conclusion that phenomenology, insofar as it attempts to go beyond the limits of language in seeking to capture the nature of reality, necessarily makes no sense. Inverting Plato's myth of the cave, Wittgenstein draws the moral that truth can only be found within the limits of language:

> If we want to imagine this language, then it is characteristic that we immediately begin to imagine the world as simpler than it is. But that speaks *for*, rather than against, the possibility of this language, since we go a determinate way to get to it.

> Or is it like this: our ordinary language is also phenomenological, only—as may be imagined—it does not permit one to separate the sensory regions, although it contains their multiplicity as a whole.

> Its space is combined visual-, taste- and kinaesthetic space; consequently I can "turn around" in this space and look at "what goes on behind me," etc.

> It is obviously possible to describe visual space. For if what ordinarily goes on in it is too complicated, then *that* already shows that the description is possible in

80. MS 107, p. 2. [German in appendix.]
81. *Philosophical Remarks*, §70; based on MS 107, p. 2. See n. 42 this chapter for a revision of this remark from the Big Typescript.
82. MS 107, p. 2. [German in appendix.]
83. MS 107, p. 3. [German in appendix.]

principle. And it is easy to think of processes in this space that are simple enough that they can easily be described.[84]

Similarly, in the *Philosophical Remarks*, Wittgenstein's critique of the fixation with finding the most direct possible description of immediate experience, "phenomenological language" in the strong sense, leads him to reiterate the need for a language for the contents of visual space, "phenomenological language" in the weak sense. He holds that "it's clear we need a way of expressing with which we can represent the phenomena of visual space, isolated as such." Wittgenstein offers "'I can see a lamp standing on the table,'" as it is ordinarily understood, as an example of a description of experience that goes beyond simply describing the content of visual space, presumably because it implicitly commits us to a hypothesis about physical objects such as the lamp and the table. He next offers "'It seems to me as if I were seeing a lamp standing on a table'" as an example of a "correct" description of visual space, but then says that form of words is still misleading, "since it makes it look as though nothing actual were being described, but only something whose nature was unclear."[85] While the talk of the "investigation of the rules for the use of our language" makes it sound as if Wittgenstein aims to do no more than describe the commitments implicit in our everyday ways of speaking, the embryonic analyses of ordinary language in the *Philosophical Remarks* actually involve a radical revision of our everyday outlook. Here, Wittgenstein's philosophy of mind is a solipsism of the present moment, his philosophy of language an extreme verificationism on which a word has a different meaning every time we associate a different criterion of verification with it. Philosophy had led him to quite extraordinary ways of conceiving of the everyday. Paradoxically, it also led him to maintain, in all sincerity, that his apparently revisionary metaphysical outlook was the product of an "absolutely *impartial*" description of the phenomena that only a metaphysician would dispute. He thought that any attempt to assert such solipsistic or verificationist theses was a mistake, an attempt to say what can only be shown. Thus he describes the solipsistic thesis that "only present experience is real" as a temptation, a temptation to be avoided, and begins his discussion of it by pointing out that it is not supposed to imply that I did not get up this morning, or that my memory of a past event is mistaken.[86] After these initial criticisms of the thesis that only the present experience is real, he acknowledges that it points toward a philosophical insight, saying that it

> appears to contain the last consequence of solipsism. And in a sense this is so; only what it is able to say amounts to just as little as can be said by solipsism.
> —For what belongs to the essence of the world simply *cannot* be said. And philosophy, if it were to say anything, would have to describe the essence of the world.
>
> But the essence of language is a picture of the essence of the world; and philosophy as custodian of grammar can in fact grasp the essence of the world, only

84. MS 107, p. 3. [German in appendix.]

85. All the quoted passages in the paragraph prior to this footnote are from *Philosophical Remarks*, §70; their source is MS 105, p. 118. In the Big Typescript, §102, p. 496, the first of these passages is rephrased as follows: "On the other hand, we need a way of expressing that represents the processes //phenomena// of visual space separated from other kinds of experiences." [German in appendix.]

86. *Philosophical Remarks*, §54. Cf. Big Typescript, §102, p. 498.

not in the propositions of language, but in rules for this language which exclude nonsensical combinations of signs.[87]

5.4 The World as Idea

We can see how Wittgenstein had arrived at the impasse of insisting that it must be possible to describe immediate experience yet entertaining doubts about whether it was really possible to do so if we review Waismann's notes of conversations during Wittgenstein's visit to Vienna for Christmas 1929, when he took part in a series of intensive discussions with the Vienna Circle, setting out and defending his recent work. The topics covered included the rejection of primary language, his conception of the relation between language and world, the distinction between visual space and Euclidean physical space, and the notion of a propositional system or calculus.[88] The following passage from the *Philosophical Remarks*, originally recorded in manuscript notes dated December 28–29, 1929, shows Wittgenstein reaffirming his conception of the world as idea even after he had explicitly repudiated the goal of a phenomenological language:

> That it doesn't strike us when we look around us, move about in space, feel our own bodies, etc., etc., shows how natural these things are to us. We do not perceive that we see space perspectively or that our visual picture is in some sense blurred towards the edges. It doesn't strike us and never can strike us because it is *the* way we perceive. We never give it a thought and it's impossible we should, since there is nothing that contrasts with the form of our world.
>
> What I wanted to say is it's remarkable that those who ascribe reality only to things and not to our ideas [*Vorstellungen*] move about so self-evidently in the world as idea and never long to escape from it.
>
> In other words, just how self-evident the given is. It would be the very devil if this were a tiny picture taken from an oblique distorting angle.
>
> This, the self-evident, *life*, is supposed to be something accidental, subordinate; while something that normally never comes into my head, reality!
>
> That is, what we neither can nor want to go beyond would not be the world.
>
> Time and again the attempt is made to use language to limit the world and set it in relief—but it can't be done. The self-evidence of the world expresses itself in the very fact that language can and does only refer to it.
>
> For since language only derives the way in which it means from its meaning, from the world, no language is conceivable which does not represent this world.[89]

Here, Wittgenstein comes as close as he can to simply saying what he wants to say, perhaps provoked into being blunter than usual by the challenges raised in his discussions with the Vienna Circle. Instead of trying to formulate rules which will show

---

87. *Philosophical Remarks*, §54. Source: MS 108, p. 2. The first ten pages of MS 108 are the source for most of §54–58 of the *Remarks*.

88. See *Ludwig Wittgenstein and the Vienna Circle*, pp. 33–96.

89. *Philosophical Remarks*, §47, based on MS 108, pp. 47–49, 28–30 December 1929. With the exception of the first paragraph, the passage is repeated verbatim in the Big Typescript, §91, pp. 428–429.

154

the structure of language and world, he simply contrasts the primary world and secondary world, describing the primary world as self-evident, the given, life, the world as idea. At the same time, he holds that none of this can be put into words, for the thesis that language must ultimately refer to the primary world is a faltering attempt to express what can only "show itself." Yet in this very passage he does just what he has said he cannot do: he "uses language to limit the world and set it in relief." He tells us that "the form of our world" includes the facts that we see space perspectivally and that the visual field is blurred toward the edges. Paradoxically, he even says that "we never give it a thought"—but then what are we supposed to be doing when we read those words?—and that it is impossible that we do, for there is no alternative to the form of our world.

While the unusually forthright exposition of his views may have been provoked by his conversations at the time, this passage expresses a position that he continued to maintain, albeit in an increasingly qualified form, for several years after it was written. It is included both in the *Philosophical Remarks*, assembled a few months later, and also in the Big Typescript, assembled several years later. But Wittgenstein's verificationist and idealist remarks from 1929 and the early 1930s are never developed into a full-fledged theory of knowledge. Of course, his methodological pronouncements run counter to any such theory: he holds that he is simply stating facts about usage that no one would dispute. When we look at what he claims our usage shows us during these transitional years, we find a very traditional picture of mind and world at work: indeed, it was only once he had brought that picture out into the open that he was able to criticize it and reject it.

In the *Philosophical Remarks*, the above-cited train of thought about the primacy of life and the world as idea leads Wittgenstein to ask whether that conception can be put into words at all. One of the problems at issue is the apparent incommensurability of the mental and physical worlds, the primary and the secondary. How could two self-contained worlds, represented by separate calculi, ever come into contact? Wittgenstein's detailed discussion of the problem turns on the differences between physicalistic and phenomenological conceptions of time. If the world as idea is not in time, not part of the temporal order of physical events, how can we grasp it in words, which do have a location and a history? "If the world of data is timeless, how can we speak of it at all?"[90] His answer in the *Philosophical Remarks* is that the world as idea and language make contact in the present moment. The two connect when what we say is made true by what we see—verified by observation. And so language, despite being spatio-temporal, is applicable to experience—it makes contact with the "stream of life" at the present moment:

> The stream of life, or the stream of the world, flows on and our propositions are so to speak verified only at instants.
> Our propositions are only verified by the present.
> So they must be constructed that they can be verified by it. And so in some way they must be commensurable with the present; and they cannot be so *in spite of* their spatio-temporal nature; on the contrary this must be related to their com-

90. *Philosophical Remarks*, §48; cf. MS 107, p. 222.

mensurability as the corporeality of a ruler is to its being extended—which is what enables it to measure.[91]

Wittgenstein holds that a principal difficulty in describing experience is that one cannot use our ordinary physicalistic terms to talk about immediate experience without systematically misdescribing it:

> It's a confusion of the time of the film strip with the time of the picture it projects. For "time" has one meaning when we conceive of memory as the source of time, and another when we conceive of it as a picture preserved from a past event.[92]

He explains the distinction between physicalistic and phenomenological time in terms of a parallel distinction between a physicalistic conception of memory as "a picture preserved from a past event" and a phenomenological conception of memory as "the source of time."

On the physicalistic conception, memory is a present picture of a past physical event, a more or less reliable representation of an independent state of affairs. We can compare what our memory tells us with independent testimony and other evidence, and it can also fade and become unreliable. Wittgenstein suggests that these facts lead us to treat memory as "somewhat secondary" when compared with present experience, as a "faint and uncertain picture of what we originally had before us in full clarity."[93] To remember is to attempt to represent an earlier experience to onself; the memory may no longer be as vivid or as detailed as the original, and there may be reason to doubt its accuracy. For instance, we say such things as "'I *only* have a *vague* memory of this house.'" In this example of what Wittgenstein calls "physical language," memories are treated as just one source of information about past events, and a potentially unreliable one, at that. From that perspective, our ordinary conception of time, on which there is a past, present, and future, is entirely acceptable. Wittgenstein next considers the objection that if this way of talking "says everything we want to say, and everything that can be said," what need is there for any other way of speaking? His response is to insist on the importance of the point that "it can also be put *differently*." Wittgenstein's second way of speaking is supposed to describe the same facts as the first, but "put the emphasis elsewhere."[94] On his alternative approach, memory is not part of the ordinary temporal order at all. Instead, it is

---

91. *Philosophical Remarks*, §48. Cf. MS 107, p. 222, dated 1 December 1929. Wittgenstein rejected a verificationist account of the relation between language and experience shortly afterward; see *Zettel*, §436. Source: MS 112, p. 230 (written in 1931). In the unpublished chapter on "Idealism, etc." in the Big Typescript, §102, p. 496, this passage is presented in scare quotes, prefaced by the words, "A thought about the representability of immediate reality through language," with the clear implication that it is a thought to be avoided. [German for the final quotation in appendix.]

92. *Philosophical Remarks*, §49. The second sentence is the first sentence of Big Typescript, §105, p. 517.

93. *Philosophical Remarks*, §52; Big Typescript, §101, p. 487. In the Big Typescript, the discussion of two different ways of conceiving of memory opens the first section of the chapter on "Idealism, etc," in a section entitled "The representation of the immediately perceived." All other quotations in this paragraph without an accompanying footnote are from *Philosophical Remarks*, §§52–53, and are repeated in the Big Typescript, §101, p. 487.

94. *Philosophical Remarks*, §53; Big Typescript, §101, p. 487.

a "kind of seeing into the past,"[95] the basis for a radically different concept of time on which we "take memory to be the source of time."[96] It is an "idea" [*Vorstellung*], a part of the world as idea. Wittgenstein takes it to be part of the logic of idea memory that the idea is the object of the memory report:

> If I describe the immediately given past, then I describe my memory, and not something which this memory signals. (For which this memory would be a symptom.)
>
> And here "memory"—like "vision" and "hearing" earlier—does not designate a psychic capacity, rather a determinate part of the logical structure of our world.[97]

Wittgenstein treats the two ways of talking as autonomous—each is internally coherent, but the two cannot be combined without creating confusion: "Both ways of talking are in order, and are equally legitimate, but cannot be mixed together."[98] Instead, we must clearly differentiate these two incommensurable conceptions of time and memory. Thus Wittgenstein holds that the physical temporality of past, present, and future cannot be applied to the world as idea:

> It's clear of course that speaking of memory as a picture is only a simile;[99] just as the way of speaking of images as "pictures of objects in our minds" (or some such phrase) is a simile. We know what a picture is, but images are surely no kind of picture at all. For, in the first case I can see the picture and the object of which it is a picture. But in the other, things are obviously quite different. We have just used a simile and now the simile tyrannizes us. While in the language of the simile, I am unable to move outside of the simile. It must lead to nonsense if you try to use the language of this simile to talk about memory as the source of our knowledge, the verification of propositions. We can speak of present, past and future events in the physical world, but not of present, past and future ideas, if what we are calling an idea is not to be yet another kind of physical object (say, a physical picture which takes the place of the body), but precisely that which is present. Thus we cannot use the concept of time, i.e. the syntactical rules that hold for the names of physical objects, in the world as idea [*Vorstellungswelt*], that is, not where we adopt a radically different way of speaking.[100]

95. *Philosophical Remarks*, §50. This is one of the few aspects of Wittgenstein's account of memory time in the *Philosophical Remarks* that he gives up in the Big Typescript. The first two paragraphs of §50 of the *Philosophical Remarks*, where he argues that memory is "a kind of seeing into the past," are scare quoted in the section of the Big Typescript on memory time. The next paragraph begins with a statement of his view:

> Our memory data are ordered; we call this order memory time, in contrast to physical time, the order of events in the physical world. Our feelings justifiably resist the expression "seeing into the past"; for it gives us a picture // for it evokes the picture // that someone sees a process in the physical world that does not now happen but rather is already over. (Big Typescript, §105, p. 520). [German in appendix.]

96. *Philosophical Remarks*, §49; Big Typescript, §105, p. 518.
97. Big Typescript, §102, p. 495. [German in appendix.]
98. *Philosophical Remarks*, §49; Big Typescript, §105, p. 518.
99. "Simile" [*Gleichnis*] in the *Philosophical Remarks* is replaced by "picture" [*Bild*] in the Big Typescript.
100. *Philosophical Remarks*, §49; Big Typescript, §105, p. 518.

Wittgenstein illustrates his claim by contrasting the open-ended past and future of physical time with memory time, which ends, or begins, in the present. The two are governed by different rules and form different systems:

> One way memory time differentiates itself from physical time is that it is a half-line whose endpoint // beginning // is the present. Naturally, the difference between memory time and physical time is a logical difference. I.e.: the two orderings could very well be designated by quite different names, and one only calls them both "time" because a certain grammatical relation obtains, just like that between cardinal and rational numbers; visual space, taste space and physical space; tones and timbres, etc., etc.[101]

From within the world as idea, one cannot compare the content of present experience with other sources of evidence: experience is all there is. Despite the apparent similarities between physical time and memory time, Wittgenstein insists that the differences between the phenomenological and physical conceptions of time make them into incommensurable systems:

> Memory time. It is (like visual space) not a part of the larger time, rather the specific order of events or situations in thought // in memory //. In this time there is, e.g., no future. Visual space and physical space, memory time and physical time, are not related as are a part of the series of cardinal numbers to the law for this series ("the whole series of numbers"); rather, like the system of cardinal numbers to the system of rational numbers. And this relation also explains the sense to the opinion that the one system includes, contains, the other.[102]

As the last passage makes clear, there is a close parallel between Wittgenstein's conceptions of memory time and physical time on the one hand and visual space and physical space on the other. He compares the phenomenological system with the cardinal numbers, the sequence of counting numbers beginning with 1,2,3 . . . , and the physical system with the rational numbers, the series of numbers that contains every fraction arranged in ascending order. An obvious objection to his analogy is that the cardinal numbers are a subset of the rational numbers: they are the set of all rational fractions whose denominator is 1. Wittgenstein's reply is that the proposed subset is still part of the system of rational numbers, and while it can be put in a one-to-one relationship with the cardinal numbers, they belong to separate and distinct systems. He makes use of precisely the same analogy in explaining his conception of the relationship between the contents of one's visual space and the physical objects one sees.

Wittgenstein holds that the word "present" is redundant in the solipsistic thesis that "only the present experience has reality," for it cannot perform its normal task of marking off the present from the past and future. The solipsist misuses physical language and so misdescribes the nature of visual space and the present moment:

> —Something else must be meant by the word, something that isn't *in* a space, but is itself a space. That is to say, not something bordering on something else (from

---

101. Big Typescript, §105, p. 521. [German in appendix.]
102. Big Typescript, §105, p. 521. [German in appendix.]

which it could therefore be limited off.) And so, something language cannot legitimately set in relief.[103]

Wittgenstein explains the conflict between these two senses of "present"—the present moment, one part of the space constituted by the physicalistic time order, and the timeless present, the neighbourless space of immediate experience—in terms of the movie metaphor. The solipsist mistakenly compares "present" experience with the frame of the film that is currently being projected, in front of those past frames which have been projected and behind those future frames which will be projected. Wittgenstein's reply is to contend that the correct analogy is with the picture on the screen, which is not part of the series of frames at all, and so "present"—and for that matter, "my," "experience," and "real"—are all inapplicable:

> The present we are talking about here is not the picture on the filmstrip that is in front of the lantern's lens right now, as opposed to the pictures before and after it, which have already been there or are yet to come; but the picture on the screen, which would illegitimately be called present, since "present" would not be used here to distinguish it from past and future. And so it is a meaningless epithet.[104]

Nor is "present" the only offending word: Wittgenstein holds that "only experience is real" and "not only experience is real" are equally nonsensical: "From the very outset 'realism,' 'idealism,' etc. are names which belong to metaphysics. That is, they indicate that their adherents believe they can say something specific about the essence of the world."[105]

In both the *Philosophical Remarks* and Big Typescript, Wittgenstein maintains that visual space only seems derivative or subjective when considered from the standpoint of the secondary language of physical space. For instance, if we describe what we see using secondary language, we will use physicalistic terms to talk of appearances, corrigible reports about how things seem to be. For instance, we look at a rod dipped in a glass of water and say that though it seems bent, it isn't really so. Wittgenstein's response to such a way of speaking, and the implicit assumption that physicalistic language is primary, is that while the physicalistic way of talking is practical and convenient, as it expresses the results of ojective measurement, it gives an unjustified priority to measurement, and so does not get at the essence of experiential phenomena:

> We talk for instance of an optical illusion and associate this expression with the idea of a mistake, although of course it isn't essential that there should be any mistake; and if appearance were normally more important in our lives than the results of measurement, then language would also show a different attitude to this phenomenon.[106]

As a corrective, Wittgenstein proposes that we consider an alternative way of speaking which does not incorporate the physicalistic bias of our ordinary ways of talking about experience:

103. *Philosophical Remarks*, §54. Source: MS 108, p. 3, 13 December 1929.
104. *Philosophical Remarks*, §54. Source: MS 108, p. 3, 13 December 1929.
105. *Philosophical Remarks*, §55. Source: MS 108, p. 5, 13 December 1929.
106. *Philosophical Remarks*, §53. Source: MS 108, p. 28, 21 December 1929. Cf. Big Typescript, §101, p. 488.

There is not—as I used to believe—a primary language as opposed to our ordinary language, the "secondary" one. But one could speak of a primary language
as opposed to ours in so far as the former would not permit any way of expressing
a preference for certain phenomena over others; it would have to be, so to speak
absolutely *impartial* [*sachlich*].[107]

Sachlich is derived from *Sache*, a rather unphilosophical word for "thing," in the sense
of the matter in hand, or a thing that one deals with every day. *Sachlich* suggests an
unbiassed, impartial report that simply states the facts. But the "impartiality" of the
primary language is that it treats all my present experience equally and refers to
nothing else; it is a language for the world as idea.

---

107. *Philosophical Remarks*, §53. Source: MS 108, p. 29, 21 December 1929. Cf. Big Typescript,
§101, p. 488.

6

The Flow of Life

6.1 Why Language Cannot Say That "All Is in Flux"

In 1929 Wittgenstein came to think of immediate experience as the primary world to which all significant discourse must refer, yet he was also convinced that the nature of the primary world necessarily eluded description. As we have seen, the resultant tension between his conviction that any attempt to formulate verificationist, idealist, or solipsist theses that describe this predicament must lead to nonsense, and his sympathy for what such formulations try to say, animates his extended discussion of the nature of lived time and the experience of the present moment. Perhaps the thesis that came closest to capturing what he wanted to say was the Heraclitean dictum that "all is in flux," a thesis he repeatedly cites in these transitional texts. Wittgenstein was well acquainted with the writings of Plato that attribute this view to Heraclitus, such as the *Cratylus* and the *Theaetetus*. In the *Cratylus*, Socrates mentions that "Heraclitus is supposed to say that all things are in motion and nothing at rest; he compares them to the stream of a river, and says that you cannot go into the same water twice."[1] Socrates treats Heraclitus' river imagery as a metaphor for the nature of the world and takes it to imply the view that everything is constantly changing, and so a world where "there is nothing stable or permanent, but only flux and motion."[2] He sums up the view he attributes to Heraclitus with the words *panta rhei*, "everything flows," or "all is in flux."

With the collapse of the Tractarian argument for the existence of simple objects and Wittgenstein's new focus on the description of immediate experience, "one cannot step twice into the same river" and "all is in flux" became natural ways of expressing his intuition that, on the one hand, the experience of the present moment is all that is real, and, on the other, that it is continually changing and eludes our grasp. In October 1929, Wittgenstein wrote:

> I feel today such a particular poverty of problems around me; a sure sign that the most important and hardest problems lie *before me*.
>
> 11.10[3]

---

1. Plato, *Cratylus*, 402b.
2. Plato, *Cratylus*, 411c.
3. As Wittgenstein followed the European convention of writing the day followed by the month, "11.10" means the eleventh of October.

The immediate finds itself in constant flux [*Fluß*]. (It has in fact the form of a stream [*Strom*].)

It is quite clear that if one wants to say here the ultimate, one must thus come to the limit of the language which expresses it.[4]

The German word for river is *"Fluß,"* which can also mean flux. As a result of this ambiguity, there is a natural transition between the notion of a river and the notion of flux in the German. Wittgenstein describes the immediately given as being in constant flux, like a stream, but concludes that one cannot actually say it, and certainly implies that one cannot draw it, either. What Wittgenstein's words on the page do say and what his drawing depicts do indirectly convey is a conception of the world that can, to a considerable extent, be stated more explicitly. At first, his drawing hardly looks like a river, for it terminates in midstream; read from left to right, it comes to a stop. I take the drawing to be a schematic illustration of the contents of consciousness: the present is the sharp line in the middle, with the specious present fading off into the past on the left. Whether or not my reading of the drawing is correct, Wittgenstein certainly did use the flux thesis to gesture at the inexpressible aspect of experience:

> The blurredness, indeterminacy of our sense impressions is not something which can be remedied, a blurredness to which a complete sharpness corresponds (or is opposed). Rather, this general indeterminacy, ungraspability, this swimming of the sense impressions, is that which has been designated by the words "all is in flux."[5]

Nevertheless, he was also convinced that the nature of experience cannot be described or pictured. For instance, he dismissed Ernst Mach's drawing of visual experience, a sketch that looks as if drawn from a point a few inches behind someone's eyes, bordered by a hazy boundary of eyelids and nose, with the words "you can't make a visual picture of the visual field."[6] This is a consequence of his Tractarian view that no general thesis about the nature of language or experience can ever be explicitly stated; such matters can only be shown or conveyed by making clear the form of our language. Thus, in the *Philosophical Remarks*, he writes:

> What belongs to the essence of the world cannot be expressed by language.
> For this reason, it cannot *say* that all is in flux. Language can only say those things we can also imagine otherwise.[7]

4. MS 107, pp. 158–159. [German in appendix.] The diagram is a schematic drawing of a pencilled diagram that Wittgenstein drew in the manuscript volume immediately between the words above and below. Reproductions of the original manuscript can be found in Stern, "Heraclitus' and Wittgenstein's River Images," p. 588 of the microfilm of the Wittgenstein *Nachlass*, or the forthcoming Oxford University Press CD-ROM edition of the *Nachlass*.

5. Big Typescript, §96, p. 448. [German in appendix.]

6. *Philosophical Remarks*, §213.

7. *Philosophical Remarks*, §54.

One other aspect to Wittgenstein's conception of the flux of experience seems to elude even the grasp of grammar: it is connected with "the feeling . . . that the present disappears into the past without our being able to prevent it," the feeling that the phenomenon, "the constant flux of appearance," slips away from us.[8] As in the attempt to grasp hold of the "present phenomenon" that ended in a "bewitched morass in which everything graspable disappears,"[9] we seem unable to reach firm ground. In the Big Typescript, Wittgenstein described the feeling of being unable to fully capture the content of experience in the following terms: "If one says that 'all is in flux,' then we feel that we are hindered from getting a firm hold on that which is actual, the actual reality."[10]

Like the solipsistic sayings, "the world is my world" and "only the present experience has reality," Wittgenstein regards "all is in flux" as a philosophical pseudo-proposition, an attempt to say the unsayable. Nevertheless, unlike his stock examples of out-and-out nonsense, such as "red is higher than green" or "the question whether the good is more or less identical than the beautiful," they are deep nonsense, for they are motivated by the desire to put "the essence of the world" into language.[11] In lectures, he said that what the solipsist is struggling to say, although strictly speaking nonsensical, expresses an "'idea . . . of enormous importance.'"[12] However, his response to the solipsist's claim that solipsism must be true, for it is impossible to imagine any alternative, ran as follows: "'If so your statement has no sense' since 'nothing can characterize reality, except as opposed to something else which is not the case.'"[13] Similarly, "all is in flux," cannot be said either, for "language can only say those things that we can imagine otherwise." The link between imagining an alternative to p and p's having a sense is the picture theory of meaning. In an appendix to the Big Typescript, Wittgenstein set out that link as follows:

> To what extent is it necessary to be able to imagine what a proposition has to say? ("Are you in pain at this location?")
>
> "Conceivable" is something similar to "imaginable." // "Conceivable" is really something similar to "imaginable." // "Conceivable" is only an extension of the concept "imaginable." (That is what my conception of the proposition as a picture wanted to say.)[14]

If p has a sense, it pictures things being arranged in a certain way, and rules out all of the possible states of affairs in which it is false. So we should also be able to imagine the states of affairs that we have ruled out. For instance, the proposition "my watch is on the table" rules out the state of affairs in which it is in my pocket, or in the drawer. But the whole point of "all is in flux" is that an alternative is meant to be inconceivable. And so it attempts to combine the facticity of an everyday proposition with the apriority of logic. But saying that we can't imagine it being otherwise

---

8. *Philosophical Remarks*, §52; Big Typescript, §91, p. 428.
9. MS 105, p. 116. See chapter 5, pp. 148–149.
10. Big Typescript, §91, p. 427.
11. "Some Remarks on Logical Form," p. 162; *Tractatus*, 4.003.
12. Moore, "Wittgenstein's Lectures in 1930–33," p. 311.
13. Moore, "Wittgenstein's Lectures in 1930–33," p. 311.
14. TS 219, p. 20. [German in appendix.]

is to rule out the possibility that the proposition is false, and in so doing we also eliminate the connection between language and world that gives the proposition its sense:

> When one wants to show the senselessness of metaphysical turns of phrase, one often says "I couldn't imagine the opposite of that," or "What would it be like if it were otherwise?" (When, for instance, someone has said that my images are private, that only I alone can know if I am feeling pain, etc.) Well, if I can't imagine how it might be otherwise, I equally can't imagine that it is *so*. For here "I can't imagine" doesn't indicate a lack of imaginative power. I can't even *try* to imagine it; it makes no sense to say "I imagine it." And that means, no connection has been made between this sentence and the means of representation by imagination (or by drawing).[15]

But how far can we rely on the imagination or our ability to produce a picture as a guide to what is and is not possible? In the *Philosophical Remarks*, Wittgenstein gives specific instances of propositions that might have been otherwise and contrasts them with propositions whose alternatives are inconceivable. Thus he writes that:

> There are, admittedly, very interesting, completely general propositions of great importance, therefore propositions describing an actual experience which might have been otherwise, but just *is as it is*. For instance, that I have only *one* body. That my sensations never reach out beyond this body (except in cases where someone has had a limb, e.g. an arm, amputated, and yet feels pain in his fingers). These are remarkable and interesting facts.
>
> But it does *not* belong in this category, if someone says I cannot remember the future. For that means nothing, and, like its opposite, is something inconceivable.
>
> That I always see with my *eyes* when I am awake is on the other hand a remarkable and interesting fact. Equally, it is important that my visual field is in a constant state of alteration.[16]

Here, too, Wittgenstein treats whether or not we can conceive of an alternative as a way of testing whether a proposition is meaningful, and he offers examples of propositions that do and do not pass the test. But we are still given no indication of how the test has been applied or how we might apply it for ourselves. Similarly, Wittgenstein asks himself, "Can I imagine experience with two bodies?", and immediately replies, "Certainly not visual experience,"[17] without offering any further justification. If Wittgenstein had chosen uncontentious examples of contingent facts of nature and logical impossibilities, then his silence would not be so troublesome. But his examples raise difficult questions about the nature of mind and body, vision and memory, on which honest disagreement is surely possible. Similarly, Wittgenstein maintains that it is impossible to see a hundred-sided polygon, take in thirty strokes in a row at one look, or see a straight line touch a circle at only one point.[18] While some people can see more clearly than others, he finds it absolutely inconceivable that someone should have a truly Euclidean visual space, one in which circles and tangents only intersect

15. *Philosophical Grammar*, §83; cf. *Philosophical Investigations*, §251–252. These two passages are an excellent example of how the source material for the *Philosophical Investigations* can be blunter than the final product.

16. *Philosophical Remarks*, §55.

17. *Philosophical Remarks*, §66; Big Typescript §104, p. 527.

18. *Philosophical Remarks*, §214; Big Typescript, §95, p. 443. See also Big Typescript, §96.

at a point instead of merging for a stretch.[19] Absolute sharpness can be neither opposed nor compared to the blurredness we experience, for the terms belong to incommensurable grammatical systems, applicable to visual space and Euclidean space
respectively: "Whatever is arranged in visual space stands in this *sort* of order *a priori*,
i.e. in virtue of its logical nature, and geometry here is simply grammar."[20] His grounds
are "grammatical": he holds that talk of such things makes no sense. It is tempting to
reply that whether or not anyone can actually do these things, we do understand what
he is saying, and so it does make sense. But to say that is to beg the question: what is
at issue is whether the words in question have any application. Presumably, to fill in
the gap between the examples and Wittgenstein's conclusions, a person would sit
down in a quiet moment and ask whether one could imagine a situation to which the
words in question would not apply. However, imagination is a dangerous guide to
logical possibility, for logic is not the only factor at work in determining the limits of
the imagination. It may be one's preconceptions that prevent one imagining an alternative. Of course, if a proposition is logically impossible, it is impossible to imagine
it—there is nothing to imagine. The obviously impossible is unimaginable and the
obviously possible is imaginable. But these observations are little help in cases where
imaginability and possibility are both equally contentious, for one can still come up
with a misleading image and so come to *think* one has imagined something that is
actually impossible. Elsewhere in the *Philosophical Remarks*, Wittgenstein is quite
willing to criticize other philosophers' claims about the limits of the conceivable:

> Philosophers who believe you can, in a manner of speaking, extend experi-
> ence by thinking ought to remember that you can transmit speech over the tele-
> phone, but not measles.
> Similarly I cannot at will experience time as bounded, or the visual field as
> homogenous, etc.[21]

In assimilating the contentious issues he wishes to resolve to those uncontentious
cases where we can all agree, Wittgenstein begs the question: How are we to determine the limits of what can be imagined, and what is the link between what can be
imagined and what is possible? For our philosophical preconceptions may affect what
we can and cannot imagine, and so the imagination is not a neutral medium with which
to test for logical possibility. Indeed, it is just as easy to imagine nonsense as it is to
say nonsense:

> It looks as if we could say: Word-language permits nonsensical combinations
> of words, but the language of imagination does not permit us to imagine anything
> nonsensical. Hence too the language of drawing doesn't permit senseless draw-
> ings. —But that isn't how it is: for a drawing can be senseless in the same way as
> a proposition. Think of a blueprint from which a turner is to work; here it is very
> easy to represent an exact analogy with a nonsensical pseudoproposition. Remem-
> ber too the example of drawing a route on a projection of the globe.[22]

19. *Philosophical Remarks*, §214; Big Typescript, §95, pp. 443–444.
20. *Philosophical Remarks*, §178; Big Typescript, §95, pp. 444–445.
21. *Philosophical Remarks*, §66. Cf. *Zettel*, §256.
22. *Philosophical Grammar*, §83. Cf. MS 110, p. 291; MS 116, pp. 75–76; *Philosophical Investigations*, §512.

There is no more guarantee that we will know how to apply an image than a picture or the original proposition. In some cases, imagination may help us see how the proposition is applied, but in others, our preconceptions may lead us astray. The following passage, which immediately precedes the discussion of solipsism in the *Philosophical Investigations*, brings out this aspect of Wittgenstein's later objections to relying on the imagination:

> There is a lack of clarity about the role of *imaginability* in our investigation. Namely about the extent to which it ensures that a proposition makes sense.
>
> It is no more essential to the understanding of a proposition that one should imagine anything in connection with it, than that one should make a sketch from it.
>
> Instead of "imaginability" one can also say here: representability in a particular medium of interpretation. And such a representation *may* indeed safely point a way to further use of a sentence. On the other hand a picture may obtrude itself upon us and be of no use at all.[23]

As we have already seen, despite the anticipation of these dangers in the passages just quoted from the *Philosophical Remarks*, the author of that work did appeal to his intuitions about what can and cannot be imagined in attempting to determine the "essence of the world":

> What belongs to the essence of the world cannot be expressed by language.
> For this reason, it cannot *say* that all is in flux. Language can only say those things we can also imagine otherwise.[24]

To sum up: Wittgenstein's thesis is that all is in flux and his metathesis is that the thesis cannot be stated, that any attempt to state it as a thesis must run up against the limits of language and misfire. Nevertheless, he tried to do it. In the next paragraph, he says "all is in flux" must be expressed in the "application" of language, the act that makes the dead words we utter or the signs we make into a living, significant language. He compares the application of language to the act that makes an evenly marked rod into a ruler, a sign into a symbol, characterizing it as a matter of *"putting language up against* reality."[25] The ruler analogy, which had played a central role in his exposition of his new conception of the role of propositional systems, is now turned in a very different direction.[26] In emphasizing the act of placing the measuring rod against the thing to be measured, Wittgenstein stresses the contribution we make in using language. Unless we give life to language by applying it, it remains a dead syntactic structure. As in the magic lantern simile, a relationship between everyday things within the world—a ruler and what it measures—is transmuted into a model for the relationship between mind and world as a whole. But in using the everyday act of making use of a ruler to articulate a quite general conception of the relation between a sign and what it stands for, Wittgenstein took away the context within which

23. *Philosophical Investigations*, §395–397.
24. *Philosophical Remarks*, §54.
25. *Philosophical Remarks*, §54. In the source manuscript, MS 108, p. 1, dated 13 December 1929, the next sentence reads: "And this application of language is the verification of the propositions." [German in appendix.]
26. See chapter 4, section 2.

the use had its life and introduced a myth of a wholly general relation between mind and world, a myth that was simultaneously protected from critical examination by the claim that it could not be put into words.

The following passage captures the interplay in Wittgenstein's work at this point between the theses that he wanted to express—the Tractarian metathesis that the truth in those theses cannot be stated but can be shown, and his gradual recognition that the tension between these views could only be resolved by a still more radical break with the philosophical tradition. Here Wittgenstein connects "all is in flux" with his sense of unclarity about where philosophy begins and considered it a possible starting point for his next book:

> If I don't quite know how to start a book, this is because I am still unclear about something. For I should like to start with what is given to philosophy, written and spoken sentences, with books as it were.
>
> And here we come on the difficulty of "all is in flux." Perhaps that is the very point at which to start.[27]

By his talk of "books, as it were," Wittgenstein means to direct our attention to language as a system of written and spoken signs that people actually use to communicate, as opposed to any idealized conception of what must accompany or animate those signs in order for them to be significant. Thus in the *Philosophical Remarks*, in response to "the apparently trivial question, what does Logic understand by a word— is it an ink-mark, a sequence of sounds, is it necessary that someone should associate a sense with it, or should have associated one, etc., etc.?", Wittgenstein replies that here "the crudest conception must obviously be the only correct one." The following paragraphs clarify what he means by his talk of "books" and connect it with his overall conception of language as a system:

> And so I will again talk about "books"; here we have words; if a mark should happen to occur that looks like a word, I say: that's not a word, it only looks like one, it's obviously unintentional. This can only be dealt with from the standpoint of a healthy human understanding. (It's extraordinary that that in itself constitutes a change of perspective.)
>
> I do not believe that Logic can talk about sentences in any other than the ordinary sense in which we say, "There's a sentence written here" or "No, that only looks like a sentence but isn't," etc., etc.
>
> The question "What is a word?" is completely analogous to "What is a chesspiece?"[28]

The final sentence is the source for the last sentence of section 108 of the *Philosophical Investigations*, a remark that contains one of the best-known formulations of

---

27. *Culture and Value*, p. 8. Source: MS 110, p. 10, 13 December 1930.

28. *Philosophical Remarks*, §18. In MS 107, p. 240, the source for the first two paragraphs quoted here, Wittgenstein wrote the English words "common sense" above the German "*gesunden Menschenverstandes*," translated here by "healthy human understanding." The earlier reference to "books" that Wittgenstein mentions is in *Philosophical Remarks*, §17: "Isn't the point that Logic is only interested in [what we say] as a part of a language system? The system our books are written in." Subsequent versions of these remarks are Big Typescript, §16, p. 71; MS 114, pp. 108–109; *Philosophical Grammar*, §77; *Philosophical Investigations*, §108.

Wittgenstein's insistence on the need for a radical change in perspective to appreciate the true significance of his later philosophy. Section 107 begins by pointing out that "The more narrowly we examine actual language, the sharper becomes the conflict between it and our requirement." By "our requirement," Wittgenstein means not only the absolute rigour that he, Frege, and Russell had demanded of formal logic, but also such impositions as the thesis of the determinacy of sense, or the doctrine of the logical independence of elementary propositions: "For the crystalline purity of logic was, of course, not a *result of investigation*: it was a requirement."[29] In the next section of the *Philosophical Investigations*, Wittgenstein elaborates his response in the following terms: "—The *preconceived idea* of crystalline purity can only be removed by turning our whole examination round. (One might say: the axis of reference of our examination must be rotated, but about the fixed point of our real need.)"[30] This is immediately followed by an amplification of the message of the draft written in 1930. Read against the backdrop of the nonspatial, nontemporal conception of immediate experience to which he had been attracted, it becomes clear that his words must have originally had a quite specific target:

> The philosophy of logic speaks of sentences and words in exactly the sense in which we speak of them in ordinary life when we say e.g. "Here is a Chinese sentence," or "No, that only looks like writing, it is actually just an ornament" and so on.
> We are talking about the spatial and temporal phenomenon of language, not about some non-spatial, non-temporal phantasm. [Note in margin: Only it is possible to be interested in a phenomenon in a variety of ways.] But we talk about it as we do about the pieces of chess when we are stating the rules of the game, not describing their physical properties.
> The question "What is a word really?" is analogous to "What is a piece in chess?"[31]

But matters were far less clear-cut in 1930. Even though he wrote then that he should like to start with "books, as it were," that philosophy should begin with our everyday use of language, what we ordinarily do and say, with whatever can be written down in a book, that train of thought leads him to propose beginning with "all is in flux"—"*Alles fliesst*"—the very words he had used to describe the fleeting, evanescent, and ungraspable character of immediate experience. At this point in his philosophical development, he remained convinced that our everyday use of language only derives its meaning from its contact with the flux of present experience, and his attempted resolution of the conflict between what he wanted to say and his recognition that such philosophical theses are nonsense remained closer to the Tractarian attempt to preserve the "truth in solipsism" than the *Investigations'* insistence on the primacy of everyday practice.

6.2 Leading Words Back from Their Metaphysical Use

In a discussion of how language represents what is seen, dated February 4, 1931, Wittgenstein once again refers to the problem of the specious present slipping away,

29. *Philosophical Investigations*, §107, in parentheses.
30. *Philosophical Investigations*, §108.
31. *Philosophical Investigations*, §108.

the river of time continually bearing experience away from us. But this time, he gives up his early river image. He writes:

> That all is in flux seems to prevent us from expressing the truth, for it as though we can't get hold of it, since it slips away from us.

> But it doesn't prevent us from expressing something. —We know what it means to want to get hold of something fleeting in a description. That happens, say, when we forget the one while we want to describe the other. But that's not what we are dealing with here. And that's how the expression /word/ "fleeting" is to be applied.

> We lead words back from their metaphysical use to their correct use in language.

> The man who said that one couldn't step twice in the same river, said something false. One can step twice into the same river.

> And that's how the solution of all philosophical difficulties looks. Their answers, if they are correct, must be everyday and ordinary. But one must only look at them in the right spirit, then it makes no difference.

> But given this answer, "But you know how sentences do it, for nothing is concealed," one would like to say: "Yes, but it all flows by so quickly and I should like to see it laid open to view, as it were."

> But here also we go wrong. For in this case, too, nothing happens which eludes us rapidly.[32]

A few pages later, he sums up this train of thought in the following terms: "The analogy of the flow /flowing/ of time is naturally misleading and, if we stick with it, must lead /bring and/ us into difficulties."[33]

In sharp contrast with his earlier work, Wittgenstein now insists that it is possible to step twice into the same river: people do step more than once into the same river and we can talk about it, just as we can talk about some things being fleeting. In each case, he holds that we should contrast cases in which we genuinely see fleeting things, or genuinely find ourselves unable to step into a river the second time, with cases in which we can encounter something a second time. As a result, Wittgenstein rejects the thesis that "all is in flux," as ungrammatical, because it misuses the term "flux." It just is not true that everything is in flux—some things, such as fast-moving rivers, are, and some things, such as the bedrock over which the river flows, are not. The philosopher attempts to apply the term to everything and creates a nonsensical proposition.

Similarly, in the *Blue Book,* Wittgenstein compares the problem of grasping the nature of the flux of experience with the problems created by popular scientists, such as Arthur Eddington, who told people that a table isn't really solid, for the wood is mainly empty space occupied by a rapidly moving cloud of electrons.[34] Here "solidity" is misapplied in the claim that the wood isn't solid, for it is quite obviously rigid

---

32. MS 110, pp. 33–35, 4 February 1931. The penultimate paragraph is an early version of the third paragraph of *Philosophical Investigations*, §435. [German in appendix.]

33. MS 110, p. 39, 5 February 1931. [German in appendix.]

34. Arthur Eddington, *The Nature of the Physical World*, pp. ix ff.

and substantial, regardless of whether or not its smallest components are evenly distributed in space. As a result, the picture of the electrons whizzing around is misapplied:

> As in this example the word "solidity" was used wrongly and it seemed that we had shown that nothing was really solid, just in this way, in stating our puzzles about the *general vagueness* of sense-experience, and about the flux of all phenomena, we are using the words "flux" and "vagueness" wrongly, in a typically metaphysical way, without an antithesis; whereas in their correct and everyday use vagueness is opposed to clearness, flux to stability, inaccuracy to accuracy, and *problem* to *solution*.[35]

The core of Wittgenstein's criticism can already be found in the *Theaetetus*: if all were in flux, one would be unable to say anything coherent at all. You couldn't even talk about the thing that is in flux, because as soon as you talk about it, it is no longer that thing but something else, for otherwise it wouldn't have been changing and so wouldn't have been in flux. In other words, the extreme flux thesis makes communication impossible. We need to recognize that only some things are in flux, that the term only makes sense in contrast with other cases where it is not applicable. In the following passage, Socrates sets out what he takes the extreme flux thesis to amount to:

> SOCRATES: Since not even this stays constant, that the flowing thing flows white, but it changes, so that there's flux of that very thing, whiteness, and change to another colour, in order not to be convicted of staying constant in that respect— since that's so, can it ever be possible to refer to any colour in such a way as to be speaking of it rightly?
>
> THEODORUS: How could it be, Socrates? Indeed, how could it be possible to do so with any other thing of that kind, if it's always slipping away while one is speaking; as it must be, given that it's in flux?[36]

Socrates goes on to argue that his conclusion is equally applicable to anything else one might say; if the flux thesis were true, then language would be useless:

> SOCRATES: We were eager to show that all things change, so that it might become clear that that answer was correct. But what has in fact become clear is, apparently, that if all things do change, then every answer, whatever it's about, is equally correct: both that things are so and that they're not so, or if you like, both that things come to be so and that they come to be not so, so as not to bring those people to a standstill by what we say.
>
> THEODORUS: You're right.
>
> SOCRATES: Yes, Theodorus, except that I said "so" and "not so." One oughtn't even to use this word "so," because what's so wouldn't any longer be changing; and, again, one oughtn't to use "not so," because that isn't a change either. No, those who state that theory must establish some other language, because as things are they haven't got expressions for their hypothesis: unless, perhaps, "not even so," said in an indefinite sense, might suit them best.[37]

35. *Blue Book*, pp. 45–46.
36. Plato, *Theaetetus*, 182d.
37. Plato, *Theaetetus*, 183a–b.

Socrates' argument anticipates one of Wittgenstein's objections to the very idea of a private language: some standard of correctness is necessary if we are to have a language at all, and a world in total flux cannot provide such a standard.

Although Wittgenstein now came to repudiate the flux thesis, instead of explicitly rejecting it while implicitly affirming it as he had done earlier, he still respected what motivated it. In a passage written shortly after the lengthy rejection of the flux thesis quoted at the beginning of this section, he wrote: "The fundamental, expressed grammatically: What about the sentence: 'One cannot step into the same river twice'?"[38]

Indeed, a couple of years after Wittgenstein repudiated his earlier river image, we find him restating his old thesis that the essence of the world cannot be expressed by language, reiterating the very words that had summed up his argument for that conclusion in his notebooks and the *Philosophical Remarks*: "What belongs to the essence of the world cannot be expressed by language. For this reason, it cannot *say* that all is in flux. Language can only say those things we could also imagine otherwise."[39] In its new setting, however, the passage is presented as a prime example of a philosophical mistake. It is the first paragraph of section 91 of the Big Typescript, a section with a lengthy title that sums up Wittgenstein's conception of how such philosophical problems arise. It reads:

> Philosophical problems don't confront us in practical life (as scientific problems do, for instance) but only if we allow our ideas about the formation of our propositions to be guided not by their practical purpose but rather certain analogies in our language.[40]

In the paragraphs that follow, Wittgenstein treats his introductory paragraph as a prototypical example of how a philosophical problem can arise from misleading linguistic analogies, rejecting his earlier attempts to talk about the relation of language and world as nonsensical. In 1929 and 1930 he had explained the thesis that one cannot say that all is in flux by invoking the inexpressible act of applying language to the world, the verification of propositions within present experience. At this stage, he was still prepared to draw a sharp distinction between a game, which he thought of as merely conventional, and real language, which in addition to its rules, outside the signs, has its application to reality. The application connects language and reality, yet cannot be stated or explained in language. When he set out these points in his lectures in the early 1930s, he stressed the crucial role of the application of language to reality in distinguishing it from a convention, speaking as if the philosopher could somehow step back from our ordinary use of language and see which conventions are applied to reality and which are not: "What distinguishes language from a game in this sense is its application to reality. . . . Conventions presuppose the application of language: they do not talk about the application of language."[41]

---

38. *Zettel*, §459. Source: MS 110, p. 155, May or June 1931.

39. Big Typescript, §91, p. 427. The same words are used in *Philosophical Remarks*, §54, the only difference being that the first sentence forms a separate paragraph.

40. Big Typescript, §91, p. 427.

41. *Wittgenstein's Lectures, Cambridge, 1930–32*, pp. 12–13. Cf. the discussion of the limits of logic in chapter 2, section 2.

In the Big Typescript, on the other hand, Wittgenstein is quite clear that there is no position outside language from which to survey the application of language to the world: that relationship is itself part of the grammar of our language: "The application of language is also described in grammar; what one would like to call the connection between language and reality."[42] Wittgenstein now insists that it is essential that the application of language be described, rather than left shrouded in the realm of the unsayable.

Typescript 212, the collection of cuttings that formed the basis for Wittgenstein's construction of Typescript 213, the finished Big Typescript, records some of the main stages in the revisions that led to the discussion of the flux thesis in the Big Typescript, moving away from the idea "all is in flux" gestured at an insight into the application of language to reality that could not be stated. Wittgenstein had his typist mark the sentence "That all is in flux must lie in the essence of the application of language to reality" with a pair of question marks and later crossed it out altogether. Thus the preparatory draft for the first two paragraphs of section 91 of the Big Typescript read as follows:

> What belongs to the essence of the world cannot be expressed by language. For this reason, it cannot *say* that all is in flux. Language can only say what we can also imagine otherwise.
> ~~That all is in flux must lie in the essence of the application of language to reality.~~ // That all is in flux must lie in the essence of the contact of language with reality. // Or better: that all is in flux must lie in the essence of language.[43]

In both drafts, the conclusion is the same: instead of looking to the specious present, the site where he had supposed that language and the world must meet, he turns our attention to the nature of language itself. And in both drafts, the second paragraph continues by offering a preliminary diagnosis of the circumstances in which the feeling that the nature of experience eludes us arises. Wittgenstein begins by reminding the reader that such thoughts do not strike us ordinarily, any more than we usually think about the blurred edges of our visual field. We only entertain thoughts about the essence of the world, or the application of language to present experience, when we try to formulate a philosophical theory. Specifically, he proposes that these misunderstandings arise when we are misled into wanting "to form propositions contrary to the grammar of time."[44] These words are a cryptic reference to the cinematic model of language and world, and the resultant distinction between experiential and physicalistic conceptions of time. Our everyday temporal terms are inapplicable to the timeless present, and if we try to talk about the fleeting or transitory nature of experience, we will run up against the grammatical distinction between the primary and the secondary.

---

42. Big Typescript, §94, p. 441. [German in appendix.] See also the criticism of the idea that language is composed of an inorganic mechanism animated by an organic meaning-giving activity in the *Blue Book*, pp. 3 ff.

43. TS 212, the immediate source for the Big Typescript; as the typescript is a collection of cuttings, it does not have page numbers. Cf. Big Typescript, §91, p. 427. Once again, these remarks immediately follow the passage from §54 of the *Philosophical Remarks*, quoted at the beginning of §1.

44. Big Typescript, §91, p. 427.

Wittgenstein goes on to describe the phenomenology of the problem in greater detail, using his description as the basis for a much more specific account of how the problem arises. On the one hand, we feel "we are hindered from getting a firm hold on that which is actual, the actual reality. The process on the screen slips away from us just because it is a process."[45] On the other hand, we do describe something, and "obviously, the description is directly connected with the picture on the screen."[46] We seem to face a dilemma: either the descriptive power of language is limited or our feeling of limitation is unjustified. Wittgenstein's answer is that we are not really losing anything—"what we could want to describe, we could describe"[47]—but that we need to understand the "false picture" that is responsible for the sense of loss if we are to agree with him. That false picture, Wittgenstein suggests, is "the picture of a filmstrip which goes by so rapidly that we don't have time to get the picture."[48] On this view, experience slips away from us like the pictures on a strip of film or a series of roadside hoardings seen from a speeding car: there really is a fleeting picture that one cannot see clearly, and if one wanted to, one could go back and take a better look at it; on the other hand, there is just nothing analogous that continually slips away from us in our everyday experience.[49] Because we project aspects of the projector and *its* operation into our understanding of ourselves, we mistakenly feel "that the present disappears into the past without our being able to prevent it," and so we suffer from the illusion that experience is slipping away from us before we can describe it fully.[50]

Wittgenstein further examines the idea of an indescribable experience in a section of the Big Typescript entitled "The representation of immediate experience." He raises the question whether any description of immediate experience can "fully describe" that experience. In other words, can any description, however circumscribed—Wittgenstein once again offers as an example "it seems that there is a lamp on the table in front of me"[51]—yield a complete description of what is experienced, or will it leave something out? He phrases the question as follows: "Is it correct to say: my visual image is so complicated it is impossible to fully describe it? That is a very fundamental question."[52] We know how to describe everyday physical objects, such as a painted picture or the lamp on the table next to me, and it is easy to imagine cases in which we cannot fully describe such an object, perhaps because the painting is too complex or the design of the lamp too strange. But these are familiar difficulties, and the kinds of further investigation they call for are also familiar. In the case

45. Big Typescript, §91, p. 427.
46. Big Typescript, §91, p. 428. Cf. MS 110, pp. 38–39, the source manuscript, dated 5 January 1931.
47. Big Typescript, §91, p. 428.
48. Big Typescript, §91, p. 428. The final phrase of this sentence is "*ein Bild aufzufassen*," which could also be translated as "to grasp a picture conceptually."
49. Big Typescript, §91, p. 428.
50. *Philosophical Remarks*, §52; Big Typescript, §91, p. 428. The first two paragraphs of §52 of the *Remarks* anticipate the more detailed treatment in the Big Typescript. For some more general criticism of talk of the "flow of time" and the misconceptions it can lead to, see the *Brown Book*, pp. 107 ff. and *Eine Philosophische Betrachtung*, pp. 156 ff.
51. Big Typescript, §101, pp. 489–490. [German in appendix.]
52. Big Typescript, §101, p. 490. [German in appendix.]

of the objects of immediate experience, on the other hand, no such investigation is supposed to even be possible. How, then, are we to conceive of an indescribable experiential content?

At this point, Wittgenstein allows an interlocutory voice to describe a case in which one might say that one's experience is indescribable: "'The flower was a reddish yellow which, however, I cannot describe more accurately (or, more accurately with words).'"[53] Wittgenstein pushes his interlocutor to explain what he means and receives the following reply: "'I see it in front of me and could paint it.'"[54] This is certainly an intelligible way of explaining why words alone might not be precise enough, for we can paint dozens of distinguishable reddish yellows. By the same token, it also means the colour isn't truly indescribable, for we now have a way of accurately describing it, once we recognize painting as part of our means of description. Wittgenstein suggests that is the idea of some further means of description which for some reason is inaccessible, rather like a ruler one always keeps at arm's length from the object to be measured, or the carrot dangling at the end of a donkey's nose, that generates the idea that there is something we are aware of but yet are unable to describe:

> If one says one couldn't describe this colour more accurately with words, then one (always) thinks of a possibility of such a description (of course, for otherwise the word //expression// "accurate description" would make no sense) and it reminds one of the case of a measurement which isn't carried out for the lack of adequate means.[55]

The feeling that we "can't get at what this colour, or a similar one, would have," or that "one can't give any description by which one could accurately reproduce the picture" arises from this misconception.[56] It leads to the illusion that there must be some form of representation that would allow us to accurately reproduce the immediately given. But we do have words to describe the way the flower looks, and if that is not enough, we can paint it. Any further form of representation we can imagine holding at arm's length, we can also imagine applying. Instead, we arrive at the idea of a more accurate reproduction of experience by imagining that there is some other method of reproduction that is currently unavailable. Here, once again, we are misled by the analogy with the investigation of such things as pictures, where new methods may indeed be discovered. In the case of visual experience:

> We can speak no *further* of the visual picture, than our language now reaches. And also *mean* (think) no more // further // than our language says // reaches //. (Not mean more than we can say.)[57]

> One of the most dangerous comparisons is that of the visual field with a painted surface (or, what comes to the same, a coloured spatial model.)

53. Big Typescript, §101, p. 490. [German in appendix.]
54. Big Typescript, §101, p. 490. [German in appendix.]
55. Big Typescript, §101, p. 490. [German in appendix.]
56. Big Typescript, §101, pp. 490–491. [German in appendix.]
57. Cf. *Tractatus*, 5.61: "We cannot think what we cannot think; so what we cannot think we cannot *say* either."

This hangs together with: Could I then recognize the visual picture "in every detail"? Or, rather, does this question make any sense?

For a painted picture or model still seems to us to be the least objectionable representation of a visual picture. But, that the question concerning "recognition in every detail" is senseless already shows how inadequate picture and model are.[58]

Wittgenstein's account of how a "false picture" had made him want to say that "all is flux" and led him to think that experience cannot be fully described illustrates how his conception of experience had been coloured by the magic lantern metaphor. Given that the words in question, taken literally, make no sense, we have to look to the analogies that motivate them if we are to understand what we were trying to say. This change in his treatment of the flux thesis turns on a new conception of the role of language in philosophy. We need to look at our use of language to understand both how we were misled into affirming that all is in flux and the true role that flux and stability do play in our lives. This positive role for language, the way language is meant to help us see these things, is intimated in the next passage, a descendant of Wittgenstein's original recantation of the flux thesis:

> We bring words back from their metaphysical to their everyday use. (The man who said one can't step twice into the same river, said something false; one *can* step twice into the same river. —And sometimes an object ceases to exist when I stop looking at it, and sometimes it doesn't. —And sometimes we *know* which colour the other sees, if he looks at this object, and sometimes we don't.) And this is how the solution of all philosophical difficulties looks. Our answers, if they are to be correct, must be everyday and trivial. —For these answers make fun of the questions, as it were.
>
> From where does our investigation get its importance, since it seems only to destroy everything interesting, that is, all that is great and important? (As it were, all the buildings; leaving behind only bits of stone and rubble.) What we are destroying is nothing but castles in the air, and we are clearing up the ground of language on which they stand.
>
> The results of philosophy are the uncovering of one or another piece of plain nonsense and bumps that the understanding has got by running up to the end [*alternate word, also in text*: limits] of language. They, the bumps, make us see the value of that discovery.[59]

In this early version of some of the central methodological passages of the *Philosophical Investigations*, he gives examples of specific philosophical problems and the platitudes he would offer in reply. In the subsequent reworking, the exposition becomes increasingly compressed and the parenthetical illustrations drop out.

---

58. Big Typescript, §101, p. 491. [German in appendix.]

59. Early Investigations, §111 (113). [German in appendix.] All three paragraphs were first drafted during 1930–1931; they are from the first stratum of drafts which ultimately led to the published *Philosophical Investigations*. Many of these remarks are about philosophical method and the nature of language. For the first paragraph, see the second paragraph of *Investigations*, §116, which is based on the first sentence alone. For the second paragraph, see *Investigations* §118. The first two sentences were composed in 1931 (MS 112, p. 229) and are also in the Big Typescript, §88; the last was added in 1937 (MS 157b, p. 33). For the third paragraph, see *Philosophical Investigations*, §119, and MS 108, p. 247, 1930.

The dual roles that are given to language in these passages—the notion of language as the stable ground on which the metaphysical cloud castles are built and the notion of language as a home from which language has gone astray—are developed further in the final version:

> When philosophers use a word—"knowledge," "being," "object," "I," "proposition," "name,"—and try to grasp the *essence* of the thing, one must always ask oneself: is the word ever actually used this way in the language [*Sprache*] which is its original home?
>
> What *we* do is to bring words back from their metaphysical to their everyday use.[60]

To understand words as they are used in philosophy we have to trace them to their use in ordinary language, back to the ways we ordinarily use them. But to understand what Wittgenstein meant by "ordinary language," one has to look at his philosophical practice. While his later remarks on philosophical method stress the importance of ordinary language, there is no new conception of the essence of language in the *Investigations*, to be set against the Tractarian conception of language as representation.

6.3 Wittgenstein's Treatment of Private Language

Philosophical interpretation of the work of a major philosopher often takes on a life of its own, so that discussion focusses on the positions taken in the most influential interpretations of certain key passages or theses. In the case of the "private language argument," a term that Wittgenstein may never even have used—it does not occur anywhere in his published writing—much of the debate is entirely independent of Wittgenstein's alleged views on the topic. This state of affairs has arisen because most philosophers have taken it for granted that Wittgenstein must be giving some argument from theses that we can all accept to the conclusion that a private language is impossible, and have only disagreed about the form the premises must take and how successful the resultant arguments actually are. As a result, they have seen Wittgenstein's treatment in the *Philosophical Investigations* of the search for a "language which describes my inner experiences and which only I myself can understand,"[61] as hinting at an argument concerning Wittgenstein's conception of the relationship between experience and language that can and should be spelled out in detail.

But it is no accident that Wittgenstein never turned section 243 ff. of the *Philosophical Investigations* into the systematic formulations of the "private language argument" that so many of his interpreters have provided. The passages in question were meant to show that the intuitions that fuel such philosophical theories are only compelling if they are left unexamined, not that some other theory is correct. A full defence of my reading, which would call for lengthy exposition and analysis of the relevant passages in the *Philosophical Investigations*, together with an evaluation of

---

60. *Philosophical Investigations*, §116. Cf. Big Typescript, §91, pp. 429–430.
61. *Philosophical Investigations*, §256.

a representative range of the wide variety of competing interpretations that have become part of the ongoing scholarly debate, cannot be undertaken here. Instead, I will limit myself to contrasting two particularly accessible introductory expositions of Wittgenstein's treatment of private language. The first is Saul Kripke's reading of Wittgenstein, presented at a Wittgenstein conference in 1976 and more fully developed in his short book, *Wittgenstein on Rules and Private Language*, which has become a well-established reference point in the literature. The second is Wittgenstein's own exposition of his approach to the topic of a "private language" in a set of notes entitled "Notes for the 'Philosophical Lecture.'"[62] The lecture in question was the annual "Philosophical Lecture" of the British Academy on a philosophical topic by a distinguished speaker for a general audience. Wittgenstein was invited to give the 1942 lecture in April 1941, but after initially accepting, he later declined, citing the pressure of other work. The exposition is often much blunter than the nuanced and elusive treatment one finds in the *Investigations*. But the less direct presentation in the *Investigations*, where Wittgenstein prefers to engage in dialogue with opposing voices and is much more reluctant to elaborate a positive view, is essentially a development of the critique of private language set out in these lecture notes.

According to Kripke, the *Philosophical Investigations* sets out a radical scepticism about meaning: he argues that Wittgenstein is committed to the thesis that there is never any fact of the matter about what a speaker's utterance means. Kripke sets out the basic structure of his reading of Wittgenstein in the following terms: "A certain problem, or in Humean terminology, a 'sceptical paradox' is presented concerning the notion of a rule. Following this, what Hume would have called a 'sceptical solution' to the problem is presented."[63] Kripke states the "sceptical paradox" he has in mind by quoting the first sentence of *Philosophical Investigations*, section 201: "This was our paradox: no course of action could be determined by a rule, because every course of action can be made out to accord with the rule."[64] Like Wittgenstein, Kripke uses a simple mathematical example to explain how his paradox arises. He introduces the notion of "quaddition," a specially constructed function which is a deviant relative of addition. Quaddition is defined in such a way that every past sum he performed was a case of both addition and quaddition, but the two functions diverge in the values they yield for some of the sums not yet considered. Kripke asks us to consider two numbers that he has not yet added, say 68 and 57; the sceptic asks him why he thinks they yield 125 rather than 5. The sceptic wants to know (a) whether there is any fact that he meant plus, not quus, in the past, (b) whether he has any reason to be so confident that he should answer "125" rather than "5." Both questions need to be answered if we are to have a reply to the sceptic. That is, we need both (a) "an account of what fact it is (about my mental state) that constitutes my meaning plus, not quus" and (b) to "show how I am justified in giving the answer '125' to '68 + 57.'"[65] Kripke argues that no such response is possible. All the past sums are equally com-

62. Ludwig Wittgenstein, "Notes for the 'Philosophical Lecture,'" ed. D. Stern, in *Wittgenstein Philosophical Occasions*, pp. 445–458.
63. Kripke, *Wittgenstein on Rules and Private Language*, pp. 3–4.
64. Kripke, *Wittgenstein on Rules and Private Language*, p. 7.
65. Kripke, *Wittgenstein on Rules and Private Language*, p. 11.

patible with the hypothesis that he used plus or quus, and anything he may have said about the nature of the rule is wide open to a further deviant interpretation. Any more basic rule we appeal to simply invites a repetition of the sceptical move.[66]

On Kripke's reading, there can be no "straight solution" to the sceptical problem, one that would show the sceptic to be wrong. As a result, the sceptic is right: there are no facts about meaning, and a person is unjustified in using one form of words rather than another. Kripke takes Wittgenstein to accept the sceptical conclusion and so maintain both (a) that there is no fact about whether plus or quus is meant and (b) that there is no justification for one response rather than another. So Kripke's Wittgenstein gives a "sceptical solution": he concedes that the sceptic is right, but maintains that our ordinary practice is justified, because it does not require the kind of justification the sceptic has shown to be untenable.[67]

On Kripke's reading of Wittgenstein, following a rule consists in doing as one's community does, and that is not something one can do by oneself. "Ultimately we reach a level where we act without any reason in terms of which we can justify our action. We act unhesitatingly but *blindly*."[68] What justifies these actions, when they are justified, is not any fact about me, but is determined by the public checks on my conformity to the rule that are provided by my linguistic community. These basic considerations about meaning are consistent with the sceptical conclusion about meaning, considered individualistically: the meaning of my words is always determined by my linguistic community. On the "community view" of meaning, it is impossible for someone to give a word meaning in isolation from the practices of a community of language users; words only have meaning in the context of the practices of a particular linguistic community. Kripke contends that this reading is strongly supported by the fact that the summary and resolution of the paradox in section 201 is followed by section 202, which reads as follows:

> And hence also "obeying a rule" is a practice. And to *think* one is obeying a rule is not to obey a rule. Hence it is not possible to obey a rule "privately": otherwise thinking one was obeying a rule would be the same thing as obeying it.

This, Kripke maintains, is Wittgenstein's principal argument against the existence of a private language: there is no fact of the matter about whether I am using a rule when I am considered individualistically; it is only my membership within a linguistic community that gives content to the notion of my being justified in using words as I do.[69] Wittgenstein's argument for the impossibility of a private language, construed by Kripke as the thesis that a person in isolation from a community could not use language, is thus already set out in section 202; the further discussion of private language in section 243 ff. is only a corollary of the prior sceptical argument about rule-following.

In response to the question why Wittgenstein never explicitly endorses Kripke's "sceptical solution," Kripke turns Wittgenstein's opposition to theses on its head:

66. Kripke, *Wittgenstein on Rules and Private Language*, pp. 16 ff.
67. Kripke, *Wittgenstein on Rules and Private Language*, p. 66.
68. Kripke, *Wittgenstein on Rules and Private Language*, p. 87.
69. Kripke, *Wittgenstein on Rules and Private Language*, p. 89.

> Had Wittgenstein—contrary to his notorious and cryptic maxim in §128[70]—stated the outcome of his conclusions in the form of definite theses, it would have been very difficult to avoid formulating his doctrines in a form that consists in apparent sceptical denials of our ordinary assertions.[71]

Like many other readers, Kripke treats Wittgenstein's opposition to theses as a device that allows Wittgenstein to avoid stating the controversial theses he supposedly really believes—the theses the reader finds in Wittgenstein's writing. Kripke does give voice to his suspicion "that to attempt to present Wittgenstein's argument precisely is to some extent to falsify it".[72] "So," he warns the reader, "the present paper should be thought of as expounding neither 'Wittgenstein's' argument nor 'Kripke's': rather Wittgenstein's argument as it struck Kripke, as it presented a problem for him."[73] In the preface, he emphasizes that his primary purpose is

> the presentation of a problem and an argument, not its critical evaluation. Primarily I can be read, except in a few obvious asides, as almost like an attorney presenting a major philosophical argument as it struck me. If the work has a main thesis of its own, it is that Wittgenstein's sceptical problem and argument are important, deserving of serious consideration.[74]

As a result, Kripke restricts his "elementary exposition" to an exposition of his interpretation of Wittgenstein's rule-following argument; evaluation is left for another occasion.

Kripke's reading of Wittgenstein on meaning has certainly succeeded in focussing critical attention on the central importance of Wittgenstein's treatment of meaning, rules and rule-following. But as an exposition of Wittgenstein's treatment of rules and private language, it must be considered a failure. Kripke failed to see that the paradox of section 201 is a problem for the voice the author argues with, the "interlocutor." The sceptical paradox only arises if one thinks of grasping a rule as a matter of being able to say something that explains the meaning of the words in question, for which Wittgenstein reserves the term "interpretation" ("*Deuten*").[75] Indeed, that is the main moral of this section of the *Philosophical Investigations*: the interlocutor's view is mistaken precisely because he views interpreting as essential to grasping a rule. Thus, despite the fact that Kripke makes so much of the first paragraph of section 201, where Wittgenstein sums up "our paradox" and his initial reply to it, he never quotes or even refers to the second paragraph, where Wittgenstein replies that the paradox is due to a mistaken conception of understanding as a matter of "interpreting," providing explanations where one substitutes one expression of a rule for another. Wittgenstein contrasts that mistaken conception and the Kripkean problems it leads to with the idea that following a rule is a practical ability:

70. "If one tried to advance *theses* in philosophy, it would never be possible to debate them, because everyone would agree to them" (*Philosophical Investigations*, §128). See p. 17.
71. Kripke, *Wittgenstein on Rules and Private Language*, p. 69.
72. Kripke, *Wittgenstein on Rules and Private Language*, p. 5.
73. Kripke, *Wittgenstein on Rules and Private Language*, p. 5.
74. Kripke, *Wittgenstein on Rules and Private Language*, p. ix.
75. "There is an inclination to say: every action according to a rule is an interpretation. But we ought to restrict the term "interpretation" to the substitution of one expression of the rule for another" (*Philosophical Investigations*, §201).

It can be seen that there is a misunderstanding here from the mere fact that in the course of our train of thought we give one interpretation after another; as if each one contented us at least for a moment, until we thought of yet another standing behind it. What this shows is that there is a way of grasping a rule which is *not* an *interpretation*, but which is expressed in what we call "obeying the rule" and "going against it" in actual cases.[76]

This way of grasping a rule without interpreting it, doing the right thing without thinking about what the words mean, is the core of Wittgenstein's response to the supposed regress of interpretations. Questions of interpretation only arise if there is reason to doubt whether one has grasped the rule, and such interpretation depends on a background of unquestioned rule-following.

In a sense, Wittgenstein provides us with what Kripke would call a "straight" solution, for he maintains that the sceptic is wrong. But it would be highly misleading to put matters this way, for Wittgenstein would have regarded Kripke's sceptical thesis and paradoxical solution as equally nonsensical consequences of a mistaken conception of language and rules. Kripke's extended discussion of the correct formulation of the sceptical doubt and the paradox of the first paragraph of section 201 is itself an exposition of the very standpoint that Wittgenstein criticizes in the second and third paragraphs of section 201.[77] In the *Philosophical Investigations*, Wittgenstein responds to the question "What is your aim in philosophy?" with "To show the fly the way out of the fly-bottle."[78] A fly-bottle is a glass bottle containing sugar-water with an entrance at the bottom, which flies never escape because they always fly upward, hitting the glass and ultimately drowning in the water. Kripke's exposition is a picture of the fly-bottle from within: because he cannot see any alternative to a conception of understanding as interpretation, he is unable to resolve the sceptical paradox.

In the *Philosophical Investigations*, Wittgenstein introduces the topic of private language by listing some of the many ways one can ordinarily talk to oneself—"a human being can encourage himself, give himself orders, obey, blame and punish himself; he can ask himself a question and answer it."[79] After observing that we can even imagine people who spoke only in monologue, he asks whether we could also imagine a language that someone could write down or express his inner experiences "for his private use." Obviously, there is a sense in which we can all do that in our ordinary language, but that is not what he has in mind: "The words of this language are to refer to what can only be known to the speaker; to his immediate, private sensations. So another person cannot understand the language."[80] In this way, the notion of a private language, a "language which describes my inner experiences and which only I myself can understand,"[81] is introduced as a seemingly natural extension of uses of language that are already familiar. But the words of that language

76. *Philosophical Investigations*, §201, second paragraph.
77. As a result, Kripke has focussed critical attention on the sceptical view that Wittgenstein opposed, an achievement in its own right.
78. *Philosophical Investigations*, §309.
79. *Philosophical Investigations*, §243.
80. *Philosophical Investigations*, §243.
81. *Philosophical Investigations*, §256.

cannot be used in the same way as we ordinarily use words to stand for sensations, for our ordinary use of such terms is tied up with the language that we use to express ourselves in public, including the "natural expressions" that enable others to under-stand what one experiences. Responding to this objection, Wittgenstein's interlocu-tor suggests that we can just attach a name to a sensation without any of the usual publicly accessible procedures: "But suppose I didn't have any natural expression for the sensation, but only had the sensation? And now I simply *associate* names with sensations and use these names in descriptions."[82] In the "Notes for the 'Philosophi-cal Lecture,'" Wittgenstein characterizes the conception of language and experience that motivates such attempts to forge a direct link between inner experience and the inner use of language in the following terms:

> We mustn't think that we understand the working of a word in lang[uage] if we say it is a name which we give to some sort of pr[ivate] experience which we have. The idea is here: we *have* something, it is as it were before the mind's eye (or some other sense) and we give it a name. What could be simpler? One might say /could put it roughly this way/: All ostensive definition explains the use of a word only when it makes one last determination, removes one last indeterminacy.[83]

In other words: any public act of ostensive definition is ambiguous until one estab-lishes a private link between the word and something within experience.

Wittgenstein opens the "Notes for the 'Philosophical Lecture'" by discussing the crucial question of what he means by "private experience." In his opening paragraph, he describes this privacy as a "superprivacy." In taking our everyday notion of pri-vacy out of context and applying it to experience as a whole, Wittgenstein charges philosophy with transmuting it into a "superconcept," a concept that is apparently significant but, because it has been deprived of the specific context that gave it its meaning, it no longer does any real work.[84] Wittgenstein describes the "essential characteristic" of privacy in the following terms: "Nobody but I can see it, feel it, hear it; nobody except myself knows what it's like. Nobody except I can get at it."[85] This is still potentially ambiguous, for there is a crucial difference between a case of everyday privacy, on which nobody can know about what I choose to keep private unless I tell them about it, and the superprivacy, on which I cannot show my feel-ings, no matter what I do:

> Privacy of feelings can mean: nobody can know them unless I show them, or: I can't really show them. Or: if I don't want to, I needn't give any sign of my feel-ing but even if I want to I can only show a sign and not the feeling.[86]

Wittgenstein argues that this ambiguity creates a dilemma for the defender of the notion of *"private* experience." If he or she means nothing more than everyday pri-vacy, then the language for talk about experience is on the same level as the rest of our language, and inner ostension plays no particularly privileged role in establish-ing the meaning of terms for what we see. If he or she means to talk of superprivacy,

82. *Philosophical Investigations*, §256.
83. *Philosophical Occasions*, pp. 447–448.
84. Cf. *Philosophical Investigations*, §97.
85. *Philosophical Occasions*, p. 447.
86. *Philosophical Occasions*, p. 447.

then the language in question has been cut off from our everyday language, but at the price of robbing it of any sense at all.

Wittgenstein's overall argument in these passages takes the form of a *reductio*. He tries to show us that his interlocutor's account of inner ostension—privately applying names to sensations—faces a dilemma, and that either horn of the dilemma leads back to ordinary language. Either the putative private linguist has tacitly presupposed the categories and techniques of our ordinary use of language in setting up the private language, and so it is not really private, or the inner ostension really is *sui generis*. In the latter case, Wittgenstein responds, nothing has been said, for no criterion has been established that would give content to the claim that what I am now experiencing is (or is not) the same as the experience to which I originally attached the name.

This is what Malcolm calls Wittgenstein's "internal" attack on private language: one assumes, for the sake of argument, that an act of private inner ostension has taken place, and then shows that the idea that one could go on to make use of such a definition in isolation from any check on one's usage is incoherent.[87] After asking us to imagine the purported private linguist using a sign on a given occasion, it is then argued that when the person next tries to use that sign, he or she will be unable to distinguish between using it correctly or incorrectly, and so nothing has been achieved. However, such arguments usually depend on an appeal to some form of verificationism, or scepticism about a solitary speaker's abilities, challenging the speaker's memory or ability to check his or her usage. All these moves depend on selectively raising sceptical questions about an individual's use of words that could just as well be applied to the community.[88] These interpretations fail because they try to do too much: they turn an objection to a theory Wittgenstein opposes—if you conceive of inner ostension as primary, and attempt to construct the outer out of the inner, you will be unable to even talk about the inner—into a freestanding argument for a positive theory of mind, a theory that is usually constructed by taking some of Wittgenstein's hints and suggestions about how to understand our use of language and turning them into a system of dogmatic theses. For instance, his remarks about the importance of use in understanding the meaning of words, or of expression in the case of first-person avowals, are frequently read as implying a "use" or "assertability condition" theory of meaning and an "expressive" theory of avowals.

One might naturally expect the internal argument against a private language to

---

87. Norman Malcolm, "Wittgenstein's *Philosophical Investigations*," pp. 65–75.

88. If the sceptical argument that a single speaker of a language can never know what he or she means is a good one, then it can equally well be levelled against a linguistic community. Conversely, if there is a solution to the sceptical problem that works for the community, then an isolated individual ought to be able to make use of it, too. In a footnote added while his book was in proof, Kripke alludes to such difficulties but leaves further discussion for another occasion (Kripke, *Wittgenstein on Rules and Private Language*, p. 146, n. 87.) The chief difficulty for defenders of the "community view" lies in justifying the claim that it is in principle impossible for a person who is not part of a community to speak a language. If one examines the standards that are supposedly set up and maintained by a linguistic community, it is not so difficult to think of cases in which an isolated person, with sufficient ingenuity and intelligence, might also satisfy those standards. See, for example, Fogelin, *Wittgenstein*, 1st ed., pp. 161–165; 2nd ed., pp. 175–183; S. Blackburn, *Spreading the Word*, ch. 3, and idem, "The Individual Strikes Back."

be complemented by an external argument that a private language could never get started. But while Malcolm is clearly in sympathy with such a train of thought, it only plays a peripheral role in his exposition.[89] If we turn to Wittgenstein's exposition, however, we will find that it does contain an external attack on private language: he not only argues "internally" that the private linguist would have no way of knowing if he or she was using a privately defined term correctly on a subsequent occasion, but "externally" that the supposed private act of ostension fails to introduce a term in the first place.

In response to his outline of the view that "we *have* something . . . before the mind's eye . . . and . . . give it a name," Wittgenstein offers some observations about what is actually involved in using a name significantly. He begins with a telegraphic summary that hints at the topics of the opening sections of the *Investigations*, in which he proposes that the conception of language as composed out of names for objects takes one of the many ways we can use words and attempts to turn it into a paradigm for understanding all uses of language: "The relation between name and object. Lang[uage-]game of builders."[90] The language-game of the builders is an example of a primitive language with an extremely limited vocabulary in which all the words function as names and is designed to jolt us out of our philosophical preconceptions about naming by getting us to imagine a language for which the name conception of meaning might actually be appropriate.

Next, Wittgenstein asks himself, "What is the relation between names and actions, names and shapes?", and replies, "The relation of ostensibly[91] defining. That's to say, in order to establish a name relation we have to establish a technique of use." This appeal to a technique of use is a central thread in Wittgenstein's discussion of naming in the "Notes for the 'Philosophical Lecture.'" Wittgenstein tries to show us that ostension in particular, and language as a whole, always depends on a practical context; so that ostensive definition, whether it concerns inner or outer objects, always depends on a prior context of practices and institutions. For a technique of use is a practice, a linguistically structured procedure that may be contingently private, in the sense that I may choose to keep it secret; if it is conceived of as "superprivate," we are simply misdescribing and misunderstanding what we ordinarily do.

Wittgenstein's point here is not that we could not go on to use a private definition consistently, but is much more elementary: that nothing one could actually do would ever amount to setting one up, for the role of training and practice in language prevent a "private linguist" from using a sign to mean anything at all, even once. This is not the epistemological problem that one would have no reliable test, or no test at all, as to whether one was using language correctly, but rather a logical problem: the stage-setting necessary for one to be able to say anything at all would not be

89. Malcolm's example of a supposedly external argument still starts from the perspective of an isolated consciousness: he cites Wittgenstein's attack on the idea that I can start from knowledge of my own case and then transfer these concepts to objects outside myself, arguing that self-ascription of conscious states only makes sense if one is prepared to ascribe them to others (Malcolm, "Wittgenstein's *Philosophical Investigations*," pp. 75–77.) But this still depends on taking the first-person predicament as primary.

90. *Philosophical Occasions*, p. 448.

91. The rest of the paragraph makes it clear that this is a slip for "ostensively," as he is talking about successful ostensive definition, not just seeming to define.

in place.[92] On this reading, the discussions of rule-following (sections 138–242) and private language (section 243 ff.) in the *Investigations* both develop aspects of the treatment of training and practice in the opening sections.[93] One of the principal aims of the opening sections of the *Philosophical Investigations* is to show that our ordinary use of language is primarily practical, a matter of skills and abilities, and cannot be understood as a matter of grasping a theory or holding that certain propositions are true. Sections 28–34, in which Wittgenstein sums up his case that public ostensive definition presupposes a prior grasp of language, closely parallels the later discussion of private ostensive definition. In both passages, he argues that the bare act of pointing does not determine a referent. Section 28 observes that "an ostensive definition can be variously interpreted in *every* case," because the hearer may take it to be defining any one of a variety of possible categories of "object": a number, a name, a colour, etc. Of course, the ostensive definition can be disambiguated by specifying the category in question, but that presupposes that the hearer grasps the relevant distinctions; it shows "the post at which we station the word."[94] One can only ask what something's name is if the question's "place is already prepared."[95]

If one is to give an ostensive definition of a term, the other terms used in the definition must be understood. For instance, to say "This is sepia," pointing to a sample of sepia in order to give an ostensive definition of sepia for someone who does not know what "sepia" means, the person would have to know that it was a colour-word, not a word for a number or a shape. We can only explain how a language works to someone who already knows how to speak. So one cannot begin with verbal explanations when teaching a first language; a child cannot first learn to use words by means of ostensive definition. Of course, we do point at objects and name them when children are learning to speak, but the child does not yet have the linguistic abilities that would be needed if it were to understand the words as an ostensive definition. In the *Philosophical Remarks*, Wittgenstein considers the role of pointing in explaining the meaning of a word by ostensive definition—explaining the meaning of a word, say "tove," by pointing at an example and saying "This is tove." But Wittgenstein goes on to argue that is not a case of bringing language into direct contact with its referent, for his hearer can only use the explanation to learn what "tove" means if he or she understands what kind of object is being pointed out. As a result:

[A]ny kind of explanation of a language presupposes a language already. And in a certain sense, the use of language is something that cannot be taught, i.e. I cannot use language to teach it in the way in which language could be used to teach someone to play the piano. —And that of course is just another way of saying: I cannot use language to get outside language.[96]

92. See Fogelin, *Wittgenstein*, 1st ed., pp. 138–152, and 2nd ed., pp. 155–165; Barry Stroud, "Wittgenstein's 'Treatment' of the Quest for 'a Language which Describes my Inner Experiences and Which Only I Myself Can Understand'"; B. Gert, "Wittgenstein's Private Language Arguments"; ter Hark, *Beyond the Inner and the Outer: Wittgenstein's Philosophy of Psychology*, p. 94 ff.

93. Cf. Kripke, *Wittgenstein on Rules and Private Language*, who does briefly discuss §1 and §§28–34, but only as partial anticipations of the sceptical paradox, subsuming the main concern of those passages into his own.

94. *Philosophical Investigations*, §29.

95. *Philosophical Investigations*, §31.

96. *Philosophical Remarks*, §6.

In the *Philosophical Investigations*, Wittgenstein calls what we actually do in such cases "ostensive teaching of words."[97] He suggests that typically the child's attention is directed at the objects in question while the appropriate word or words are uttered, thus training it to use the words correctly; only later can questions arise about what words mean, once the context of our linguistic practices has been put in place by means of teaching "him to use the words by means of *examples* and *practice*."[98] He describes the activities involved in such teaching in the following terms:

> I do it, he does it after me; and I influence him by expression of agreement, rejection, expectation, encouragement. I let him go his way, or hold him back; and so on.
> Imagine witnessing such teaching. None of the words would be explained by means of itself; there would be no logical circle.[99]

In short, the language learner is initially *trained* to make certain responses under certain circumstances, to react in the right way. The teacher brings it about that the learner makes some of the right moves. In *Zettel*, Wittgenstein sums up his predicament here in the following terms: "I cannot describe how (in general) to employ rules, except by *teaching, training* you to employ rules."[100] On this view of language learning and teaching, naming and ostension are relatively sophisticated skills that can only come into play once much else is already in place. For instance, someone who asks what an object is called must be able to point to the object in question or otherwise draw attention to it, and make clear that it is the object's *name* which is desired, not what kind of object it is, or any of the indefinitely many other questions that could be asked. These tacitly presupposed skills can be made explicit, if need be. For instance, instead of asking "What is that called?" one might ask "What's the name of the thing I'm pointing to?" But that would presuppose, in turn, that one understands how to use such a question; nor would the original question have been made fully explicit. In short, one cannot learn a first language by ostensive definition of names, because ostensive definition presupposes that we already have a linguistic framework in place:

> Naming is not so far a move in the language-game—any more than putting a piece on the board is a move in chess. We may say: *nothing* has so far been done, when a thing has been named. It has not even *got* a name except in the language-game.[101]

Explicit linguistic acts such as giving an ostensive definition or interpreting a rule are only possible within the context of a great deal of practical linguistic ability.

In section 257, Wittgenstein makes it clear that the same problems arise in the case of inner ostension:

> When one says "He gave a name to his sensation" one forgets that a great deal of stage-setting in the language is presupposed if the mere act of naming is to make sense. And when we speak of someone's giving a name to pain, what is presup-

---

97. *Philosophical Investigations*, §6.
98. *Philosophical Investigations*, §208.
99. *Philosophical Investigations*, §208.
100. *Zettel*, §318; *Remarks on the Philosophy of Psychology*, II §413. 1948.
101. *Philosophical Investigations*, §49.

posed is the existence of the grammar of the word "pain"; it shows the post where the new word is stationed.

In the "Notes for the 'Philosophical Lecture'" this appeal to the "grammar of the word 'pain'" is foreshadowed in Wittgenstein's reference to "techniques of use." In a passage that is probably directed at Russell, although it seems to anticipate Kripke, he characterizes the view that "it is a peculiar process of christening an object which makes a word the word for an object" as a kind of "superstition."[102] Instead, it is only possible to actually name something, as apart from going through a ceremony that one thinks of as attaching a name to an object within a practical and linguistic context. Such a "technique of use" is always potentially public:

> So it's no use saying that we have a private object before the mind and give it a name. There is a name only where there is a technique of using it and that technique can be private; but this only means that nobody but I can know about it, in the sense in which I can have a private sewing machine. But in order to be a private sewing machine, it must be an object which deserves the name "sewing machine," not in virtue of its privacy but in virtue of its similarity to sewing machines, private or otherwise.[103]

"Technique of use," as the term is used in the "Notes for the 'Philosophical Lecture,'" does not neatly map onto any one of Wittgenstein's terms in the *Philosophical Investigations*. The English translation uses the term "technique" in a variety of contexts. It covers both the "technique of use" the private linguist fantasizes about, as in section 262: "Is it to be assumed that you invent the technique of using the word; or that you found it ready-made?"[104] but also the "*customs* (uses, institutions)" that Wittgenstein insists are constitutive of any language at all.

Near the beginning of the "Notes for the 'Philosophical Lecture,'" Wittgenstein makes it clear that he considers the myth of private inner ostension itself is to be understood as a misunderstanding of our ordinary (potentially public) techniques of use, techniques that must be established by *training* children to use words in certain ways before explanations of meaning can gain a foothold:

> How a kind of object is hypostatised for a technique of use. This word refers to this → object, that word to that → object. Explanation of the object referred to, not by pointing, but by explaining a technique. Colour words, shape words, etc.
>
> Under what circumstances pointing can explain, i.e. convey the use of a word.

102. Cf. *Philosophical Investigations*, §49, §110, on superstition, and the following passage from the "Notes for Lectures on 'Sense Data' and 'Private Experience'", p. 290:

> But what is it like to give a sensation a name? Say it is pronouncing the name while one has the sensation and possibly concentrating on the sensation,—but what of it? Does this name thereby get magic powers? And why on earth do I call these sounds the 'name' of the sensation? I know what I do with the name of a man or of a number, but have I by this act of "definition" given the name a use? "To give a sensation a name" means nothing unless I know already in what sort of a game this name is to be used.

103. *Philosophical Occasions*, p. 448.

104. The German is *Technik dieser Anwendung*; "technique of this application" would be a better translation.

Not to a baby. *It* learns by being drilled. There is, therefore, no occult act of *naming* an object that in itself can give a word a meaning.[105]

Toward the end of the manuscript, Wittgenstein returns to these issues once more when he criticizes the idea that understanding a word consists in the ability to produce a mental image or picture of the appropriate sort. But while he is quite prepared to concede that there is a connection between understanding and imagining, he rejects any theory along these lines as a prototypical philosophical error:

> When we philosophise we are constantly bound to give an account of our technique of the usage of words and this technique we know in the sense that we master it, and we don't know it in the sense that we have the very greatest difficulty in surveying it and describing it.[106]

6.4 "Words Only Have Meaning in the Flow of Life"

The later Wittgenstein argues that philosophical theses, such as the claim that it is impossible to step twice into the same river, or to see someone else's sensation, arise out of a misunderstanding of grammatical platitudes. The impossibilities in question are not a reflection of the nature of things, but rather a shadow cast by the structure of our language. Thus, Wittgenstein advises:

> Instead of "one cannot," say: "it doesn't exist in this game." Instead of: "one can't castle in draughts"—"there is no castling in draughts"; instead of "I can't exhibit my sensation"—"in the use of the word 'sensation,' there is no such thing as exhibiting what one has got"; instead of "one cannot enumerate all the cardinal numbers"—"there is no such thing here as enumerating all the members, even if there is an enumerating of members."
>
> The proposition "sensations are private" is like: One plays patience by oneself.[107]

These ordinarily unproblematic impossibilities only become philosophically troubling if one divorces them from the particular linguistic context that made it impossible to say those things. This is the heart of Wittgenstein's later response to the Tractarian question: What are the limits of thought; what determines whether an utterance makes sense? His answer is that what we think and say can only be understood in its everyday context, our ordinary use of words. A philosopher might well ask: What are those circumstances, the conditions under which words can be used intelligibly, and what limitations do they impose? In this way, one can start constructing a philosophical theory of the very kind that Wittgenstein was opposing. The problem arises because there is no sharp boundary separating background and foreground, and we can always bring aspects of the background into the foreground by considering what would happen if they were no longer in place. For instance, we can con-

---

105. *Philosophical Occasions*, p. 447.
106. *Philosophical Occasions*, p. 456.
107. MS 116, p. 178, 1937–1938. [German in appendix.] The second remark is an early version of *Philosophical Investigations*, §248.

sider what would happen if I were to find a chasm rather than a corridor on opening my office door, or people were no longer able to follow the line of a pointing finger as they do at present. But such examples do not show that the background as a whole can be brought into the foreground, or that the background consists of tacit presuppositions that are shown to be true by the language we speak, much as the preconditions for the possibility of language are shown on the Tractarian view. That train of thought is briefly sketched in the following remarks from *On Certainty*:

> Certain events would make put me in a position in which I could not go on with the old language-game any further. In which I was torn away from the *sureness* of the game.
> Indeed, doesn't it seem obvious that the possibility of a language-game is conditioned by certain facts?
> In that case it would seem as if the language-game must *"show"* the facts that make it possible. (But that's not how it is.)[108]

The danger that Wittgenstein points to in the last paragraph is closely related to the "dogmatism" that enabled him to move from compelling examples to supposedly universal insights about the nature of language in the *Tractatus*: we may be tempted to turn the obvious regularities of our everyday lives into a mythology about what makes those lives possible.

In *On Certainty*, Wittgenstein repeatedly explores that temptation by considering particular examples of facts that we ordinarily take for granted and how they can be foregrounded by a philosophical sceptic or a case where the ordinary course of events is disrupted. For instance, in sections 310–317 he discusses the case of a pupil who will not let anything be explained to him because he continually interrupts with doubts about the existence of things, the meaning of words, and the like. Wittgenstein observes that the teacher will feel that the questions are not legitimate, that the student has not learned how to ask questions. In the classroom, such a question is out of place precisely because it is not an ordinary question about an empirical state of affairs, but rather challenges the methods that we take for granted in everyday inquiry. The next day's notes begin with a terse summary of that line of response: "'The question doesn't arise at all.' Its answer would characterize a *method*."[109] But he then goes on to reflect on the lack of a sharp boundary between empirical propositions and rules, and the misleadingly tidy view he had just set out:

> Isn't what I am saying: any empirical proposition can be transformed into a postulate—and then becomes a norm of representation. But I am suspicious even of this. The sentence is too general. One almost wants to say "any empirical proposition can, theoretically, be transformed . . .", but what does "theoretically" mean here? It sounds all too reminiscent of the *Tractatus*.[110]

This concern for the way theory can reconstitute itself out of antitheoretical observations motivates a subsequent use of the passage quoted above where Wittgenstein proposes replacing talk of an impossibility with the observation that what is said to

108. *On Certainty*, §§617–618, 23 April 1951.
109. *On Certainty*, §318, 12 March 1951.
110. *On Certainty*, §321, 12 March 1951. Cf. §§400–402.

be impossible is not part of the game in question. In this new context, that passage is included in a discussion of the idea that thought and language require particular circumstances, a context, if they are to make sense:

> We only speak of "thinking" in quite particular circumstances.
>
> How then can the sense and the truth (or the truth and the sense) of sentences collapse together? (Stand or fall together?)
>
> And isn't it as if you wanted to say: "If such-and-such is not the case, then it makes no *sense* to say it is the case?"
>
> Like this, e.g.: "If all moves were *always* false, it would make no sense to speak of a 'false move.'" But that is only a paradoxical way of putting it. The non-paradoxical way would be: "The general description . . . makes no sense."
>
> Instead of "one cannot," say: "it doesn't exist in this game." Not: "one can't castle in draughts" but—"there is no castling in draughts"; and instead of "I can't exhibit my sensation"—"in the use of the word 'sensation,' there is no such thing as exhibiting what one has got"; instead of "one cannot enumerate all the cardinal numbers"—"there is no such thing here as enumerating all the members."
>
> Conversation, the application and interpretation of words flows on, and only in the flow [*Fluß*] does a word have its meaning.
> "He has gone away." —"Why?" What did you mean, when you uttered the word "why"? What did you *think* of?[111]

In his final remark, Wittgenstein first states the thesis that words only have meaning in the flow, the river, of conversation, and then illustrates it with a brief conversational exchange. The exchange is a capsule reference to a train of thought that occurs repeatedly throughout his later philosophical writing, in which he counters the demand that there must be some occurent state of affairs which accounts for our words' meaning, something going on in the speaker's head or mind that explains why those words are significant.[112] Wittgenstein counsels that we look instead to the practical context, the stream of thought and activity, in which a given use of words is embedded: "Words only have meaning in the river of thought and life."[113] The river image returns in a very different form: words no longer have meaning in virtue of their application to the flux of present experience; instead, the significance of a particular utterance is a matter of its location within the stream of conversation, our ordinary use of language. Thus, in the following passage, Wittgenstein describes a snippet of conversation and points out that nothing in particular need go on in the speaker's mind in order for the speaker's words to be significant:

> What does someone mean when he says "I think he's pretending"? —Well, he's *using a word* which is used in such-and-such situations. Sometimes he will continue the game by making conjectures about the other person's future behaviour; that doesn't have to happen.

---

111. *Zettel*, §§130–135. In the collection of fragments which form the basis for the published work, the previously quoted paragraph (§134) is typewritten, while the remainder of the fragment (§§130–133 and §§135–137) is a handwritten addition to the sheet on which §134 was typed.

112. See chapter 4, section 4.

113. *Zettel*, §174. See also *Remarks on the Philosophy of Psychology*, I §240.

There's some behaviour and some conversation taking place. A few sentences back and forth; and a few actions. That might be all.
(Words only have meaning in the river [*Fluβ*] of life.)[114]

Wittgenstein also responds to the claim that one can't look inside another's mind by pointing out that inner experience, which he had once equated with life, only has meaning in virtue of its place in our lives as a whole: "What goes on inwardly, too, only has meaning in the river of life."[115]

Wittgenstein's conception of life is now social, not solipsistic; while he could have accepted the words just quoted in early 1929, when he was still working within a Tractarian framework, they would have referred to the stream of consciousness, not the course of ordinary life.[116] In *On Certainty*, Wittgenstein sets out his later river image at length, both as an illustration of the nature of the boundary between everyday empirical claims and the words we use to describe their background, and to indicate why it is so hard to describe that background:

> But I did not get my picture of the world by satisfying myself of its correctness; nor do I have it because I am satisfied of its correctness. No: it is the inherited background against which I distinguish between true and false.
>
> The propositions describing this world-picture might be part of a mythology. And their role is like that of rules of a game; and the game can be learned purely practically, without learning any explicit rules.
>
> It might be imagined that some propositions, of the form of empirical propositions, were hardened and functioned as channels for such empirical propositions as were not hardened but fluid; and that this relation altered with time, in that fluid propositions hardened, and hard ones became fluid.
>
> The mythology may change back into a state of flux, the river-bed of thoughts may shift. But I distinguish between the movement of the waters on the river-bed and the shift of the bed itself; though there is not a sharp division of the one from the other.
>
> But if someone were to say "So logic too is an empirical science" he would be wrong. Yet this is right: the same proposition may get treated at one time as something to test by experience, at another as a rule of testing.
>
> And the bank of the river consists partly of hard rock, subject to no alteration or only to an imperceptible one, partly of sand, which now in one place now in another gets washed away, or deposited.[117]

In this passage, Wittgenstein sketches a world-picture, a graphic depiction of his understanding of the world and our place in it. His recourse to imagery here is a consequence of his conception of a world-picture: although it can be described, the propositions describing it are more like a myth, or the rules of a game we know but

114. *Last Writings on the Philosophy of Psychology*, I §913, early 1949.
115. *Last Writings on the Philosophy of Psychology*, II p. 30.
116. Cf. Malcolm's use of Wittgenstein's later references to the stream of life to draw a sharp contrast between his earlier and later philosophy in the epilogue to *Nothing Is Hidden*. Unaware of this ambiguity, he insisted that "'Words have their meaning only in the flow of life' is not a possible remark within the framework of the *Tractatus*" (p. 238).
117. *On Certainty*, §§94–99, 1950.

have never articulated, than a traditional analysis. This is not only because the rules are implicit and normative, rather than explicit and factual, but because any explicit formulation of our world-picture will be no more than an approximation to the ways of acting in which it is embedded. These practices have a flexibility that resists being captured by any set of necessary and sufficient conditions.

Part of the flexibility of our practices consists in their indeterminacy: although we all agree in some of our judgments, the borderline between the empirical and the methodological is not sharply demarcated, and will change over time. The distribution of sand on the river bed alters, and even the underlying rock will eventually be worn away, but these changes cannot be assimilated to the flow of the waters. In this image, the water's continual flow is not treated as a model of the nature of all things. Instead, it is used as an object of comparison,[118] as a way of bringing out the continuum that connects our world-picture, the inherited background that we take for granted in judging truth and falsity, and the particular truths and falsehoods we discuss. Unlike Wittgenstein's earlier river image, his later image accommodates both change and persistence, for he now holds that change is possible only against a background: in talking of change, one must hold some things constant, at least for the present. Both of Wittgenstein's river images imply the indeterminacy of the world we live in and the impossibility of fully grasping it in language. But while the early Wittgenstein explains this in terms of the fleeting character of present experience, continually carried away by the river of time, the later Wittgenstein points to the primacy of the background and its indeterminacy: "If a pattern of life is the basis for the use of a word then the word must contain some amount of indefiniteness. The pattern of life, after all, is not one of exact regularity."[119] Thus, for very different reasons, both the early and the late Wittgenstein are driven to the Heraclitean conclusion that the nature of language can only be shown. In the *Tractatus*, that conclusion leads to a conception of philosophy on which the nature of language, logic and the world must be accepted as a given; but in Wittgenstein's later work, the view that the nature of language can only be shown is illustrated by a close examination of our linguistic practice: "Am I not getting closer and closer to saying that in the end logic cannot be described? You must look at the praxis of language, then you will see it."[120]

Wittgenstein's later river image is an image of movement and activity; but it is not an image in which all is in flux. In this image, the river's banks and bed are fixed, at least for the present, and for the most part. In other words, at any given time, one must take some things for granted, and that taken for granted background limits what one can say and do. But here we are on the brink of a crucial misunderstanding, for talk of a "background" makes it sound as if there is some specific thing to be referred to with a definite article, the Background, something like the scenery on a stage, that makes it possible for actions on that stage to have the significance that they do. That conception of (the capital-B) Background, the regress-stopper at the end of a search for the basis for what we ordinarily take for granted, is hinted at in the following remark from the early 1930s: "Perhaps what is inexpressible (what I find myste-

118. Cf. *Philosophical Investigations* §§130–131, and Early Investigations §107 (109), quoted and discussed in chapter 1, pp. 20–21 and chapter 4, p. 103.
119. *Last Writings on the Philosophy of Psychology*, I §211; cf. §§243–247.
120. *On Certainty*, §501, 11 April 1951.

rious and am not able to express) is the background against which whatever I could express has its meaning."[121] In a related remark from the 1914–1916 notebooks, Wittgenstein attempts to dispel the mystery by proposing that while the background of any particular thought may be inexpressible and mysterious at the time it is thought, it can itself be made the subject of a later act of reflection: "Behind our thoughts, true and false, there is always to be found a dark background, which we are only later able to bring into the light and express as a thought."[122]

With the advent of the calculus conception of language and the associated critique of the idea of hidden rules or underlying mental processes, Wittgenstein became deeply suspicious of the idea that linguistic practice is only a surface phenomenon, animated by a dark and mysterious background. Instead, he conceived of the relevant context as simply being a matter of being able to use the words in question, a skill that simply consists in having learned to play the game, or use the appropriate calculus:

> The understanding of language, as of a game, seems like a background against which a particular sentence acquires meaning. —But this understanding, the knowledge of the language, isn't a conscious state that accompanies the sentences of the language. Not even if one of its consequences is such a state. It's much more like the understanding or mastery of a calculus, something like the *ability* to multiply.
>
> . . . In our study of symbolism there is no foreground and background; it isn't a matter of a tangible sign with an accompanying intangible power or understanding.[123]

Just as Wittgenstein's transitional rejection of his earlier image of the river of life is directed against a quite specific use of that image, and actually paves the way for his later use of river imagery, so too his rejection of the idea that a dark and inaccessible background animates our everyday use of language makes it possible for a very different conception of foreground and background to return in his later work. His later notion of a background is not something apart from or prior to our lives; instead, it is the pattern of those lives themselves, the "praxis of language" in all its detail and complexity:

> We judge an action according to its background within human life, and this background is not monochrome, but we might picture it as a very complicated filigree pattern, which, to be sure, we can't copy, but which we can recognize from the general impression it makes.
>
> The background is the bustle of life. And our concept points to something within *this* bustle.
>
> And it is the very concept "bustle" that brings about this indefiniteness. For a bustle only comes about through constant repetition. And there is no definite starting point for "constant repetition." . . .
>
> How could human behaviour be described? Surely only by showing the actions of a variety of humans, as they are all mixed up together. Not what *one* per-

---

121. *Culture and Value*, p. 16. Source: MS 112, p. 1, 5 October 1931.
122. *Notebooks 1914–1916*, p. 36, 8 December 1914.
123. *Philosophical Grammar*, §12; §43.

son is doing *now*, but the whole hurly-burly, is the background against which we
see an action, and it determines our judgement, our concepts, and our reactions.[124]

Characteristically, Wittgenstein refuses to turn his conception of the primacy of
praxis into a doctrine. Instead, he establishes it indirectly, throughout the *Philosophical
Investigations* and his subsequent writing, by giving examples of our agreement in
the use of language, showing how these practices are part of what he calls "our natural history" and how they depend on "certain very general facts of nature."[125] In a
preparatory draft for Part II of the *Investigations*, he lists some of these everyday
practices, and insists they must be treated as a given:

> Instead of the unanalysable, specific, indefinable: the fact that we act in such-
> and-such ways, e.g. *punish* certain actions, *establish* the state of affairs thus and
> so, *give orders*, render accounts, describe colours, take an interest in others' feel-
> ings. What has to be accepted, the given—it might be said—are facts of living
> //forms of life.//[126]

They have to be treated as a given because any explanation of what words mean
presupposes that their background is, for the most part, already in place. If we try to
specify everything one has to know in order to understand statements about punish-
ing a specific action, establishing a state of affairs obtains, or simply ordering someone to open the door, those sentences will also have to be understood, and that will
presuppose further practical abilities on the part of the reader.

---

124. *Remarks on the Philosophy of Psychology*, II §§624–626, §629. The last of these remarks
has also been published as *Zettel*, §567.
125. See *Philosophical Investigations*, §25, §142, the remark without a number on p. 56, and p. 230.
126. *Remarks on the Philosophy of Psychology*, I §630. The last sentence is an early version of a
remark in *Philosophical Investigations*, II, p. 226.

Appendix: Passages from the
Unpublished Wittgenstein Papers
(*Nachlass*)

This appendix provides the German for all passages from the unpublished Wittgenstein papers that are translated in the text. Each passage is identified by chapter and footnote; the number usually locates the place in the text where the passage occurs, but on some occasions, it refers to a passage in the footnote itself. While I have tried to provide accurate transcriptions, I have not attempted to show as much information about the text as can be found in the Bergen Wittgenstein Archive transcriptions; for instance, passages that Wittgenstein marked for insertion are simply included in the appropriate place, and erasures are only shown where they seem particularly important. Occasionally, the transcriptions are slightly longer than the translated passages (for instance, when part of a sentence is translated, I have supplied the whole of the original sentence.)

As sections 86–93 of the Big Typescript have been published in both English and German, with the original pagination clearly marked, and are now easily available in *Philosophical Occasions*, the German for quotations from these sections is not included in this appendix.

Chapter 1

4. Rhees "Correspondence and Comment" p. 153. Rhees quotes from the *Nachlass*, saying that this passage was written in 1948, "roughly two and a half years before his death," but does not give a page reference.

Ich habe kein Recht, der Öffentlichkeit ein Buch zu geben, worin einfach die Schwierigkeiten, die ich empfinde, ausgedrückt und durchgekaut sind. Denn diese Schwierigkeiten sind zwar für mich interessant, der in ihnen steckt, aber nicht notwendigerweise für die Andern. Denn sie sind Eigentümlichkeiten *meines* Denkens, bedingt durch *meinen* Werdegang. Sie gehören, sozusagen, in ein Tagebuch, nicht in ein Buch. Und wenn dies Tagebuch auch einmal für jemand interessant sein könnte, so kann ich's doch nicht veröffentlichen. Nicht meine Magenschwerden sind interessant sondern die Mittel—if any— die ich gegen sie gefunden habe.

26. Big Typescript, §94, p. 438
Irrtümliche Anwendung unserer physikalischer Ausdrucksweise auf Sinnesdaten. "Gegenstände," d.h. Dinge, Körper im Raum des Zimmers—und "Gegenstände" im

Gesichtsfeld; der Schatten eines Körpers an der Wand als Gegenstand! Wenn man gefragt wird: "existiert der Kasten noch, wenn ich ihn nicht anschaue," so ist die korrekte Antwort: "ich glaube nicht, dass ihn jemand gerade dann wegtragen wird, oder zerstören."

69. MS 121, pp. 98–99

Man sagt, Sinnesdaten sind primärer als physikalische Gegenstände—aber unsre Notation mittels "physikalische Gegenstände" soll sich doch am Schluß auf Sinnesdaten beziehen. Es kann also wohl nur eine *Notation* primär und eine sekundär sein. Und warum soll man die Notation die einzig sich bewährt hat nicht die primäre nennen. Oder: wozu hier überhaupt von primär und sekundär reden? Denn liegt ein Mißverständnis zu Grunde. Wenn man sagt der "physikalische Gegenstand" sei nur eine logische Konstruktion aus Sinneseindrücken errichtet, so ist, was man konstruiert hat, doch nur ein Sprachspiel.

80. MS 110, p. 239

In der Philosophie werden wir durch einen Schein getäuscht. Aber dieser /ein/ Schein ist auch etwas, und ich muß ihn einmal ganz klar mir vor Augen stellen, ehe ich sagen kann, daß es nur ein Schein ist.

96. TS 219, p. 6

Der Mensch mit "gesundem Menschenverstand," wenn er einen früheren Philosophen liest, denkt (und nicht ohne Recht): "lauter Unsinn!"—wenn er mich hört, so denkt er: "lauter fade Selbstverständlichkeiten!" Wieder mit Recht. Und so hat sich der Aspekt der Philosophie geändert. (Ich will sagen: "so schaut dieses eine Ding von verschiedenen Standpunkten aus.")

Chapter 3

77. Big Typescript, §97, p. 463

In *Wirklichkeit* aber bezieht sich doch das Wort "Gesichtsraum" nur auf eine Geometrie, ich meine auf einen Abschnitt der Grammatik unserer Sprache.

78. Big Typescript, §97, pp. 463–464

Es ist nun wichtig, dass der Satz "das Auge, womit ich sehe, kann ich nicht unmittelbar sehen" ein verkappter Satz der Grammatik, oder Unsinn ist. Der Ausdruck "näher am (oder, weiter vom) sehenden Auge" hat nämlich eine andere Grammatik, als der "näher an dem blauen Gegenstand, welchen ich sehe." Die visuelle Erscheinung, die der Beschreibung entspricht "A setzt die Brille auf," ist von der grundverschieden, die ich mit den Worten beschreibe: "ich setze die Brille auf." Ich könnte nun sagen: "mein Gesichtsraum hat Ähnlichkeit mit einem Kegel," aber dann muss es verstanden werden, dass ich hier den Kegel als Raum, als Repräsentanten einer Geometrie, nicht als Teil eines Raumes (Zimmer) denke.

91. Big Typescript, §104, pp. 508–509

Die Subjekt-Objekt Form bezieht sich auf den Leib und die Dinge um ihn, die auf ihn wirken.

In der nicht-hypothetischen Beschreibung des Gesehenen, Gehörten—diese Wörter bezeichnen hier grammatische Formen—tritt das Ich nicht auf, es ist hier von Subjekt und Objekt nicht die Rede.

Der Solipsismus könnte durch die Tatsache widerlegt werden, dass das Wort "ich" in der Grammatik keine zentrale Stellung hat, sondern ein Wort ist, wie jedes andere Wort.

Wie im Gesichtsraum, so gibt es in der Sprache kein metaphysisches Subjekt.

/Die Schwierigkeit, die uns das Sprechen über den Gesichtsraum ohne Subjekt macht und über *"meine* und *seine* Zahnschmerzen,"* ist die, die Sprache einzurenken, dass sie richtig in den Tatsachen sitzt./

96. Big Typescript, §104, p. 514

Wir wollen doch einfach zwei verschiedene Erfahrungsgebiete trennen; wie wenn wir Tasterfahrung und Gesichtserfahrung an einem Körper trennen. Und verschiedener kann nichts sein, als die Schmerzerfahrung und die Erfahrung, einen menschlichen Körper sich winden sehen // zu sehen//, Laute ausstossen zu hören, etc. Und zwar besteht hier kein Unterschied zwischen meinem Körper und dem des Andern, denn es gibt auch die Erfahrung, die Bewegungen des eigenen Körpers zu sehen und die von ihm ausgestossenen Laute zu hören.

98. Big Typescript, §104, p. 512

"Wie ein Satz verifiziert wird, —das sagt er": und nun sieh Dir daraufhin die Sätze an: "Ich habe Schmerzen," "N hat Schmerzen."

114. Big Typescript, §101, p. 493

Wenn ich mich mit der Sprache dem Andern verständlich mache, so muss es sich hier um ein Verstehen im Sinne des Behaviourism handeln. Dass er mich verstanden hat, ist eine Hypothese, wie, dass ich ihn verstanden habe.

"Für wen würde ich meine unmittelbare Erfahrung beschreiben? Nicht für mich, denn ich habe sie ja; und nicht für jemand andern, denn der könnte sie nie aus der Beschreibung entnehmen?" —Er kann sie soviel und so wenig aus der Beschreibung entnehmen, wie aus einem gemalten Bild. Die Vereinbarungen über die Sprache sind doch mit Hilfe von gemalten Bildern (oder was diesem gleichkommt) getroffen worden. Und, unserer gewöhnlichen Ausdrucksweise nach, entnimmt er doch aus einem gemalten Bild etwas.

119. MS 120, pp. 87–88; MS 116, pp. 225–226

Man kann sagen: wenn wir philosophieren, feiert nicht nur unsre Sprache, sondern auch unser Blick. Denn während ich den Ofen heize, sehe ich ihn anders, als wenn ich beim Philosophieren auf ihn starre, denke ich nicht an den "visuellen Ofen," der Sinnesdatum, etc.

Ein Philosoph, der beim Philosophieren immer ein Auge zudrückte, könnte von andern Anschauungen gefangen werden, als der, welcher immer mit beiden schaut.

[*The next remark is in MS 116, p. 226, taken from MS 120, p. 89.*]

Wer sagt, man könne nicht zweimal in den gleichen Fluß steigen, kann nur unter sehr besonderen Umständen so empfinden; d.h., nur unter diesen Umständen versucht sein, es zu sagen. // steigen, kann nur unter *besonderen* Umständen so empfinden; d.h., nur unter ganz bestimmten Umständen versucht sein, dies zu sagen.

121. MS 112, pp. 54–55

/Es ist seltsam, dass ich geschrieben habe, der Gesichtsraum hat nicht die Form

und nicht, er habe nicht die Form

und dass ich das Erste geschrieben habe, ist sehr bezeichnend./

Chapter 4

43. Early Investigations, §107 (109)

Nur so nämlich können wir der Ungerechtigkeit, oder Leere unserer Behauptungen entgehen, indem wir das Vorbild als das, was es ist, als Vergleichsobjekt—sozusagen als Maßstab—hinstellen; und nicht als das Vorurteil, dem die Wirklichkeit entsprechen *müsse*. (Ich denke an die Betrachtungsweise Spenglers.) Hierin nämlich liegt der Dogmatismus, in den unsre Philosophie so leicht verfallen kann.

Es ist wahr: eine Maßeinheit ist gut gewählt, wenn sie viele der Längen, die wir mit ihr messen wollen, in ganzen Zahlen ausdrückt. Aber der Dogmatismus behauptet, jede Länge *müsse* ein ganzes Vielfaches unserer Maßeinheit sein.

48. MS 110, pp. 229–230

Es wäre wichtig, den Fehler allgemein auszudrücken, den ich in allen diesen Betrachtungen zu machen neige /geneigt bin/. Die falsche Analogie aus den er entspringt. . . .

Ich glaube, jener Fehler liegt in der Idee, daß die Bedeutung eines Wortes eine Vorstellung ist, die das Wort begleitet.

Und die Conception hat /steht/ wieder mit der des Bewußt-Seins zu tun /in Verbindung/. Dessen, was ich immer "das Primäre" nannte.

49. MS 110, pp. 233–234

Denn die Frage ist eben ob unter der "Bedeutung in dem man ein Wort gebraucht" ein Vorgang verstanden werden soll den wir beim Sprechen oder Hören des Wortes erleben.

Die Quelle des Fehlers scheint die Idee von *Gedanke* zu sein *der den Satz begleitet.* Oder der seinem ~~symbolisch~~ Ausdruck vorangeht.

52. TS 235, §§36–37

"*Was geht da vor sich,* wenn man versteht, denkt, fühlt, sich etwas verstellt, etc.?"

Um ein philosophisches Problem zu lösen, muß man sich von der Fragestellung abwenden, die sich uns am stärksten aufdrängt. Diese Fragestellung ist das Problematische.

53. MS 110, pp. 230–231

Wenn ich nämlich über die Sprache–Wort, Satz etc.—rede, muß ich die Sprache des Alltags reden. —Aber gibt es denn eine andere?

Ist diese Sprache etwa zu grob, materiell für das, was wir sagen wollen? Und kann es eine andere geben? Und wie merkwürdig, daß wir dann mit der unseren dennoch /überhaupt/ etwas anfangen können.

Es ist doch klar, daß jede Sprache die dasselbe leistet, dieselbe sein müßte. Daß also unsere gewöhnliche nicht schlechter ist, als irgend eine andere.

54. MS 157b, pp. 10–13

Es zeigte sich nämlich daß ich nicht einen allgemeine Begriff vom Satz und der Sprache *hatte*.

Ich mußte das und das als Zeichen anerkennen (Sraffa) und konnte doch keine Grammatik dafür angeben. Verstehen und Wissen der Regeln.

Das Pneumatische am Verstehen verschwand ganz und damit das Pneumatische des Sinnes.

Zuerst erschienen die strenge Regeln als etwas /noch/ im Hintergrund, im /nebulosen/ Mediums des Verstehens versteckt; und man konnte sagen: sie *müssen* da sein—oder ich sehe sie, sozusagen durch ein dickes Medium hindurch, aber ich sehe sie. Sie waren also *konkret*. Ich hatte ein Gleichnis gebraucht (von der Projektionsmethode, etc.) aber durch die grammatische Täuschung des einheitliches Begriffes erschien es nicht als Gleichnis. Das Wort "eigentlich."

Je offenbarer diese Täuschung wird, je klarer es wird daß Sprache eine Familie ist, desto klarer wird es daß jenes scheinbar Konkrete, eine Abstraktion, eine Form war und daß wenn wir vorgeben sie seien überall zur Stelle, unsere Aussagen leer und sinnlos werden. Daß wir nur mehr logische Possen treiben.

Wir sehen, daß wir uns an die Beispiele klammern müssen, um nicht haltlos herumzutreiben.

Unsere Betrachtungen aber verlieren nun nicht etwa ihre Bedeutung, sondern diese liegt nun ganz auf den Mißverständnisse die uns irreführen.

58. Big Typescript, §20, p. 81

Der Sinn des Stazes, keine *Seele*.

Die Methode des Messens, z.B. des räumlichen Messens, verhält sich zu einer bestimmten Messung genau so, wie der Sinn eines Satzes zu seiner Wahr- oder Falschheit.

Der Sinn eines /des/ Satzes ist nicht pneumatisch, sondern ist das, was auf die Frage nach der Erklärung des Sinnes zur Antwort kommt. Und—oder—der eine Sinn unterscheidet sich vom andern, wie die Erklärung des einen von der Erklärung des andern.

Welche Rolle der Satz im Kalkül spielt, das ist sein Sinn.

Der Sinn steht (also) nicht *hinter* ihm (wie der psychische Vorgang der Vorstellungen etc.).

60. MS 108, p. 277

Denken nenne ich das was sich durch eine Sprache ausdrücken läßt. Dann muß es in diese Sprache aus einer *anderen* übersetzt werden. Ich will sagen: alles Denken muß dann in Zeichen vorsichgehen.

Wenn man aber sagt: "Wie soll ich wissen was er meint ich sehe ja nur seine Zeichen" so sage ich: "Wie soll *er* wissen was er meint, er hat ja auch nur seine Zeichen."

Die Frage "*wie* ist das gemeint," hat nur Sinn wenn es heißt "es ist *so* gemeint." Dieses "so" ist ein sprachlicher Ausdruck.

Chapter 5

28. MS 107, p. 205

Die phänomenologische Sprache oder "primäre Sprache" wie ich sie nannte schwebt mir jetzt nicht als Ziel vor; ich halte sie jetzt nicht mehr für möglich. Alles was möglich und nötig ist, ist das Wesentliche *unserer* Sprache von ihrem Unwesentlichen zu sondern.

30. MS 107, p. 176

Die Annahme daß eine phänomenologische Sprache möglich wäre und die eigentlich erst das sagen würde was wir in der Philosophie ausdrücken müssen /wollen/ ist—glaube ich— absurd. Wir müssen mit unserer gewöhnlichen Sprache auskommen und sie nur richtig verstehen. D.h. wir dürfen uns nicht von ihr verleiten lassen Unsinn zu reden.

Ich meine: was ich Zeichen nenne muß das sein was man in der Grammatik Zeichen nennt, etwas auf dem Film nicht auf der Leinwand.

37. MS 107, pp. 223–224

Das Phänomen ist nicht Symptom für etwas anderes sondern ist die Realität.

Das Phänomen ist nicht Symptom für etwas anderes was den Satz erst wahr oder falsch macht sondern ist selbst das was ihn verifiziert.

38. MS 107, p. 233

In der Zeit ausgedehnt betrachtet ist die Anwendung der Wörter leicht zu verstehen dagegen finde ich es unendlich schwierig den Sinn im Moment der Anwendung zu verstehen.

Was heißt es z.B. einen Satz als ein Glied eines Satzsystems /Systems von Sätzen/ zu verstehen?

42. Big Typescript, §102, p. 496

(Wir befinden uns mit unserer Sprache (als physischer Erscheinung) sozusagen nicht im Bereich des projizierten Bildes auf der Leinwand, sondern im Bereich des Films, der durch die Laterne geht.)

45. Big Typescript, §102, p. 495

Wir stellen uns das Erleben wie einen Filmstreifen vor, so dass man sagen kann: dieses Bild, und kein anderes, ist in diesem Augenblick vor der Linse.

Aber nur im Film kann man von einem in diesem Moment gegenwärtigen Bild reden; nicht, wenn man aus dem physikalischem Raum und seiner Zeit in den Gesichtsraum und seine Zeit übergeht.

47. Big Typescript, §107, p. 528

Erfahrung ist nicht etwas, das man durch Bestimmungen von einem Anderen abgrenzen kann, was nicht Erfahrung ist; sondern eine logische Form.

48. TS 219, p. 20

Erfahrung als logische Form. Erfahrung im Gegensatz wozu?

49. MS 105, p. 108

Die phänomenologische Sprache beschreibt genau dasgleiche wie die gewöhnliche, physikalische. Sie muß sich nur auf das beschränken was verifizierbar ist.

Ist das überhaupt möglich?

50. MS 105, p. 108

Vergessen wir nicht daß die physikalische Sprache auch wieder nur die primäre Welt beschreibt und nicht etwa eine hypothetische Welt. Die Hypothese ist nur eine Annahme über die praktischste /richtigste ?/ Art der Darstellung.

Ist nun dieses Hypothetische jeder Darstellung der Welt wesentlich?

51. Big Typescript, §101, p. 491
Phänomenologische S̲p̲r̲a̲c̲h̲e̲: Die Beschreibung der unmittelbaren Sinneswahrnehmung, ohne hypothetische Zutat.

53. Big Typescript, §101, pp. 491–492
Wenn etwas, dann muss doch wohl die Abbildung durch ein gemaltes Bild oder dergleichen eine solche Beschreibung der unmittelbaren Erfahrung sein. Wenn wir also z.b. in ein Fernrohr sehen und die gesehene Konstellation aufzeichnen oder malen.

58. Big Typescript §101, p. 492
Denken wir uns sogar unsere Sinneswahrnehmung dadurch reproduziert, dass zu ihrer Beschreibung ein Modell erzeugt wird, welches von einem bestimmten Punkt gesehen, diese Wahrnehmungen erzeugt; das Modell könnte mit einem Kurbelantrieb in die richtige Bewegung gesetzt werden und wir könnten durch Drehen der Kurbel die Beschreibung herunterlesen. (Eine Annäherung hierzu wäre eine Darstellung im Film.)
Ist *das* keine Darstellung des Unmittelbaren—was sollte eine sein? —Was noch unmittelbarer sein wollte, müsste es aufgeben, eine Beschreibung zu sein. Es kommt dann vielmehr statt einer Beschreibung jener unartikulierte Laut heraus, mit dem manche Autoren die Philosophie gerne anfangen möchten. ("Ich habe, um mein Wissen wissend, bewusst etwas" Driesch.)

71. Big Typescript §102, p. 495
Was wir die Zeit im Phänomen (*specious present*) nennen können, liegt nicht in der Zeit (Vergangenheit, Gegenwart und Zukunft) der Geschichte, ist keine Strecke der Zeit. Während, was wir unter "Sprache" verstehen, // Während, der Vorgang der "Sprache" // in der homogenen geschichtlichen Zeit abläuft. (Denke an den Mechanismus zur Beschreibung der unmittelbaren Wahrnehmung.)

72. MS 105, pp. 116–118
Es ist als käme ich mit der phänomenologische Sprache in einen verzauberten Sumpf wo alles erfaßbare verschwindet.

Angenommen die Welt bestünde aus einem gleichbleibende Gesichtsfeld wäre es dann nicht möglich sie zu beschreiben.

Z.B. in der Mitte eines roten Gesichtsfeldes ist ein blauer kreisförmiger Fleck.

Obwohl auch hier, das, was beim Lesen des Satzes vorsichgeht nicht im Satz beschrieben sein kann.
Aber von welcher Wichtigkeit kann denn diese Beschreibung des gegenwärtigen Phänomens sein? Es scheint als wäre die Beschäftigung mit dieser Frage geradezu kindisch und wir /ich/ in eine Sackgasse hineingeraten. Und doch ist es eine bedeutungsvolle Sackgasse, denn in sie lockt es Alle zu gehen, als wäre dort die letzte Lösung des philosophischen Problems zu suchen.

74. Big Typescript, §102, p. 496
(Von welcher Wichtigkeit ist denn diese Beschreibung des *gegenwärtigen* Phänomens, die für uns gleichsam zur fixen Idee werden kann. Dass wir darunter leiden, dass die Beschreibung nicht das beschreiben kann, was beim Lesen der Beschreibung vor sich geht.
Es scheint, als wäre die Beschäftigung mit diese Frage geradezu kindisch und wir in eine Sackgasse hineingeraten. Und doch ist es eine bedeutungsvolle Sackgasse, denn in sie lockt es Alle zu gehen; als wäre dort die letzte Lösung der philosophischen Probleme zu suchen.

—Es ist, als käme man mit dieser Darstellung des gegenwärtigen Phänomens in einen verzauberten Sumpf, wo alles Erfassbare verschwindet.)

76. MS 107, p. 1
Es ist nicht notwendig ausschaltende Experimente (etwa Gedankenexperimente zu machen). Der Gesichstraum so wie er ist hat seine selbständige Realität.
Er selbst enthält kein Subject. Er ist autonom.

Er läßt sich unmittelbar beschreiben (aber wir sind weit davon entfernt eine Ausdrucksweise zu kennen die ihn beschreibt). Die gewöhnliche physikalische Sprache bezieht sich auf ihn in einer *sehr* komplizierten und uns instinktiv bekannten Weise.

77. MS 107, p. 1
Der entscheidende Moment für eine Sprache ist ihre Anwendung. Das Denken mit ihrer Hilfe.

78. MS 107, p. 1
Die Betrachtungsweise die gleichsam in einen Talkessel hinunter führt aus dem kein Weg in die freie Landschaft führt ist die Betrachtung der Gegenwart als des einzig Realen. Dieses Gegenwart in ständigen Fluß oder vielmehr in ständigen Veränderung begriffen läßt sich nicht fassen. Sie verschwindet ehe wir daran denken können sie zu erfassen. In diesem Kessel bleiben wir in einem Wirbel von Gedanken verzaubert stecken.

79. MS 107, pp. 1–2
Der Fehler muß sein daß wir versuchen die fliehende Gegenwart mit der wissenschaftlichen Methode zu erfassen. Das muß so sein als wollten wir die Festigkeit eines Balkons losgelöst von ihm erfassen. Sie gleichsam aus ihm herausdestillieren.

80. MS 107, p. 2
Dieses Unmögliche zu versuchen, davor muß uns die Erkenntnis retten daß wir Unsinn reden wenn wir versuchen unsere Sprache in diesem Unternehmen zu verwenden.

82. MS 107, p. 2
Was ich nicht denken darf, kann die Sprache nicht ausdrücken. Das ist unsere Beruhigung.

Wenn man aber sagt: Der Philosoph muß aber eben in diesen Kessel hinuntersteigen und die reine Realität selbst erfassen und ans Tageslicht ziehen so lautet die Antwort daß er dabei die Sprache hinten lassen müßte und daher unverrichteter Dinge wieder heraufkommt.

83. MS 107, p. 3
Und doch kann es eine phänomenologische Sprache geben. (Wo muß diese Halt machen?)

84. MS 107, p. 3
Wenn wir uns diese Sprache vorstellen wollen so ist es charakteristisch daß wir gleich anfangen uns die Welt einfacher vorzustellen als sie ist. Aber das spricht nicht gegen sondern *für* die Möglichkeit dieser Sprache denn wir gehen einen bestimmten Weg um zu ihr zu kommen.

Oder ist es so: Unsere gewöhnliche Sprache ist auch phänomenologisch, nur erlaubt sie es begreiflicherweise nicht die Sinnesgebiete deren gesamte Mannigfaltigkeit die ihre ist zu trennen.
Ihr Raum ist der kombinierte Gesichts-, Tast- und Muskelgefühls Raum darum kann ich mich in diesem Raum "umdrehen" und schauen "was hinter mir vorgeht" etc.

Es ist offenbar möglich den Gesichtsraum zu beschreiben. Denn ist das was gewöhnlich in ihm vorgeht zu kompliziert so sagt *das* schon daß die Beschreibung prinzipiell möglich ist. Und es ist leicht sich Vorgänge in diesem Raum zu denken die einfach genug sind um sich leicht beschreiben zu lassen.

85. Big Typescript, §102, p. 496
Andererseits brauchen wir eine Ausdrucksweise, die Vorgänge // Phänomene // des Gesichtsraums getrennt von der Erfahrungen anderer Art darstellt.

91. Big Typescript, §102, p. 496
"Ein Gedanke über die Darstellbarkeit der unmittelbaren Realität durch die Sprache:"

95. Big Typescript, §105, p. 520
Die Daten unseres Gedächtnisses sind geordnet; diese Ordnung nennen wir Gedächtniszeit, im Gegensatz zur physikalischen Zeit, der Ordnung der Ereignisse in der physikalischen Welt. Gegen der Ausdruck "Sehen in die Vergangenheit" sträubt sich unser Gefühl mit Recht; denn es gibt uns ein Bild davon // denn es ruft das Bild hervor //, dass Einer einen Vorgang in der physikalischen Welt sieht, der jetzt gar nicht geschieht, sondern schon vorüber ist.

97. Big Typescript, §102, p. 495
Wenn ich die unmittelbar gegebene Vergangenheit beschreibe, so beschreibe ich mein Gedächtnis, und nicht etwas, was dieses Gedächtnis anzeigt. (Wofür dieses Gedächtnis ein Symptom wäre.)

Und "Gedächtnis" bezeichnet hier—wie früher "Gesicht" und "Gehör"—auch nicht ein psychisches Vermögen, sondern ein bestimmten Teil der logischen Struktur unserer Welt.

101. Big Typescript, §105, p. 521
Die Erinnerungszeit unterscheidet sich unter anderem dadurch von der physikalischen, dass sie ein Halbstrahl ist, dessen Endpunkt // Anfangspunkt // die Gegenwart ist. Der Unterschied zwischen Erinnerungszeit und physikalischer Zeit ist natürlich ein logischer. D.h.: die beiden Ordnungen könnten sehr wohl mit ganz verschiedenen Namen bezeichnet werden und man nennt sie nur beide "Zeit," weil eine gewisse grammatische Verwandtschaft besteht, ganz wie zwischen Kardinal- und Rationalzahlen; Gesichtsraum, Tastraum und physikalischem Raum; Farbtönen und Klangfarben, etc., etc.

102. Big Typescript, §105, p. 521
Gedächtniszeit. Sie ist (wie der Gesichtsraum) nicht ein Teil der grossen Zeit, sondern die spezifische Ordnung der Ereignisse oder Situationen im Gedächtnis // in der Erinnerung //. In dieser Zeit gibt es z.B. keine Zukunft. Gesichtsraum und physikalischer Raum, Gedächtniszeit und physikalische Zeit, verhalten sich zueinander nicht wie ein Stück der Kardinalzahlenreihe zum Gesetz dieser Reihe ("der // zur // ganzen Zahlenreihe"), sondern, wie das System der Kardinalzahlen zu dem, der rationalen Zahlen. Und dieses Verhältnis erklärt auch den Sinn der Meinung, dass der eine Raum den andern einschliesst, enthält.

Chapter 6

4. MS 107, pp. 158–159
Ich fühle heute eine so besondere Armut an Problemen um mich; ein sicheres Zeichen daß *vor mir* die wichtigsten und härtesten Probleme liegen.

11.10

Das unmittelbare ist in ständigem Fluß begriffen. (Es hat tatsächlich die Form eines Stroms.)

Es ist ganz klar, daß wenn man hier das Letzte sagen will man eben auf die Grenze der Sprache kommen muß, die es ausdrückt.

5. Big Typescript, §96, p. 448
Die Verschwommenheit, Unbestimmtheit unserer Sinneseindrücke ist nicht etwas, dem sich abhelfen lässt, eine Verschwommenheit, der auch völlige Schärfe entspricht (oder entgegensteht). Vielmehr ist diese allgemeine Unbestimmtheit, Ungreifbarkeit, dieses Schwimmen der Sinneseindrücke, das, was mit dem Worte "alles fliesst" bezeichnet worden ist.

14. TS 219, p. 20
Inwiefern ist es nötig, sich, was ein Satz sagt, vorstellen zu können? ("Hast Du an dieser Stelle Schmerzen?")

"Denkbar" ist etwas ähnliches wie "vorstellbar." // "Denkbar" ist wirklich etwas Ähnliches wie "vorstellbar." // "Denkbar" ist nur eine Ausdehnung des Begriffs "vorstellbar." (Das ist es, was meine Auffassung des Satzes als eines Bild sagen wollte.)

25. MS 108, p. 1
Und dieses Anlegen der Sprache ist die Verifikation der Sätze.

32. MS 110, pp. 33–35
Daß alles fließt scheint uns am Ausdruck der Wahrheit zu hindern, denn es ist als ob wir sie nicht auffassen könnten da sie uns entgleitet.

Aber es hindert uns eben nicht am Ausdruck. —Was es heißt, etwas entfliehendes in der Beschreibung festhalten zu wollen, wissen wir. Das geschieht etwa, wenn wir das eine vergessen, während wir das andere beschreiben wollen. Aber darum handelt es sich doch hier nicht. Und so ist der Ausdruck /das Wort/ "entfliehen" anzuwenden.

Wir führen die Wörter von ihrer metaphysischen wieder auf ihre richtige Verwendung in der Sprache zurück.

Der Mann, der sagte, man könne nicht zweimal in den gleichen Fluß steigen, sagte etwas falsches. Man kann zweimal in den gleichen Fluß steigen.

Und so sieht die Lösung aller philosophischen Schwierigkeiten aus. Ihre Antworten müssen wenn sie richtig sind hausbacken und gewöhnlich sein. Aber man muß sie nur im richtigen Geist anschauen dann macht das nichts.

Aber auf die Antwort "Du weißt ja wie es der Satz macht, es ist ja nichts verborgen" möchte man sagen: "ja, aber es fließt alles so rasch vorüber und ich möchte es gleichsam breiter auseinandergelegt sehen."

Aber auch hier irren wir uns. Denn es geschieht dabei auch nichts was uns durch die Geschwindigkeit entgeht.

33. MS 110, p. 39
Das Gleichnis vom Fluß /Fließen/ der Zeit ist natürlich irreführend und muß uns wenn wir daran festhalten in Verlegenheit führen. /bringen landen./

42. Big Typescript, §94, p. 441
In der Grammatik wird auch die Anwendung der Sprache beschrieben; das, was man den Zusammenhang zwischen Sprache und Wirklichkeit nennen möchte.

43. TS 212
Was zum Wesen der Welt gehört, kann die Sprache nicht ausdrücken. Daher kann sie nicht *sagen*, dass Alles fliesst. Nur was wir uns auch anders vorstellen könnten, kann die Sprache sagen.
~~Dass alles fliesst, muss in dem Wesen // im Wesen // der Anwendung der Sprache auf die Wirklichkeit liegen.~~ // Dass alles fliesst, muss im Wesen der Berührung der Sprache mit der Wirklichkeit liegen. // Oder besser: dass Alles fliesst, muss im Wesen der Sprache liegen.

51. Big Typescript, §101, pp. 489–490
So kann der Satz "es scheint vor mir auf dem Tisch eine Lampe zu stehen" nichts weiter tun, als meine Erfahrung (oder, wie man sagt, unmittelbare Erfahrung) zu beschreiben.

52. Big Typescript, §101, p. 490
Ist es richtig zu sagen: Mein Gesichtsbild ist so kompliziert, es ist unmöglich, es ganz zu beschreiben? Dies ist eine sehr fundamentale Frage.

53. Big Typescript, §101, p. 490
"Die Blume war von einem rötlichgelb, welches ich aber nicht genauer (oder, nicht genauer mit Worten) beschreiben kann." Was heisst das?

54. Big Typescript, §101, p. 490
"Ich sehe es vor mir und könnte es malen."

55. Big Typescript, §101, p. 490
Wenn man sagt, man könnte diese Farbe nicht mit Worten genauer beschreiben, so denkt man (immer) an eine Möglichkeit einer solchen Beschreibung (freilich, denn sonst hätte das Wort // der Ausdruck // "genaue Beschreibung" keinen Sinn) und es schwebt einem dabei der Fall einer Messung vor, die wegen unzureichender Mittel nicht ausgeführt wurde.

56. Big Typescript, §101, pp. 490–491
Es ist mir nichts zur Hand, was diese oder eine ähnliche Farbe hätte.
Wenn man sagt, man könne das Gesichtsbild nicht ganz beschreiben, meint man, man kann keine Beschreibung geben, nach der man sich dieses Gesichtsbild genau reproduzieren könnte.

58. Big Typescript, §101, p. 491
Wir können von dem Gesichtsbild nicht *weiter* reden, als unsere Sprache jetzt reicht. Und

auch nicht mehr // weiter // *meinen* (denken), als unsere Sprache sagt // reicht //. (Nicht mehr meinen, als wir sagen können.)

Einer der gefährlichsten Vergleiche ist der des Gesichtsfelds mit einer gemalten Fläche (oder, was auf dasselbe hinauskommt, einem farbigen räumlichen Modell.)

Hiermit hängt es zusammen: Könnte ich denn das Gesichtsbild "mit allen Einzelheiten" wiedererkennen? Oder vielmehr, hat diese Frage überhaupt einen Sinn?

Denn als einwandfreiste Darstellung des Gesichtsbildes erscheint uns immer noch ein gemaltes Bild oder Modell. Aber, dass die Frage nach dem "Wiedererkennen in allen Einzelheiten" sinnlos ist, zeigt schon, wie inadäquat Bild und Modell sind.

59. Early Investigations, §111 (113)

Wir führen die Wörter von ihrer metaphysischen, wieder auf ihre alltägliche Verwendung zurück. (Der Mann, der sagte, man könne nicht zweimal in den gleichen Fluß steigen, sagte etwas Falsches; man *kann* zweimal in den gleichen Fluß steigen. —Und ein Gegenstand hört manchmal auf zu existieren, wenn ich aufhöre ihn zu sehen, und manchmal nicht. —Und wir *wissen* manchmal, welche Farbe der andere sieht, wenn er diesen Gegenstand betrachtet, und manchmal nicht.) Und so sieht die Lösung aller philosophischen Schwierigkeiten aus. Unsere Antwörten müssen, wenn sie richtig sind, gewöhnliche und triviale sein. —Denn diese Antworten machen sich gleichsam über die Fragen lustig.

Woher nimmt die Betrachtung ihre Wichtigkeit, da sie doch nur alles Interessante, d.h. alles Große und wichtige, zu zerstören scheint? (Gleichsam alle Bauwerke; indem sie nur Steinbrocken und Schutt übrig läßt.) Aber es sind nur Luftgebäude, die wir zerstören, und wir legen den Grund der Sprache frei, auf dem sie standen.

Die Ergebnisse der Philosophie sind die Entdeckung irgendeines schlichten Unsinns und Beulen, die sich der Verstand beim rennen an das Ende [*alternate word, also in text*: Grenze] der Sprache geholt hat. Sie, die Beulen, lassen uns den Wert jener Entdeckung erkennen.

107. MS 116, pp. 177–178

Statt: "man kann nicht," sage: "es gibt in diesem Spiel nicht": Statt "man kann im Damespiel nicht rochieren"—"es gibt in Damespiel kein Rochieren"; statt "ich kann meine Empfindung nicht vorzeigen"—"es gibt in der Verwendung von 'ich habe die Empfindung . . .' kein Vorzeigen dessen, was 'man hat'"; statt "man kann nicht alle Kardinalzahlen aufzählen"—"es gibt hier kein Aufzählen aller Glieder, wenn auch ein Aufzählen von Gliedern."

Der Satz "Empfindungen sind privat" ist von der Art: Patience spielt man allein.

Bibliography

Primary Sources

Wittgenstein, Ludwig. "A Lecture on Ethics." *Philosophical Review* 74 (1965): 3–12. Reprinted in *Philosophical Occasions*.

Wittgenstein, Ludwig. *Culture and Value*. Edited by G. H. von Wright, translated by P. Winch. Oxford: Blackwell, 1980.

Wittgenstein, Ludwig. Early Investigations. Unpublished typescript, edited by G. H. von Wright and H. Nyman. University of Helsinki, Helsinki: photocopy, 1979.

Wittgenstein, Ludwig. *Eine Philosophische Betrachtung*. Edited by Rush Rhees. Frankfurt am Main: Suhrkamp, 1970.

Wittgenstein, Ludwig. *Last Writings on the Philosophy of Psychology*. Vol. 1, *Preliminary Studies for Part II of the "Philosophical Investigations."* Edited by G. H. von Wright and H. Nyman, translated by C. G. Luckhardt and M. A. E. Aue. Chicago: University of Chicago Press, 1982.

Wittgenstein, Ludwig. *Last Writings on the Philosophy of Psychology*. Vol. 2, *The Inner and the Outer*. Edited by G. H. von Wright and H. Nyman, translated by C. G. Luckhardt and M. A. E. Aue. Chicago: University of Chicago Press, 1992.

Wittgenstein, Ludwig. *Letters to C. K. Ogden*. Edited by G. H. von Wright. Oxford: Blackwell, 1973.

Wittgenstein, Ludwig. *Letters to Russell, Keynes and Moore*. Edited by G. H. von Wright and B. F. McGuinness. Oxford: Blackwell, 1974.

Wittgenstein, Ludwig. *Ludwig Wittgenstein and the Vienna Circle: Conversations Recorded by Friedrich Waismann*. Edited by B. F. McGuinness, translated by J. Schulte and B. F. McGuinness. Oxford: Blackwell, 1979. German edition, with the same pagination: *Ludwig Wittgenstein und der Wiener Kreis: Gespräche aufgezeichnet von Friedrich Waismann*, edited by B. F. McGuinness. Oxford: Blackwell, 1967.

Wittgenstein, Ludwig. *Notebooks 1914–1916*, 2nd ed. Edited by G. H. von Wright and G. E. M. Anscombe, translated by G. E. M. Anscombe. Chicago: University of Chicago Press, 1979.

Wittgenstein, Ludwig. "Notes for Lectures on 'Sense Data' and 'Private Experience,'" in *Philosophical Occasions*, pp. 200–288.

Wittgenstein, Ludwig. *On Certainty*. Edited by G. E. M. Anscombe and G. H. von Wright, translated by G. E. M. Anscombe and D. Paul. Oxford: Blackwell, 1969.

Wittgenstein, Ludwig. *Philosophical Grammar*. Edited by R. Rhees, translated by A. Kenny. Berkeley: University of California Press, 1974. German edition: *Philosophische Grammatik*. Oxford: Blackwell, 1969.

Wittgenstein, Ludwig. *Philosophical Investigations*, 2nd ed. Edited by G. E. M. Anscombe and R. Rhees, translated by G. E. M. Anscombe. Oxford: Blackwell, 1967. German text and English translation on facing pages.

Wittgenstein, Ludwig. *Philosophical Occasions: 1912–1951*. Edited by J. Klagge and A. Nordmann. Indianapolis, IN: Hackett, 1993.

Wittgenstein, Ludwig. *Philosophical Remarks*. Edited by R. Rhees, translated by R. Hargraves and R. White. Oxford: Blackwell, 1975. German edition: *Philosophische Bemerkungen*. Oxford: Blackwell, 1964.

Wittgenstein, Ludwig. "'Philosophie' §§86–93 (S. 405–435) aus dem sogenannten 'Big Typescript' (Katalognummer 213)," edited by H. Nyman. *Revue Internationale de Philosophie* 43 (1989): 175–203. English translation by C. G. Luckhardt and M. A. E. Aue, as "Philosophy: Sections 86–93 (pp. 405–435) of the so-called 'Big Typescript' (Catalog Number 213)." *Synthese* 87 (1991): 203–226. Reprinted in *Philosophical Occasions*.

Wittgenstein, Ludwig. *Preliminary Studies for the "Philosophical Investigations" Generally Known as "The Blue and Brown Books,"* 2nd ed.; references in the footnotes are to the *Blue Book* or the *Brown Book*. Oxford: Blackwell, 1969.

Wittgenstein, Ludwig. *Prototractatus*. Edited by B. F. McGuinness et al., translated by Pears and McGuinness. Ithaca, NY: Cornell University Press, 1971.

Wittgenstein, L. *The Published Works of Ludwig Wittgenstein*. Clayton, GA: InteLex (electronic text database), 1993.

Wittgenstein, Ludwig. *Remarks on the Foundations of Mathematics*, 2nd ed. Edited by G. E. M. Anscombe, R. Rhees, and G. H. von Wright; translated by G. E. M. Anscombe. Cambridge, MA: MIT Press, 1978.

Wittgenstein, Ludwig. *Remarks on the Philosophy of Psychology*, Vol. 1. Edited by G. E. M. Anscombe and G. H. von Wright, translated by G. E. M. Anscombe. Chicago: University of Chicago Press, 1980.

Wittgenstein, Ludwig. *Remarks on the Philosophy of Psychology*, Vol. 2. Edited by G. H. von Wright and H. Nyman, translated by C. G. Luckhardt and M. A. E. Aue. Chicago: University of Chicago Press, 1980.

Wittgenstein, Ludwig. "Some Remarks on Logical Form." *Proceedings of the Aristotelian Society*, Suppl. Vol. 9 (1929): 162–171. Reprinted in *Philosophical Occasions*.

Wittgenstein, Ludwig. *Tractatus Logico-Philosophicus*. Translated by C. K. Ogden. London: Routledge and Kegan Paul, 1922; second rev. ed., with corrections, 1933.

Wittgenstein, Ludwig. *Tractatus Logico-Philosophicus*. Translated by David Pears and Brian McGuinness. London: Routledge and Kegan Paul, 1961.

Wittgenstein, Ludwig. *Wittgenstein's Lectures, Cambridge, 1930–32*. From the notes of John King and Desmond Lee, edited by Desmond Lee. Oxford: Blackwell, 1980.

Wittgenstein, Ludwig. *Wittgenstein's Lectures, Cambridge, 1932–1935*. From the notes of Alice Ambrose and Margaret Macdonald, edited by Alice Ambrose. Chicago: University of Chicago Press, 1979.

Wittgenstein, Ludwig. *Wittgenstein's Published Writings in Electronic Form*. Edited by H. Kaal and A. McKinnon. Montreal: Inter Editions, 1990.

Wittgenstein, Ludwig. *Zettel*. Edited by G. E. M. Anscombe and G. H. von Wright, translated by G. E. M. Anscombe. Chicago: University of Chicago Press, 1980.

Secondary Sources

Anscombe, G. E. M. "On the Form of Wittgenstein's Writing." In *Contemporary Philosophy: A Survey*. Vol. 3, edited by R. Klibansky, 373–378. Florence: La Nuova Italia, 1969.

Baker, Gordon. "*Verehrung* und *Verkehrung*: Waismann and Wittgenstein." In *Wittgenstein: Sources and Perspectives*, edited by C. G. Luckhardt. Ithaca, NY: Cornell University Press, 1979, pp. 242–285.

Baker, G. & Hacker, P. *Wittgenstein: Understanding and Meaning. An Analytical Commentary on the* Philosophical Investigations. Vol. 1. Chicago: University of Chicago Press, 1980.

Baker, G. & Hacker, P. *Wittgenstein: Rules, Grammar and Necessity. An Analytical Commentary on the* Philosophical Investigations. Vol. 2. Oxford: Blackwell, 1985.

Beck, L. W. "Kant's Letter to Marcus Herz." *Philosophical Forum* 13 (1955): 96–110.

Blackburn, S. "The Individual Strikes Back." *Synthese* 58 (1984): 281–303.

Blackburn, S. *Spreading the Word*. Oxford: Clarendon, 1984.

Bouwsma, O. K. *Wittgenstein: Conversations, 1949–1951*. Edited by J. L. Craft and R. E. Hustwit. Indianapolis, IN: Hackett, 1986.

Cavell, Stanley. *The Claim of Reason*. Oxford: Oxford University Press, 1979.

Copi, I., & Beard, R., eds. *Essays on Wittgenstein's Tractatus*. New York: Macmillan, 1966.

Descartes, René. *Meditations on First Philosophy*. Translated by J. Cottingham. Cambridge: Cambridge University Press, 1986.

Dreyfus, Hubert. "Holism and Hermeneutics." *Review of Metaphysics* 34 (1980): 3–23.

Driesch, Hans. *Wirklichkeitslehre*. Leipzig: Emmanuel Reinicke, 1922.

Driesch, Hans. *Ordnungslehre*, 2nd ed. Jena: Eugen Diederichs, 1923.

Drury M. O'C. "Conversations with Wittgenstein." In *Ludwig Wittgenstein: Personal Recollections*, edited by Rush Rhees, pp. 112–189. Totowa, NJ: Rowman and Littlefield, 1981.

Eddington, Arthur. *The Nature of the Physical World*. Cambridge: Cambridge University Press, 1928.

Edwards, J. C. *Ethics Without Philosophy. Wittgenstein and the Moral Life*. Gainesville, FL: University of Southern Florida Press, 1982.

Engelmann, Paul. *Letters from Ludwig Wittgenstein*. Edited by B. F. McGuinness, translated by L. Furtmüller. Oxford: Blackwell, 1967.

Fogelin, Robert. *Wittgenstein*. London: Routledge & Kegan Paul, 1976, rev. 2nd ed., 1987.

Frege, Gottlob. *Grundgesetze der Arithmetik*, 2 vols. Hildersheim: Olms, 1962.

Frege, Gottlob. *Translations from the Philosophical Writings of Gottlob Frege*. Edited by P. Geach and M. Black. Oxford: Blackwell, 1960.

Garver, Newton. "Neither Knowing nor Not Knowing." *Philosophical Investigations* 7 (1984): 206–224.

Gert, B. "Wittgenstein's Private Language Arguments." *Synthese* 68 (1986): 409–439.

Goldfarb, Warren. "I Want You to Bring Me a Slab. Remarks on the Opening Sections of the 'Philosophical Investigations.'" *Synthese* 56 (1983): 265–282.

Griffin, J. *Wittgenstein's Logical Atomism*. Oxford: Oxford University Press, 1964.

Hacker, P. M. S. *Insight and Illusion: Themes in the Philosophy of Wittgenstein*. Oxford: Clarendon, 1972; rev. 2nd ed., 1986.

Hallett, G. *A Companion to Wittgenstein's "Philosophical Investigations."* Ithaca, NY: Cornell University Press, 1977.

Heidegger, Martin. *Being and Time*. Translated by J. Macquarrie and E. Robinson. New York and Evanston: Harper and Row, 1962.

Hertz, Heinrich. *The Principles of Mechanics*. Translated by D. E. Jones and J. T. Walley. New York: Dover, 1956.

Hilmy, S. S. *The Later Wittgenstein: The Emergence of a New Philosophical Method*. Oxford: Blackwell, 1987.

Hintikka, J. "An Impatient Man and His Papers." *Synthese* 87 (1991): 183–202.

Hintikka, M. B. & Hintikka, J. *Investigating Wittgenstein*. Oxford: Blackwell, 1986.

Huitfeldt, Claus. "Das Wittgenstein-Archiv der Universität Bergen. Hintergrund und erster Arbeitsbericht." *Mitteilungen aus dem Brenner-Archiv* 10 (1991): 93–106. Pages 93–104 are a translation of Huitfeldt (forthcoming).

Huitfeldt, Claus. "The Wittgenstein Archives at the University of Bergen—Background and First Work Report." *Philosophy and Computing*, forthcoming.

Huitfeldt, Claus & Rossvaer, Viggo. *The Norwegian Wittgenstein Project Report 1988*. Bergen: Norwegian Computing Center for the Humanities, 1989.

Hylton, Peter. "The Nature of the Proposition and the Revolt Against Idealism." In *Philosophy in History*, edited by R. Rorty, J. B. Schneewind, and Q. Skinner. Cambridge: Cambridge University Press, 1984, pp. 375–397.

Ishiguro, H. "Use and Reference of Names." In *Studies in the Philosophy of Wittgenstein*, edited by Peter Winch. London: Routledge & Kegan Paul, 1969.

Johannessen, K. S. "The Concept of Practice in Wittgenstein's Later Philosophy." *Inquiry* 31 (1981): 357–369.

Kant, Immanuel. *Critique of Pure Reason*. Translated by Norman Kemp Smith. London: Macmillan, 1933.

Kant, Immanuel. *Kant—Philosophical Correspondence 1759–99*. Edited and translated by Arnulf Zweig. Chicago: University of Chicago Press, 1967.

Kenny, A. "From the Big Typescript to the *Philosophical Grammar*." *Acta Philosophical Fennica* 28 #1–3 (1976): 41–53. Reprinted in Kenny, *The Legacy of Wittgenstein*, pp. 24–37.

Kenny, A. *The Legacy of Wittgenstein*. Oxford: Blackwell, 1984.

Kenny, A. *Wittgenstein*. Harmondsworth: Penguin, 1973.

Kripke, Saul. *Wittgenstein on Rules and Private Language*. Cambridge, MA: Harvard University Press, 1982.

Leibniz, G. W. *Philosophical Essays*. Edited and translated by R. Ariew and D. Garber. Indianapolis, IN: Hackett, 1989.

Malcolm, Norman. *Ludwig Wittgenstein: A Memoir*, 2nd ed. Oxford: Oxford University Press, 1984.

Malcolm, Norman. *Nothing Is Hidden: Wittgenstein's Criticism of His Early Thought*. Oxford: Blackwell, 1986.

Malcolm, Norman. "Wittgenstein's *Philosophical Investigations*." In *Wittgenstein: The Philosophical Investigations*, edited by G. Pitcher. Garden City, NY.: Doubleday, 1966, pp. 65–103.

Maury, André. "Sources of the Remarks in Wittgenstein's *Zettel*." *Philosophical Investigations* 4 (1981): 57–74.

Maury, André. "Sources of the Remarks in Wittgenstein's *Philosophical Investigations*." *Synthese* 98 (1994): 349–378.

McDonough, Richard. *The Argument of the* Tractatus. Buffalo NY: SUNY Press, 1986.

McGuinness, Brian. "The So-Called Realism of the *Tractatus*" in *Perspectives on the Philosophy of Wittgenstein*, edited by I. Block. Cambridge: MIT Press, 1981, pp. 60–73.

McGuinness, Brian. *Wittgenstein: A Life. Young Ludwig: 1889–1921*. London: Duckworth, 1988.

Monk, Ray. *Ludwig Wittgenstein: The Duty of Genius*. New York: Free Press, 1990.

Moore, G. E. "Wittgenstein's Lectures in 1930–33." Published in three parts in *Mind* 63–64 (1954–1955). Reprinted in *Philosophical Papers*. London: Allen & Unwin, 1959. References are to the reprint.

Nagel, Thomas. "Physicalism." *Philosophical Review* 74 (1965): 339–356.

Pascal, Fania. "Ludwig Wittgenstein, A Personal Memoir." In *Ludwig Wittgenstein: Personal*

Recollections, edited by Rush Rhees, pp. 26–62. Totowa, NJ: Rowman and Littlefield, 1981.

Pears, David. *Bertrand Russell and the British Tradition in Philosophy*. London: Fontana, 1967.

Pears, David. "The Logical Independence of Elementary Propositions." In *Perspectives on the Philosophy of Wittgenstein*, edited by I. Block. Cambridge: MIT Press, 1981, pp. 74–84.

Pears, David. *The False Prison*, Vols. 1 and 2. Oxford: Clarendon, 1987, 1988.

Perry, John. "The Problem of the Essential Indexical." *Noûs* 13 (1979): 3–21.

Pichler, Alois. *Ludwig Wittgenstein, Culture and Value: A List of Source Manuscripts*. Bergen: Working Papers from the Wittgenstein Archives at the University of Bergen, no. 1, 1991.

Plato, *Cratylus*. Translated by Benjamin Jowett. In *Plato: The Collected Dialogues*, edited by Edith Hamilton and Huntington Cairns. Princeton: Princeton University Press, 1963, pp. 422–474.

Plato, *Theaetetus*. Translated by John McDowell. Oxford: Clarendon, 1973.

Ramsey, Frank. "Critical Notice of the *Tractatus*." *Mind* 32 (1923): 465–478.

Ramsey, Frank. *Philosophical Papers*, edited by D. H. Mellor. Cambridge: Cambridge University Press, 1990.

Ramsey, Frank. Unpublished manuscripts, University of Pittsburgh collection.

Rhees, Rush. Preface to "Conversations on Freud." In *Lectures and Conversations on Aesthetics, Psychology and Religious Belief*, edited by Cyril Barrett. Oxford: Blackwell, 1966, pp. 41–42.

Rhees, Rush. "Correspondence and Comment." *The Human World* 15–16 (1974): 153–162.

Rhees, Rush. "The Language of Sense Data and Private Experience," Parts I and II. *Philosophical Investigations* 7 (1984): 1–45, 101–140.

Russell, Bertrand. "On Propositions: What They Are and How They Mean." *Proceedings of the Aristotelian Society*, Suppl. Vol. (1919): 1–43. Reprinted in *Logic and Knowledge*.

Russell, Bertrand. "The Philosophy of Logical Atomism." In *Logic and Knowledge*, edited by R. C. Marsh, pp. 177–281. London: Allen and Unwin, 1956.

Russell, Bertrand. *The Autobiography of Bertrand Russell*, Vol. 2. London: Allen and Unwin, 1968.

Schopenhauer, Arthur. *The World as Will and Representation*, translated by C. J. F. Payne. New York: Dover, 1969.

Searle, John. *Intentionality: An Essay in the Philosophy of Mind*. Cambridge: Cambridge University Press, 1983.

Sluga, Hans. "Subjectivity in the *Tractatus*." *Synthese* 56 (1983): 123–139.

Spinoza, Benedict. *Ethics. On the Improvement of the Understanding; The Correspondence*, translated by R. H. M. Elwes. New York: Dover, 1977.

Stern, David. "'What is the ground of the relationship of that in us which we call "representation" to the object?' Reflections on the Kantian Legacy in the Philosophy of Mind." In *Doing Philosophy Historically*, edited by P. Hare, 216–230. Buffalo NY: Prometheus Press, 1988.

Stern, David. "Heraclitus' and Wittgenstein's River Images: Stepping Twice into the Same River." *Monist* 74 (1991): 579–604.

Stern, David. "The 'Middle Wittgenstein': From Logical Atomism to Practical Holism." *Synthese* 87 (1991): 203–226.

Stern, David. "A New Exposition of the 'Private Language Argument': Wittgenstein's Notes for the 'Philosophical Lecture'." *Philosophical Investigations* 17 (1994): 552–565.

Stern, David. "Recent Work on Wittgenstein, 1980–1990." *Synthese* 98 (1994): 415–458.

Stern, David. "Review of *The Published Works of Ludwig Wittgenstein.*" *Canadian Philosophical Reviews* 14 (1994): 77–80.

Stern, David. "The Availability of Wittgenstein's Philosophy." In *The Cambridge Companion to Wittgenstein*, edited by Hans Sluga and David Stern. New York: Cambridge University Press, 1996.

Stroud, Barry. "Wittgenstein's 'Treatment' of the Quest for 'a Language Which Describes My Inner Experiences and Which Only I Myself Can Understand.'" In *Epistemology and Philosophy of Science, Proceedings of the 7th International Wittgenstein Symposium*, edited by P. Weingartner and J. Czermak, 438–445. Vienna: Hölder-Pichler-Tempsky, 1983.

ter Hark, M. *Beyond the Inner and the Outer: Wittgenstein's Philosophy of Psychology.* Dordrecht, Holland: Kluwer, 1990.

Tugendhat, Ernst. *Self-Consciousness and Self-Determination.* Translated by Paul Stern. Cambridge, MA: MIT Press, 1986. Translation of *Selbstbewußtsein und Selbstbestimmung.* Frankfurt am Main: Suhrkamp, 1979.

von Wright, G. H. "A Biographical Sketch." *Philosophical Review* 64, #4 (1955): 527–545. Reprinted in N. Malcolm, *Ludwig Wittgenstein: A Memoir.*

von Wright, G. H. "The Wittgenstein Papers." *Philosophical Review* 78 (1969): 483–503. The latest revisions are in *Philosophical Occasions.*

von Wright, G. H. *Wittgenstein.* Oxford: Blackwell, 1982.

von Wright, G. H. "The Troubled History of Part II of the *Investigations*," *Grazer Philosophische Studien* 42 (1992): 181–192.

Index

Ludwig Wittgenstein has been abbreviated as LW. Material from the appendix is not included in the index.

Visual space, 92, 94. *See also* Eye; Visual
  field
  geometry of, 75, 84, 112, 142, 163–64
  grammar of, 75, 164
  as primary, 11, 86–87, 150–59
  and self, 74–76, 79, 84
  and time, 146–47
von Ficker, Ludwig, 8, 70
von Hayek, F. A., 113*n*
von Wright, Georg Henrik
  conversation with LW, 35, 107*n*
  numbering system for *Nachlass,* 4*n*
  on picture theory, 35
  typescripts from *Philosophical
    Investigations* period, 96–98

Waismann, Friedrich, 15, 91, 93, 95, 99,
    101, 137
Will, 25–26, 74
Wittgenstein, Ludwig. *See also* Early
    writings; Later writings; 1929
    writings
  in Cambridge, 91–92
  collaboration with Waismann on
    exposition of *Tractatus,* 93, 95
  context provided by oeuvre of, 6–7, 146
  conversation with Bouwsma, 140
  conversation with Malcolm, 63, 107*n*
  conversation with Ramsey, 3, 91–92,
    104
  conversation with Vienna Circle, 3, 11,
    91, 93, 100, 140, 153
  conversation with von Wright, 35, 107*n*
  conversation with Waismann, 101
  criticism of Russell, 39, 47*n*, 55, 60–61,
    64
  falling out with Waismann, 95
  idealism of, 127
  learns Russian, 95
  philosophy's hold over, 19–20
  Ramsey visits in 1920s, 91
  reads Kant, 112
  reads Plato, 160

relations with Russell (1929–1930), 43,
    92, 93
  as teacher and architect in Austria, 91
  travels to Norway, 95
  vacations in Vienna, 93
Wittgenstein Archives (University of
    Bergen), 5*n*
World. *See also* Ordinary language;
    Primary/secondary distinction
  as composed of facts, 53, 66, 72, 82
  and conventions, 48–49, 63, 65, 68,
    102–3
  essence of, 45, 77, 152, 158, 161, 165,
    170–71
  of experience ("my world"), 11–12, 70–
    71, 73–78, 81–82
  as hypothesis, 78, 111–12
  as idea, 153–59
  inexpressibility, 81–82
  in itself and as spatio–temporal, 9–14
  Kantian conception of, 65
  and language, 38–41, 43–46, 48–49, 53–
    69, 81–82, 102–3
  life equated with, 69, 73–74
  limits of, 9–10, 65, 71, 74–75, 77
  logical form as structure of, 66, 120–21
  picture theory, 38–41, 43–46
  simple objects, 53–63
  visual-field analogy, 75
  "the world as I found it," 73, 76, 144
  world–picture, 189–90

Zettel
  background, 191–92
  flux thesis, 170, 188
  justification of grammar, 114
  philosophical method, 20
  picture theory, 39–40
  relation to sources and *Philosophical
    Investigations,* 97–98
  rule-following, 118
  teaching of language, 30, 41–42, 184
  verification, 115

Index of Quotations

MS 105
(p.)
108,   143
116,   162
116–18,   149

MS 107
(p.)
1,   150
1–2,   150
2,   151
3,   151, 152
158–59,   161
176,   137
205,   136
223–24,   139
233,   122, 139
240,   166

MS 108
(p.)
1,   165
277,   110

MS 110
(p.)
33–35,   168
39,   168
229–30,   105
230–31,   107
233–34,   106
239,   25

MS 112
(p.)
54–55,   87
93,   19

MS 116
(p.)
178,   186

MS 120
(p.)
87–88,   86
89,   86

MS 121
(p.)
98–99,   22

MS 148
(p.)
21,   21

MS 150
(p.)
59,   29

MS 157b
(p.)
10–13,   107

Notebooks 1914–1916
(p.)
2,   61
3,   61, 62
7,   38, 48
32,   99
36,   191
45,   62
47,   63
51,   72
52,   72
60,   60
61,   59
63,   58
64,   62
67,   59, 62
68,   59
69,   62
70,   63
73,   74, 75
80,   73
82,   76
83,   9
94,   37

On Certainty
(§)
37,   42
139,   120
204,   127
318,   187
321,   187
501,   190
617–18,   187
94–99,   189

Philosophical Grammar
(§)
2,   120
12,   191
27,   120
43,   191
48,   118
52,   118, 119, 120
83,   25, 163, 164
84,   109
85,   105
90,   54
99,   118
115,   20

(p.)
211,   64
244,   117
301,   114

*Philosophical In-
vestigations*
(p.)
ix,   97
ix–x,   4

(§)
1,   119
6,   184
18,   28
29,   183
31,   183
38,   86
46,   55
49,   184
65,   121
66,   163
81,   104
85,   125
87,   126
93–96,   40
98,   138
104,   43
107,   167
108,   17, 167
109,   24, 108
115,   43
116,   23, 175
119,   19
123,   18, 29